Edward J. Mullen,
James R. Dumpson,
and Associates

EVALUATION
OF SOCIAL
INTERVENTION

WITHDRAWN

Jossey-Bass Inc., Publishers
San Francisco • Washington • London • 1972

The Jossey-Bass Behavioral Science Series

General Editors

WILLIAM E. HENRY, *University of Chicago*

NEVITT SANFORD, *Wright Institute, Berkeley*

Special Adviser in Social Work

MARTIN B. LOEB, *University of Wisconsin*

To Virginia Garretson,
a volunteer committed to
effective community service

Preface

During the past decade, many experimental evaluations of social work intervention have been reported, raising question about the relevance and effectiveness of conventional social work methods and pointing toward promising new approaches. The contributors to *Evaluation of Social Intervention* review the findings of thirteen of these major experiments as well as other evaluations of professional social work intervention they consider relevant. Each contributor addresses himself to a selected topic and focuses on the implications of the studies for that particular aspect of social work education. The thirteen evaluations of professional social work intervention reviewed meet three criteria: the study is a relevant and major evaluation of the effects of social work intervention; the study used an experimental research design; and the study has potential for contributing to the redesign of social work programs and curricula.

Evaluation of Social Intervention is addressed not only to social work educators and students but to everyone associated with social work, including planners, administrators, practitioners, and researchers. Thus, we have divided this book into two main parts. Experimental evaluations and evaluative research methodology are

critically examined in Part One. The implications of these findings
and of evaluative research methodology for social intervention and
education for effective social intervention are discussed in Part Two.

The book is further divided into fourteen chapters. In Chapter One, we review evaluations of social work and related interventions within a historical context, as well as discussing the effects of allied counseling and psychotherapeutic efforts. The chapter concludes
with some reflections on the practical implications of various studies
and identifies the micro-, mezzo-, and macrosystem levels of social
intervention.

Ludwig Geismar, in Chapter Two, summarizes thirteen
studies, discussing them within a descriptive framework of method
and theory pertinent to evaluative research. He summarizes each
study under the headings of problem investigated, research setting,
goal, program of intervention, and results. In conclusion, Geismar
asks some discerning questions and urges the profession to assume
responsibility for building research into practice. He observes that
"the argument that evaluation must take second place is unconvincing in light of some of the foregoing findings."

Chapters Three and Four address problems in carrying out
evaluative research, pinpointing implications for practice and education. Wyatt Jones and Edgar Borgatta, in Chapter Three, after
reviewing some criteria on which evaluations should be assessed,
call our attention to an emerging need—evaluating the effects of
large-scale programs on total population groups and communities.
They imply that the problems of evaluating impact on individuals
and families seem small when compared with the control and measurement of variables relating to community structure and institutional change. They suggest that methods other than classical statistical ones may be desirable in future evaluative research. Finally,
Jones and Borgatta point out that difficulties of evaluative research
at conventional levels may lead to research at other levels, such as
social system analyses with agencies as elements.

James Breedlove, in Chapter Four, agrees with Jones and
Borgatta that improved research technology and goal specification
will enhance evaluative studies. However, Breedlove claims that
problems of evaluative research are essentially a consequence of

failure to give serious, concentrated attention to practice theory development and testing. In addition to specifying the tasks and levels of evaluative research, Breedlove analyzes and suggests ways to improve practice theory.

In Part Two, Harold Lewis, in Chapter Five, discusses epistemologic stumbling blocks to the effective and efficient use of new knowledge and values in redesigning professional intervention programs and curricula. In so doing, he analyzes the organizing rubrics for curricula, the structure of knowledge and values in a professional practice, and the principles of curriculum design and development. While Chapter Five focuses on professional education, it should interest anyone concerned with professional interventions since the concepts discussed are broadly applicable.

Viewing social intervention from a systems perspective, we address ourselves to three levels of system intervention—macrosystem, mezzosystem, and microsystem. Walter Walker and Gene Webb, in Chapters Six and Seven, discuss macrosystem intervention and education. Walker defines macrosystems as large, complex social systems, and macrosystem interventions as those which affect a large, geographically scattered population. Training for macrosystem practice requires a massive input of products from a variety of disciplines and viewpoints, and several means for achieving this training are presented.

John Turner defines mezzosystem social work as "efforts to initiate, design, create, influence, manage, and evaluate programs and policies affecting the well-being of people as executed locally. As such it works primarily with institutions and their subunits *in behalf of* individuals, families, and groups." Turner sees the mezzosystem practitioner as the middleman in accountability for human services. At a time when local social intervention is viewed by many as of primary importance, given the attempt of the profession to deal with the problems of large urban centers, the analyses presented by Turner and Simon Slavin, in Chapters Eight and Nine, are most timely.

Carol Meyer, in Chapter Ten, speaks of the microsystem as small units—the individual, the family, and the small group—each viewed systematically and transactionally. This chapter and Chapter Eleven, by Helen Perlman, are major analyses of the effects of social work intervention on the microsystem level and present useful guidelines for curriculum revision.

Werner Boehm and Donald Feldstein, in Chapters Twelve and Thirteen, address the continuum in social work education, discussing the training and utilization of social welfare manpower. Their common theme is that it is time to rethink levels of education for social welfare practice and to plan for their rational integration.

Chapter Fourteen expresses our overall reaction to the issues discussed in *Evaluation of Social Intervention* and pinpoints several priority areas for action.

Acknowledgments

Stimulated by the research findings of the past decade over 125 representatives from graduate and undergraduate schools of social work, student associations, and public and private social agencies met for two days at Fordham University to consider these evaluations and to deliberate on their implications for social work education. Known as the Fordham Symposium, this gathering was convened by the faculty of the School of Social Service and a planning committee composed of social work educators from numerous universities, with the cooperation of the Council on Social Work Education. The Ittleson Family Foundation funded the entire undertaking, of which *Evaluation of Social Intervention* is an outgrowth.

The symposium and the preparation of this book were enriching and exciting experiences, and we are deeply indebted to the symposium planning committee members: Werner Boehm, James Breedlove, Stanley Budner, Helen Dermody, Samuel Finestone, Lowell Iberg, Paul Kirkham, Rosa Marin, Patricia Morisey, Victoria Olds, Mary Ann Quaranta, Robert Roberts, Belén Serra, John Turner, and Kermit Wiltse.

We are grateful to the individual authors, who not only reviewed the studies but also undertook the painstaking task of synthesizing their findings and communicating the results of that synthesis. While the contributions of the individual symposium participants to *Evaluation of Social Intervention* are not specifically identified, we are grateful to them for their critical and productive consideration and discussion.

The enthusiastic support the symposium received from the faculty of the Fordham University School of Social Service from the time sponsorship was presented until the closing session is deeply appreciated. The faculty, with the alumni association, the student body, and the university administration, provided the atmosphere and facilities that made the gathering a success.

For the initial suggestion that a conference of social work educators be held, we are indebted to the State Communities Aid Association, and the continued guidance and interest of the association, expressed through Lowell Iberg, its deputy director, were most helpful.

Finally, and most importantly, the generous support of the Ittleson Family Foundation and the assistance of William T. Beaty II, secretary of the foundation, are gratefully acknowledged. We are deeply impressed by their foresight in recognizing the need for this reexamination and, again, are grateful for their support.

Appreciation is expressed to Virginia Seymour and the clerical staff of the Fordham University School of Social Service for their assistance in making the symposium possible. And to Edith Oxley for her personal commitment to this book and her investment of countless hours in seeing it through many phases, including editing and typing the final manuscript, we are most grateful.

We trust that the combined efforts of all these individuals and groups will result in a serious rethinking of social interventions within the context of evaluative research. The thoughts expressed in the following pages, we believe, represent a step in that direction. We trust that the reader will add to these thoughts as new findings are forthcoming.

New York City   EDWARD J. MULLEN
September 1972   JAMES R. DUMPSON

Contents

xiii

Contributors

WERNER W. BOEHM, *dean and professor, Graduate School of Social Work, Rutgers University*

EDGAR F. BORGATTA, *distinguished professor of sociology, Queens College, City University of New York*

JAMES L. BREEDLOVE, *professor, School of Social Work, Portland State University*

JAMES R. DUMPSON, *dean and professor, Graduate School of Social Service, Fordham University*

DONALD L. FELDSTEIN, *director, Center for Social Work and Applied Social Research, Fairleigh Dickinson University*

LUDWIG L. GEISMAR, *professor of social work and sociology and director of the Social Work Research Center, Graduate School of Social Work, Rutgers University*

WYATT C. JONES, *professor of social research, Heller Graduate School, Brandeis University, and research sociologist, Veterans Administration*

HAROLD LEWIS, *dean and professor, School of Social Work, Hunter College, City University of New York*

CAROL H. MEYER, *professor, School of Social Work, Columbia University*

EDWARD J. MULLEN, *professor, Graduate School of Social Service, Fordham University, and director of research and evaluation, Community Service Society of New York*

HELEN HARRIS PERLMAN, *Samuel Deutsch Distinguished Service Professor, School of Social Service Administration, University of Chicago*

SIMON SLAVIN, *dean and professor, School of Social Administration, Temple University*

JOHN B. TURNER, *dean and professor of social work, School of Applied Social Sciences, Case Western Reserve University*

WALTER L. WALKER, *professor, School of Social Service Administration, and vice-president for planning, University of Chicago*

GENE E. WEBB, *professor, School of Social Work, Western Michigan University*

Evaluation of
Social Intervention

Is Social Work
on the Wrong Track?

Edward J. Mullen, James R. Dumpson

What does research tell us about the effectiveness of professional social work intervention? In raising this question, we recognize that the value of social work intervention is currently disputed.

Social work is reviewed in this chapter within the contexts of research findings about the effectiveness of related human service efforts. Therefore, while we will focus primarily on effectiveness as it relates to professional social work intervention, we refer throughout to evaluations of psychotherapeutic and counseling interventions as well. We do not equate social work intervention with psychotherapy or counseling but, rather, recognize that they have conventionally been considered intimately related to some social work methods. Although we believe that evaluations of broad societal interventions conducted by professions allied with social work should be included in this analysis, no relevant experimental evalua-tions meeting our criteria are available. These case examples pre-sented were chosen because of their historical significance and also to provide the reader with a feel for evaluations.

The effectiveness of professional social work intervention has been a matter of concern for at least forty years. As long ago as 1931, Richard C. Cabot, in his presidential address to the Na-tional Conference on Social Work, urged the profession to begin assessing the results of its programs. Cabot not only admonished the profession for not undertaking evaluations but developed and financed the now famous Cambridge-Somerville Youth Study (Powers and Witmer, 1951), one of the first controlled studies evaluating the effectiveness of therapeutic interventions. Cabot based this study on the assumption that many delinquent or poten-tially delinquent boys would become constructive citizens if pro-vided with the continued friendship of adults who were deeply interested in them and who could secure for them needed commu-nity services. Thus, Cabot established an agency and engaged a staff of social workers to help a group of 325 six- to ten-year-old boys over an eight year period (1937–1945). An equal number of boys had been randomly assigned to a control group after having been matched on a large number of variables. Each boy in the ex-perimental group was assigned to one of ten social workers. The treatment offered was chosen by each counselor and ranged from being a big brother to conducting psychoanalytically oriented inter-views. During World War II, a shift toward orthodox child guid-ance center tactics occurred.

Since this was a study of delinquency prevention, its results were shown in the boys' delinquency records. During the course of the experiment, ninety-six experimental boys had court appearances for 264 offenses, while ninety-two control boys had court appear-ances for 218 offenses. This lack of difference between the experi-mental and control groups repeated itself on most other indicators of delinquency examined. The inescapable conclusion was that treat-ment did not reduce the incidence of adjudged delinquency. Of considerable interest in this study was the lack of correspondence between the measured outcome and the positive evaluations of the program made by the counselors and the boys. The counselors firmly believed that they had substantially aided about two-thirds of the boys; and more than half the boys at the terminal interview said they had been helped.

The results of the Cambridge-Somerville Youth Study, reported in 1951, appeared immediately prior to publication of an article by Eysenck (1952) in which he argued that no evidence proved psychotherapy with neurotics to be more effective than no treatment at all. Thus, he offered survey data showing that the expected recovery rate from psychoneurosis without psychotherapy was 72 per cent, compared with 64 per cent with eclectic treatment and 44 per cent with psychoanalysis. He concluded: "There thus appears to be an inverse correlation between recovery and psychotherapy; the more psychotherapy, the smaller the recovery rate" (p. 322).

In arriving at these conclusions, Eysenck reviewed five studies classified as psychoanalytic and nineteen studies classified as eclectic, contrasting them with recovery rates for neurotics receiving either custodial care or the care of a general physician. His report set off violent and stormy reactions; however, at the time, critics failed to produce contradictory evidence.

Levitt (1957) reported on children diagnosed as neurotic, eighteen evaluations being conducted at case closing and seventeen at follow-up. He compared these thirty-five studies with similar evaluations of untreated children and found that two-thirds of the children at closing and three-quarters at follow-up showed improvement. Roughly the same percentages were found for untreated control groups, leading Levitt to conclude that the results "fail to support the view that psychotherapy with 'neurotic' children is effective" (p. 195). In 1960, Eysenck revised his original study and, again reviewing the literature, became more firmly convinced of his earlier conclusions, no longer limiting them to neurotics. On the basis of four additional controlled studies he stated: "The results . . . show that whatever effects psychotherapy may have are likely to be extremely small. . . . It rather seems that psychologists and psychiatrists will have to acknowledge the fact that current psychotherapeutic procedures have not lived up to the hopes which greeted their emergence fifty years ago" (p. 720).

While the studies reviewed by Eysenck and Levitt were

primarily assessing the effectiveness of psychotherapy, comparable evaluations of social work were developing. In 1965, the Russell Sage Foundation published a report entitled *Girls at Vocational High: An Experiment in Social Work Intervention* (Meyer and others, 1965). The goals of the study presented were to determine whether potentially problematic subjects can be identified and helped before they develop problems, and the extent to which social casework is effective in prevention when applied to such subjects. The report describes a four-year experiment with New York City Vocational high school girls whose earlier performance and behavior at school pointed to potential delinquency. Various students were referred to an agency which offered them individual or group counseling services by professional social workers. A control group was selected from the same pool of potential problem cases so that girls who received services could be compared with similar girls who did not. One hundred and eighty-nine girls were assigned to the experimental group and 192 to the control group. Investigators examining the differences between the experimental and control groups in such areas as school completion, academic performance, school-related behavior, out-of-school behavior, and self-reports, stated: "We must conclude that, with respect to all of the measures we have used to examine effects of the treatment program, only a minimal effect can be found" (Meyer and others, 1965, p. 204). Nor was this minimal effect or difference between the groups of statistical significance.

This study sparked a controversy over the effectiveness of traditional social work counseling services. In the foreword to the report, Leonard S. Cottrell, Jr., of the Russell Sage Foundation asks, "Is social work on the wrong track?" and comments that "the issue is whether or not the social work profession can continue to maintain that the individual casework, clinical approach is its central method for dealing with the kinds of problems presented by the population dealt with in this experiment" (Meyer and others, 1965, pp. 3–4).

While *Girls at Vocational High* has been perhaps the most publicized and discussed evaluation of social work intervention, a close second is undoubtedly *The Chemung County Evaluation of*

Casework Service to Multiproblem Families (Brown, 1968), published one year after *Girls at Vocational High*. The Chemung County Study assessed the effects of intensive social casework on a group of fifty multiproblem families, in contrast with the effects of normal public assistance services given a control group of fifty similar families. The intensive service was given by experienced caseworkers who had earned the M.S.W. degree. Caseloads in the experimental group were limited to less than half the usual number carried by public assistance workers, and use of other community services was emphasized. The treatment phase ran thirty-one months. Evaluators found that while the experimental group attained a slightly better degree of family functioning, its margin of progress over the control group was not significant.

Some evaluators speculated that one reason the Chemung County Study failed was that it intervened in families already chronically dependent and multiproblem, that results might have been different if intervention had occurred earlier when the families began depending on public assistance. The Community Service Society of New York published the results of an experiment testing this belief (Mullen and others, 1970). In this experiment, the New York City Department of Social Services and the Community Service Society combined their resources to help approximately 100 families who, for the first time, were dependent on public assistance. In addition to financial and supportive assistance by the Department of Social Services, these families received social casework services from the Community Service Society. The objective was to demonstrate the effectiveness of a collaborative approach with newly dependent families to prevent individual and family disintegration, and to assist them in their economic, psychological, and social functioning. It was expected that this demonstration could facilitate the establishment of similar services for public assistance families on a larger scale.

A major concern in setting up the experiment was the rapidly increasing number of families and individuals becoming dependent on public economic assistance. It was feared that prolonged economic dependency would produce injurious effects in these individuals as well as in society and that, without counseling, many newly dependent families would be unable to cope with such effects. Eventually, it was assumed, many would enter a chronic state of economic, psychological, and social dysfunctioning.

Thus, one approach to the prevention of chronic dysfunctioning, in addition to the financial and material assistance provided by the Department of Social Services, would be professional casework service to help families cope with the situation that precipitated their need for public assistance and their new condition of economic dependence. It was believed that professional caseworkers, with their skills of psychological and family counseling, would help families with potential for economic independence achieve that independence and prevent disintegration during the crisis period.

Each of the four Community Service Society Family Service Centers was paired with a public Social Service Center covering the same geographical area. Each pair offered their combined services to approximately twenty-five families over a period of about fourteen months. To evaluate the project, an after-test experimental design was used. Families applying to the Department of Social Services for the first time were randomly assigned to either an experimental or contrast group. Families in the experimental group received both Community Service Society and Department of Social Services assistance, while families in the contrast group received only the normal Department of Social Services assistance. From November 1966 through December 1967, 118 families were assigned to the experimental service and eighty-two to the contrast service. At the close of the experiment, trained research interviewers interviewed each family at home, recording their self-reports in eleven areas. These self-reports were the primary source of data.

The hypothesis was that individuals and families in the experimental group would report more improvement or less deterioration or both in their economic and general psychosocial functioning during the course of the project and a more adequate level of functioning at the time of the research interview than would those in the contrast group. Twenty-seven specific hypotheses in eleven areas were examined in the investigation of this general hypothesis, and eighty-three specific comparisons were explored and taken as indicators of these twenty-seven hypotheses.

However, the evaluation did not validate the study hypothesis. The families in the experimental group, while functioning at a slightly higher level, were not functioning significantly better at the conclusion of this project than were those in the contrast group. Furthermore, the public-private collaboration initially envisioned did not occur as extensively as planned.

The response to these and a number of similar social work evaluations reported during the sixties stimulated calling the Fordham Symposium to assess the implications of these evaluations for social work education. The response to the invitation was indicative of the degree of widespread concern: over 125 universities and organizations directly involved in social work education attended and spent two days deliberating on the findings of thirteen evaluations, including the last three mentioned. The remaining ten evaluations were included in the symposium review for a total of thirteen reports. These thirteen evaluations are systematically reviewed in the following chapter. If we add to this list three additional reports (Krause and others, 1971; Olson, 1970; Wilson, 1967), we can bring under this review sixteen experimental studies of social work intervention—all originally reported during the 1960s and most since 1965.

Of these sixteen studies, nine (Behling, 1961; Brown, 1968; Geismar and others, 1970; Krause and others, 1971; Kühl, 1969; Mullen and others, 1970; Olson, 1970; Reid and Shyne, 1969; Wilson, 1967) can be roughly classified as having used the casework method as the primary intervention. Among these, some utilized M.S.W. caseworkers, while others used either a combination of M.S.W. and B.A. practitioners or B.A. practitioners only. Two (McCabe and others, 1967; Meyer and others, 1965) of the sixteen projects utilized casework and group methods as their primary intervention. In both instances, the group methods were employed by M.S.W. caseworkers. Three (Geismar and Krisberg, 1967; Marin, 1969; United Community Services of the Greater Vancouver Area, 1968–1969) of the sixteen studies used all three social work methods: casework, group work, and community organization. One additional study (Blenkner and others, 1964) used a combination of casework and public health nursing service, and the remaining project (Schwartz and Sample, 1970) used a team approach that included M.S.W.s, B.A.s, and individuals with less than a college level of education.

Another informative way of classifying these sixteen studies is by the target population, admittedly an ambiguous term. However, for our purposes, we classified these studies into four categories. The largest number, twelve, is concerned with the problems of a poverty population (Behling, 1961; Brown, 1968; Geismar and Krisberg, 1967; Kühl, 1969; Marin, 1969; McCabe and others, 1967; Meyer and others, 1965; Mullen and others, 1970; Olson, 1970; Schwartz and Sample, 1970; United Community Services of the Greater Vancouver Area, 1968–1969; Wilson, 1967); seven of these twelve (Behling, 1961; Brown, 1968; Marin, 1969; Mullen and others, 1970; Olson, 1970; Schwartz and Sample, 1970; Wilson, 1967) deal solely with individuals or families receiving public assistance. The thirteenth study (Geismar and others, 1970), intended to serve a group of families across socioeconomic levels, reports that the majority of families turned out to be of low socioeconomic status. Three of the studies (Blenkner and others, 1964; Krause and others, 1971; Reid and Shyne, 1969) deal with a range of families cutting across socioeconomic levels with at least two of these three composed primarily of middle-class families.

A final method for classifying these projects is according to results. At the risk of oversimplifying, the sixteen studies can be grouped into three categories in terms of overall success in supporting the major study hypotheses. Using this approach, we find that six of the sixteen (Blenkner and others, 1964; Brown, 1968; Krause and others, 1971; Marin, 1969; Meyer and others, 1965; Mullen and others, 1970) cannot statistically demonstrate overall support for the major study hypotheses (37.5 per cent). Three of these have already been commented on. Four of the sixteen (Behling, 1961; Geismar and Krisberg, 1967; Schwartz and Sample, 1970; Wilson, 1967) report general success in supporting the major hypotheses (25 per cent). The remaining six (Geismar and others, 1970; Kühl, 1969; McCabe and others, 1967; Olson, 1970; Reid and Shyne, 1969; United Community Services of the Greater Vancouver Area, 1968–1969) have mixed results (37.5 per cent); that is, the outcomes supported some of the predictions but not others, or while the overall results may have been either positive or negative, other factors modify the conclusions.* By matching outcome with method and type of population, we find no patterns that allow us to distinguish outcome by either methods employed or populations served. However, as Geismar notes, some positive and mixed outcome studies do offer interesting leads as to successful interventions.

We do want to take note of recent developments in evaluations of psychotherapeutic interventions. A third survey of published psychotherapeutic studies was reported by Eysenck (1965), this time including eleven controlled studies. His conclusions about the ineffectiveness of conventional psychotherapy had not changed, but new evidence was cited in favor of behavior therapy based on learning theory.

Truax and Carkhuff (1967), reviewing controlled outcome research concerning the effects of psychotherapy, note that "the weight of evidence, involving very large numbers of clients or therapists, suggests that the average effects of therapeutic intervention (with the average therapist or counselor) are approximately equivalent to the random effects of normal living without treatment" (p. 12). While Truax and Carkhuff arrive at rather negative conclusions, they do suggest that there is some evidence that certain exceptional therapists may be quite effective and urge that the work of such therapists be examined.

Meltzoff and Kornreich (1970) published a report that seems to contradict the Eysenck, Levitt, Truax and Carkhuff conclusions. They reviewed 101 separate investigations (plus twenty-five evaluations of therapeutic programs) and concluded that 80 per cent yielded positive results and 20 per cent yielded negative results. The authors consider only fifty-seven of these 101 studies to have used adequate research designs, and, of these, forty-eight showed statistically significant positive effects of psychotherapy. About half of the negative-result studies with adequate designs were failures of verbal therapies to bring about improvement

---

* The differences between our classification of outcome and that presented by Geismar in the following chapter are partially due to a difference in definition of outcome categories used in the two schemes as well as the number of studies included in each review. The general conclusions reached are similar.

in chronic schizophrenic patients, and another one-third were failures with delinquency, drug addiction, and enuresis. The reviewers conclude that, "far more often than not, psychotherapy of a wide variety of types and with a broad range of disorders has been demonstrated under controlled conditions to be accompanied by positive changes in adjustment that significantly exceed those that can be accounted for by the passage of time alone" (Meltzoff and Kornreich, 1970, p. 175).

Thus, the emerging picture of professional intervention is far from clear. The evidence does not definitely indicate that such intervention is effective or ineffective. We are now confronted with a large number of outcome evaluations and have not had the wisdom, skill, or time as professionals to assess and integrate their meaning. Our immediate task is to determine the reasons for our failures and the meaning of our successes. The subsequent chapters assess the implications of these findings.

Questions for Evaluators

Many projects fail to reach their goals because the following question has been inadequately considered: On what basis and toward what end will who do what to whom, for how long, with what effect, at what cost, and with what benefits? This criticism applies not only to the negative-outcome projects, but to many of those with positive outcomes as well, for even if the effects are judged to be positive, we are usually not sure why. Most of the positive-outcome studies did not adequately define and measure the nature of the interventions; thus, how are we to repeat or learn from successful programs?

On what basis? asks why the intervention is being under·taken, what assumptions are involved, what the theoretical underpinning is. We find that few studies clearly address themselves to this question but move ahead presuming an understanding and consensus.

Toward what end? asks what the specific targets for change are. What does the program hope to accomplish? What are its goals? How feasible are they, and to what extent are they mutually consistent?

Who? asks which individuals are best suited to deliver the particular intervention. Why this agency? Why a caseworker or a group worker or a psychiatrist or a public health nurse? Why not another agency or a paraprofessional or a friend or a local gatekeeper?

Do what? asks why this intervention and not another. Why a collaborative program, a family service program, a family-centered program, a neighborhood-centered program?

To whom? requests that we define our reasons for selecting a particular type of individual, family, group, neighborhood, or area for intervention. Why newly dependent welfare families? Why not underemployed working families? Why families in Harlem? Why not families in Chinatown? Why not a particular system or institution?

For how long? pinpoints the issue of time and asks should time limits be set. How soon will the change objectives be reached? How long must the program continue if it is to reach these objectives?

With what effect? asks what specific outcomes can be expected during the time set. What criteria of goal achievement can be observed?

At what cost and with what benefits? raises a value issue. Cost is usually the easiest part of the question to answer. However, a value decision normally needs to be made, namely, does the cost justify the projected benefits within the limits of priorities? What are the human costs, what unintended negative consequences may occur? How can benefits be assessed?

The studies reviewed answer these questions with varying degrees of thoroughness. Most avoid them or raise them only superficially. To the extent a particular project addressed itself to these points, to that extent can we have confidence in its results and benefit from its experience.

Micro-, Mezzo-, and Macrosystems

Microsystem problems are those in which the determining forces seem to be within the boundaries of either an individual or a small group directly experiencing the problem. In such cases, large social systems do not seem to play a significant determining role. The study conducted at the Community Service Society by Reid and Shyne (1969) provides excellent examples of families with microsystem problems. Such problems can be further classified as encompassing instrumental or expressive areas of functioning or both. Instrumental microsystem problems are those involving the maintenance or improvement of physical and environmental conditions and the means of attaining desirable goals (such as health and household practices and aspects of child care). Expressive microsystem problems refer to behavior aimed at the achievement of basic satisfactions and goals.

Mezzosystem problems are those in which the determining forces seem directly to involve not only human systems (individuals and small groups) but social systems (geographic localities such as neighborhoods and communities). Such problems intimately involve not only the people in these areas but also in a determining sense their institutions, structures, and processes. Excellent examples of promising interventions with mezzosystem problems are the Vancouver Area Development Project (United Community Services of the Greater Vancouver Area, 1968–1969) and the New Haven Neighborhood Improvement Project (Geismar and Krisberg, 1967).

Macrosystem problems are those in which the critical determining factors extend beyond given individuals, groups, or localities and, as Walter Walker notes in Chapter Six, occur on the broadest level of social organization involving large geographically scattered populations. None of the evaluations reviewed offers examples of interventions on this level.

This classification of problems assumes a systems framework and artificially establishes relative parameters which are not readily apparent in actual situations. An excellent discussion of system levels within the context of general systems theory is presented by Boulding (1956) and Miller (1965, 1970). The term *level* appears often in the systems literature. Boulding developed a general typology which presented nine levels of systems—each representing a higher order of complexity. In general, the term level refers to the complexity of the system process. In Boulding's framework each new level of system presents a fundamental characteristic which is added to the structure or the dynamics of the system process. A system has been defined as "a complex of elements in mutual interaction" (Allport, 1960, p. 302) or "a set of objects together with relationships between the objects and between their attributes" (Hall and Fagen, 1956, p. 18).

Macrosystem and mezzosystem problems do have an impact on microsystems, and, therefore, to say that a situation represents a macrosystem or a mezzosystem problem is also to say that there are usually individuals needing assistance. However, their situation should not be defined as caused by them or under their personal control. Most unsuccessful studies failed to clarify the nature of the target problems and often seemed to equate microsystem with mezzo- or macrosystem problems. The successful outcomes seem to have occurred where the nature of the problem was appropriately viewed. For example, the CSS-DSS Study (Mullen and others, 1970), in our opinion, did not appropriately perceive the target problem, but defined a macrosystem problem as a microsystem problem and intervened accordingly. No relevant difference in outcome among the evaluations of microsystem, mezzosystem, or macrosystem problems occurred when they were appropriately defined. Rather, given an appropriate problem definition, differential outcomes seem dependent on the nature of the interventions, which may be classified as those using microsystem influence, mezzosystem influence, or a combination of both.

Projects using conventional psychological methods such as those developed within traditional social casework or traditional psychoanalytic method and concerned with microsystem problems produced discouraging outcomes in relation to the goals cited. Successful outcomes associated with microsystem influence are reported in projects using interventions that were time limited and task structured and were focused on explicit target problems. With such interventions, target problems are located, are agreed to by both the intervener and intervenee (sometimes only implicitly), and are judged to be achievable given the resources of the two. Further, these interventions seem almost exclusively devoted to problem reduction, even though the client's behavior or his situation may need to undergo change in order to alleviate the problem. These target problems also seem to be relatively limited and specific in nature. A time limit involves two considerations: it structures the task, and it assumes most change in such problems occurs rather rapidly and that extended intervention reaches a point of diminishing or negative returns.

Task-structured intervention implies that an intervener and intervenee agree to a specific task or set of tasks; the intervener's role becomes one of facilitating the intervenee's achievement of that task (Reid, 1971). This approach to microsystem influence is approached in a Community Service Society study, the Casework Methods Project (Reid and Shyne, 1969), and seems to characterize some behavioral modification models. Changes achieved in these models seem to lie for the most part in the instrumental areas of functioning rather than in expressive areas (Geismar, 1971). In those projects appropriately using mezzosystem interventions, the most promising interventions are characterized by multiservices occurring in the midst of relevant forces (such as neighborhood forces), utilizing a variety of levels of trained staff, and occurring within a systems frame of reference (Geismar and Krisberg, 1967).

Therefore, we need to further refine and develop appropriate paradigms of microsystem influence for problems whose determining forces primarily encompass individuals or small groups. We also need to develop appropriate mezzosystem and macrosystem interventions for broad social system problems. This is the challenge of today. The social welfare field and its associated professions must move from a fixed service delivery stance to one characterized by experimentation, model development, and evaluation. As Cabot challenged over forty years ago, "Let us criticize and reform ourselves before a less gentle and appreciative body takes us by the shoulders and pushes us into the street" (1931, p. 24).

2

Thirteen
Evaluative Studies

Ludwig L. Geismar

This book is one of the daring professional endeavors, for here we have the unusual spectacle of a helping profession willing to risk itself—and helping professions as a group are not noted for a readiness to put their reputations on the line—by examining the evidence available at this time on the outcome of its work. The profession is taking two risks. It is exposing the vast and well-institutionalized undertaking of social work to critical scrutiny when the results could prove unfavorable, and it is uncovering the armamentarium of evaluation, which may turn out to be feeble or invalid.

The total scientific effort has been modest in scope as the small amount of adequate research ruled out the necessity for a sampling technique. Though small, the number of experimental evaluations represents a substantial advance in scientific productivity over what existed in the early 1960s (Lagey and Ayres, 1962). The projects dealt with in this book are not necessarily the best or com-

15

pletely representative of all such endeavors published and unpublished, but they reflect fairly well the state of the art in the sixties. Thus, Wyatt Jones, Edgar Borgatta, and James Breedlove, in the following two chapters, take a critical look at the methodology that has been employed in social work research and propose new approaches suited to the complex changes accompanying programs of intervention. Whatever the shortcomings of the studies reviewed here, and Jones, Borgatta, and Breedlove note that the authors themselves were conscious of the hazards of the methodologies and cognizant of the limitations of the studies, they still convey a substantive message to the profession in general and social work education in particular.

The Projects

Area Development Project (ADP) (United Community Services of the Greater Vancouver Area, 1968–1969). This study investigated the so-called multiproblem families who constituted about 3 per cent of the families of Vancouver, British Columbia, but who required a disproportionate share of the public and private health and welfare services in the community. The problems involved socioeconomic deprivation and human distress, and the project was carried out under the auspices of the United Community Services, financial support coming from the national and provincial governments and several private foundations. Project families were located in a predominantly lower-class neighborhood of the city. United Community Services collaborated with local health and welfare agencies to improve the families' social functioning through a multiservice program and the coordination of community services for multiproblem families.

A coordinated three-year program of casework, group work, and neighborhood and community organization services was extended to ninety-two multiproblem families selected from the rosters of community agencies. The basis for the selection was past service from these agencies indicating that there were severe and chronic family difficulties. These families were compared on outcome with 122 control families who were given the ordinary community services. Assignment to the two groups was made by random selection. The experimental treatment services were rendered by social workers loaned to the project by local cooperating agencies. They carried reduced caseloads. The results of the project, as assessed by the St. Paul Scale of Family Functioning, showed that integrated and multifaceted services were significantly more effective than the usual agency services in five out of eight areas of social functioning.

Casework Methods Project (CMP) (Reid and Shyne, 1969). This study contrasted two structures for the interpersonal treatment of complex psychosocial problems: continued, or open-ended, service (CS) and planned short-term service (PSTS). The subjects were intact families who came voluntarily to the agency. The study occurred at the Community Service Society (CSS) of New York City. The project was a collaborative undertaking by the CSS Department of Family Services (now known as the Department of Program Operations) and the CSS Institute of Welfare Research (now known as the Department of Research and Evaluation), and received federal financial support. Tested was the widely held assumption that extended services, based on psychoanalytic theory, are more likely to meet the needs of these clients than is short-term treatment that rests on no special theories but is basically an abbreviated version of long-term treatment.

The two services were furnished to 120 families, first-time applicants to the agency, relatively young, and generally free of gross psychopathology. The project families were assigned randomly to either the brief or extended treatment programs. The mean number of interviews was seven for PSTS and twenty-six for CS. The worker-client exchanges had a psychosocial focus with emphasis on the functioning of the client and others in family roles. By and large, the two treatment approaches did not differ sharply with regard to the use of casework techniques, although the brief treatment tended to extensive use of direction. Results were measured, in part, by the analysis of tape-recorded interviews by research observers, caseworkers, and clients; the evaluation occurred during the treatment and a six-month follow-up period. Sixteen key ratings were chosen covering changes in family problems, functioning of family members, quality of various aspects of family life, and so forth. Short-term service clients exhibited more favorable outcomes than did open-ended service clients, with some statistically significant differences. In the absence of a true control group, no conclusion could be reached as to the absolute effectiveness of the service, although the change data, particularly on the brief service cases, suggest more positive outcomes than do some other social work evaluations. This study also examined differences in process and outcome between the modifying and supportive methods of casework as well as between single- and multiple-client interviews; however no meaningful differences were found.

Chemung County Study (Brown, 1968). The question in this study (similar to that in the Area Development Project) was whether professional caseworkers have greater success than untrained workers in rehabilitating multiproblem families on public assistance. Chemung County, New York, whose principal city is Elmira (population 50,000) was the setting of the project, which, with federal funds, was completed by the State Communities Aid Association and the County of Chemung Department of Social Services. Its goal was improvement in the families' social functioning through the intensive casework services of professional social workers.

The intensive casework services were judged by experts to be "slightly above average for regular assistance workers and slightly below average for trained caseworkers" (p. 14). Caseworkers made twice as many contacts with families in the demonstration program as with families in the control group. Median weeks of service were ninety-eight for the demonstration and ninety-six for the control groups. The research subjects were families on public assistance who had previously received services from several agencies for an extended time period. Each of the 150 participating families was randomly assigned to a treatment group, a before-after control group, or an after-only (hidden) control group. Before and after measurement (and after measurement of the hidden control group) was based on the St. Paul Scale of Family Functioning, used independently by two coding teams, and the CSS Movement Scale. All forms of measurement yielded essentially similar results: the demonstration group showed a small but statistically nonsignificant margin of improvement over the control groups.

Community Service Society of New York–New York City Department of Social Services Collaborative Demonstration Project (CSS-DSS Study) (Mullen and others, 1970). This study was concerned with the psychosocial and economic situation of new public assistance families. The Community Service Society (CSS) of New York and the New York City Department of Social Services (DSS) collaborated to help a group of New York City families dependent for the first time on public assistance. The goal was to demonstrate the effectiveness of a joint approach in preventing individual and family disorganization and in assisting families to achieve economic independence and an adequate level of psychosocial functioning.

DSS supplied the conventional income maintenance and other basic services, and CSS provided professional casework counseling. An experimental group of 105 families and a control group of sixty-eight families, randomly assigned from the caseloads of a number of DSS district offices, received service for a maximum of fourteen months. A public assistance worker and a professionally trained CSS caseworker jointly aided the experimental group families. Routine public assistance service was given the control group cases. An after test, using structured interviews in the homes of the study families, provided the evaluative data on the psychosocial and economic changes of these families; included in the evaluation were the clients' assessments of their changes. The interview questionnaire contained scales as well as discrete items. Although four of eighty-three comparisons showed significant differences in the expected direction (three of these four showed that more experimental than control families reported receiving professional and organizational help during the previous fourteen months, items thought to reflect CSS service), the evaluation as a whole did not support the hypothesis postulating better functioning for the experimental families.

A Comprehensive Program for Multiproblem Families (Marin, 1969). The focus of this study was similar to that of the Area Development Project and the Chemung County Study, namely, multiproblem families, but in a different cultural setting, Puerto Rico. The multiproblem families had been receiving continued child welfare services without apparent rehabilitation or solution of problems. A demonstration center administered by the Division of Public Welfare of Puerto Rico, and located in San Juan, was the project setting. The study, a collaboration of the Division of Public Welfare and the School of Social Work of the University of Puerto Rico, was financed in part by a federal grant.

The goal was to use family-centered treatment as a means of bringing about significant changes in the social functioning of the multiproblem families.

Family-centered services, including casework, group work, and community organization, were extended over a two-year period to 120 experimental group families. These had been chosen randomly from a pool of 240 active cases, recipients of continued child welfare services for five years or more in the metropolitan area of San Juan. The other 120 families were assigned to the control group and received the regular services of the Division of Public Welfare. Methods of evaluation taking the form of before-after tests (except for half the control group which received after-only measurement) covered seventy-seven different variables of an objective as well as subjective nature, including attitude scales and projective tests. Although more treatment families showed positive than negative change and more change variables appeared in the positive than the negative column, differences between the experimental and control groups failed to support the hypothesis of greater effectiveness of the demonstration program.

Experimental Study to Measure the Effectiveness of Casework Service (Behling, 1961). The problem of concern in this study was chronic dependence of individuals and families on relief. The setting was the Welfare Department of Franklin County, Ohio, which administers economic assistance to destitute residents of Columbus and Franklin County. The study was done in collaboration with Ohio State University and was presented as a doctoral thesis in the Department of Sociology and Anthropology. The project goal was the achievement of improved psychological and social well-being through intensive casework services to public assistance clients.

The program consisted of intensive casework, defined as services rendered to a small caseload (about fifty cases—roughly half the size of the usual public assistance load), given to two hundred public assistance cases over a fifteen-month period. The study sample consisted of four hundred clients (70 per cent of whom were families) who were assigned, two hundred each, to experimental and control groups through a matching procedure utilizing twelve demographic and service factors. Control group cases received the routine services of the department. Experimental group workers were selected on the basis of their representativeness of the total staff of public assistance workers. Measurement by means of the CSS Movement Scale supported the major study hypothesis postulating greater movement or improvement of a social and psychological nature in the experimental group as compared with the control group. Differences were statistically significant. Contrary to expectations, greater positive change was also associated with greater relief costs and more cases receiving assistance in the treatment group.

Rutgers Family Life Improvement Project (FLIP) (Geismar and others, 1970). The apparently limited effectiveness of remedial casework intervention stimulated this project to test preventive intervention as a means to help young families cope with developmental problems and the difficulties of urban living. The setting was Newark, New Jersey, in an agency operated by the Graduate School of Social Work of Rutgers University. The five-year operation was federally financed and housed in the building of the Child Service Association of Newark. The project goal was to moderate a trend toward social malfunctioning during the early years of young families.

The program encompassed giving information, advice, advocacy, counseling in interpersonal problems, vocational guidance, assistance in finding jobs and housing, and so forth, with each service pattern adapted to the specific needs and problems of a particular family. The study sample, 555 young Newark families with a first child born in 1964 or before April 30, 1965, was selected randomly from the Vital Statistics Register and divided evenly into treatment and control groups. One hundred and seventy-seven treatment group families and 175 control group families finished the five-year project. The treatment and evaluation period extended over three years. Measurement with the aid of the St. Paul Scale of Family Functioning applied through a panel technique of interviewing (carried out at periodic intervals) revealed greater improvement or less deterioration in social functioning in the treatment group in seven out of eight areas. Child care, health practices, and housing showed statistically significant differences, but total score changes were not statistically significant. Other indices measuring changes in the families' social and economic status were, for the most part, in the hypothesized direction but not statistically significant.

Familycenter Project (Kühl, 1969). The concern of this project was multiproblem families in Copenhagen, characterized as a group by greater social and legal deviance than most North American samples reported in the literature. The Danish National Institute of Social Research directed this two-year project, which was financed by the city of Copenhagen. Services to the treatment group were rendered at a family center by a team of social workers under the direction of a psychologist. The goal was the social rehabilitation of multiproblem families by a sociopedagogical effort.

The investigation included 140 families with at least two children under eighteen who met one or more of the selection criteria—a record of public support, problem children, and deviant parental behavior. Seventy families assigned to the service group were matched with seventy so-called social twins for sex and age of head of household, education, number of children, and types of problems. Assignments to either the experimental or control group were done by random procedure. Families in the experimental group were seen by members of the family center team, whose service included giving advice and support, coordinating the families' dealings with social agencies, alleviating pressing problems, and making efforts to modify client attitudes toward children, work, and community resources. Before-and-after outcome measurement was based on a rating of functioning in eleven areas of family life. The researchers found moderate improvement spread over most areas of social functioning, but major improvement was registered only in employment and housing. The total movement for the experimental group showed that they experienced greater improvement than the control group at the 7 per cent level of statistical significance.

Girls at Vocational High (Meyer and others, 1965). This project focused on adolescent girls with school problems who were psychologically troubled, unmanageable at home, and prone to engage in deviant behavior. The New York Youth Consultation Service (YCS), working in collaboration with a New York vocational high school, provided the setting for the treatment program. The Russell Sage Foundation furnished the scientific direction, assisted by the faculty and students of New York University, as well as financial support (with the help of other foundations). By means of casework and group counseling services, the project aimed to help the girls adjust and lessen their deviant behavior.

Potential problem cases among four groups of girls entering a vocational high school were identified. Experimental and control cases were selected by random procedure, and, over the course of the four-year research, 189 girls were referred for service at YCS and studied, while 192 control cases were only studied. Services consisted of casework and group work with an increasing emphasis on the latter as the program progressed. Evaluation was based on a large array of data including academic performance, conduct at school, out-of-school behavior, health record, out-of-wedlock pregnancies, various attitude scales, personality tests, and sociometric information. Treatment cases were also studied by means of a variety of client-rating procedures including the CSS Movement Scale. The results showed that the services provided the experimental cases had little impact, and only a few of the differences between the experimental and control subjects were statistically significant.

Midway Project (Schwartz and Sample, 1970). This study dealt with chronic shortages and ineffective use of professional social workers in public assistance. It was conducted at the Midway Research and Training District Office, operated jointly by the School of Social Service Administration of the University of Chicago and the Cook County Department of Public Aid. The project, which received federal financial support, aimed to upgrade client functioning by improving staff attitudes and upgrading performance as the result of improved utilization of available social workers.

The research program, which lasted twenty-six months, tested four patterns of service delivery. The first pattern, the work group form of organization, was based on the traditional worker-supervisor relationship, and the group was served by a central filing and clerical staff. The second pattern was an experimental team operating as an autonomous unit, served by a unit clerk, with specialization of team members and restructured responsibilities of workers and supervisors. Each type of work organization employed Plan A and Plan B of service: Plan A, with ninety cases per worker, concentrated on financial need and crisis situations and only residually on counseling and rehabilitation; Plan B, with forty-five cases, focused not only on financial assistance but also on many other services needed by the client. Out of 314 clients in the project receiving a year or more of services, 163 were families, and the rest were individuals. An additional 261 cases, with less than a year of service, were included in the initial and follow-up study. Supervisors and work loads were randomly distributed.

The effects of the program on volume of work, worker activity, and morale were measured by work statistics and attitude scales. Findings, by and large, favored the experimental team in regard to morale in Plan A as well as the combined results of Plans A and B; and members of teams also tended to show a high level of activity in Plan B, but not in Plan A. However, these results were not statistically significant. Outcome data, obtained by a specially designed schedule covering eighteen areas of individual and family functioning, indicated that clients served by experimental teams showed greater improvement or less deterioration than those served by conventional work groups. Differences were statistically significant (the researchers defined significance as rejection of the null hypothesis at the 10 per cent level) for all clients under Plan A and Plan B separately and in combination and for individual clients under Plan A and families under Plan B. Work groups having both the team form of organization and low caseloads effected greater client change than did groups having one or neither of these advantages, although the team form of organization alone produced more than 90 per cent of the benefits obtained through the caseload reduction program (Schwartz and Sample, 1967) and produced superior results over the reduced caseload approach at a lower financial cost.

New Haven Neighborhood Improvement Project (NIP) (Geismar and Krisberg, 1967). This study, like several of the previously reviewed studies, focused on the lower-class, multiproblem family living in a low-income housing project, in this instance the Farnam Courts Housing Project of New Haven, Connecticut. The study was sponsored by the Community Council of Greater New Haven and financially supported by federal funds and local foundations. It hoped to improve the social functioning of Farnam Courts residents in general and the most malfunctioning families in particular. NIP, over a three-year period, sought to effect these changes through various services, including open-door casework for all residents, intensive casework for problematic families, a nursery school for all preschoolers, a youth neighborhood center, scout and 4H activities, social and educational activities for adults (including English and Spanish classes), a senior citizens' group, neighborhoodwide cultural events and entertainment, and community organizational activities.

Systematic evaluation by means of an experimental-control design was extended to only thirty problematic families in Farnam Courts and to a matched group of fifty-one of the most problematic AFDC families living in other low-cost housing projects and not receiving NIP-type services. The St. Paul Scale of Family Functioning was applied to the treatment group at the beginning of the study and at three six-month intervals, and to the control group at the start of the research and at two nine-month intervals; thus, the evaluation period covered eighteen months. Treatment families had improved in family functioning over nearly seven scale steps on the average (mean per family) at the final evaluation. Control group cases registered a one-step rise over the first nine-month period, then a drop of three-quarters of a scale step, resulting in a net gain of one-quarter of a scale step. The differences were statistically highly significant. However, a comparison between Farnam Courts and comparable housing projects on changes in delinquency rates and the economic dependency of residents produced inconclusive results.

Pursuit of Promise (McCabe and others, 1967). This project was concerned with the intellectually superior slum-bred child who stands little chance of living up to his potential because of the handicaps inherent in his environment. The study involved six elementary schools near the East Harlem Demonstration Center of the Community Service Society (CSS) Department of Public Affairs. The project, evaluated by the CSS Department of Research and Evaluation, aimed to improve or lessen the deterioration of the scholastic and social functioning of these children.

The children were selected on the basis of various intelligence tests from grades two to four and assigned randomly to either an experimental or a control group. The project lasted a little over three years, and forty-two children in the experimental and twenty-five children in the control group completed it. The program of intervention for the experimental group included group activities designed to strengthen their egos, help them to identify with successful adults, and promote educational achievement and aspirations; discussions with the parents to engage their support of the program and of the educational goals of their children; and casework services to encourage group attendance and help with practical problems. Events such as open houses for parents and children developed a family frame of reference for the program. The before-after design of the study utilized fifty-eight measures, twenty-eight of which were concerned with intellectual, academic, or ego functioning; twenty-two reflected parental functioning; and eight dealt with functioning of the family as a whole. Statistical analysis revealed significant differences in reading ability for both black and Puerto Rican children (there were too few whites to merit separate analysis) in the experimental group. On one ego scale (soundness of judgment), black children in the control group showed significantly greater change. By and large, Puerto Rican youngsters in the experimental group scored greater gains than did their counterparts in the control group. The reverse was true for black children, although both black experimental and control subjects improved their scores during the study period. For Puerto Rican mothers and fathers, experimental-control differences were not statistically significant and relative gains favored sometimes one group and sometimes the other. In family functioning there was but one statistical difference (degree of organization) in favor of black controls only, while other measures gave an edge to both the Puerto Rican experimental group and the black control group. The investigator attributed the unexpectedly good showing of black control subjects to the effect of forces beyond the control of the experimentor.

Serving the Aging (Blenkner and others, 1964). The concern of this study was the inadequate services for the aging in the metropolis. The setting was the Community Service Society (CSS) of New York City, and the research was directed by the CSS Department of Research and Evaluation with financial support from a private foundation. Several modes of service to the aging were compared with respect to their effect upon recipients and their relative benefit versus no service.

From the noninstitutionalized population aged sixty and over in three boroughs of New York City, two samples were drawn, one consisting of applicants for agency service (within a specified period), the other nonapplicants. Three hundred and thirty-two cases were selected by random sampling and stratified random sampling and assigned to three types of service: 142 to DO service, an ongoing service without time limitation at one of the CSS district offices; 139 to Special Services for the Aging (SSA) Short-Term Service, given at the central offices of the agency and limited to four in-person interviews over a two-month period; and forty-two to SSA Collaborative Service, also provided at the central offices but without time or interview limits and involving collaboration between a caseworker and a public health nurse. The latter two represent the experimental programs in the present study. Information on the participant sample was compared with that on the 133 nonparticipants six months after the treatment period. Most of the data on which the evaluation study is based were collected over a two-year period.

Change during service, evaluated by the CSS Movement Scale, gave a slight edge to SSA Short-Term Service over the DO and the SSA Collaborative Service. Outcome at follow-up, based on physical and mental health, mortality, morale, satisfaction, adjustment, social participation, and so forth, does not support the hypothesis that either experimental program is demonstrably superior to the DO service. On only some variables did the participants of one program or another attain the normative level of problems or functioning of the aged as determined by measurement of the nonapplicant population. In view of the greater problemicity of the applicant population at the start of the study, this finding cannot be interpreted to denote failure of the programs; but the exact meaning of the results is unclear.

Method and Theory

Experimental Designs. One must distinguish in these thirteen studies between those which used a more or less classical experimental-control design and those which used an alterntaive. The classical design is not the only method of scientifically evaluating outcome; in fact, as Jones and Borgatta indicate in Chapter Three, the experimental-control design has limitations as a measure of program outcome. It does, nevertheless, have the advantage of tightness of control, which some of the other traditional evaluative techniques lack.

In these thirteen studies, only four used the classical experimental design in which an experimental or treatment group is compared with a control or untreated group by means of a before-and-after evaluation. The studies following this pattern closely were Girls at Vocational High, Pursuit of Promise, Serving the Aging, and Family Life Improvement Project (FLIP). All the remaining projects save one, the Casework Methods Project, employed what has come to be known as the comparative design (Kahn, 1960), an adaptation of the classical experimental design to the conditions prevailing in program research in the helping professions. The comparative design is resorted to where ethical considerations preclude depriving people of needed service or where it is impossible to locate groups that have not received some form of service. The use of the comparative design, which employs comparison or contrast groups (Kahn, 1960), can be justified by arguing that the significance of experimental results can be appraised by comparing an experimental program with a conventional one rather than with a situation, held atypical in any case, in which no service is rendered. This argument makes certain assumptions regarding the utility or nonutility of existing services. The projects employing the comparative design did so because access to cases for purposes of sampling, interviewing, observation, and collection of data required using the auspices of an organization rendering some form of service to every case.

The Casework Methods Project used an alternate service design, a modification of the comparative design, the difference merely being one of degree. The comparative design contrasts an experimental program wtih a conventional one which seems to have little desirable input. The traditional programs are public assistance services, statutory programs generally requiring an eligibility review, means test, and periodic visits by untrained investigators. The essential service component is the monetary grant—usually far from adequate. Other transactions in the conventional service are designed to protect the agency or society more than the client; thus, this service appears to fulfil only the bare minimum legal requirements.

The situation is quite different in the alternate service design, which, in the CMP, involved contrasting the usual agency service with an innovative helping approach thought to offer certain advantages of speed and economy. The latter, far from being seen as a minimal investment in the client, was even more effective in bringing about client change than was the usual agency service.

The use of the alternate service design in the aforementioned study (though it does not detract from the value of the practice research; in fact, this project is among the most rigorously designed and executed in the field of social work) makes evaluation of outcome difficult, for no conventional baseline exists against which to assess results. That is a pity, for the less systematic evidence suggests that the degree of positive outcome registered is greater than it is in many other studies using the same or comparable instruments (Reid and Shyne, 1969).

Theoretical Frameworks. Although social researchers tend to distinguish between theoretical and evaluative research (the former testing hypotheses relevant to some larger body of theory and the latter assessing the practical value of some action program) (Hyman, 1955; Suchman, 1967), the distinction is mainly one of emphasis rather than of quality. The objective of theoretical research is to gather knowledge regardless of whether this knowledge has immediate practical application. Evaluative research "is more likely to be aimed at achieving some practical goal—its major emphasis is upon utility" (Suchman, 1967, p. 75).

Advocates of evaluative research rarely play down the importance of theory in evaluation studies. Serious investigators are not likely to look upon their endeavor as a purely ad hoc undertaking with no rationale for applying a particular set of actions or with no effort to tie their work to that of others. The difference is usually in the range and depth of the theory guiding the study and the degree of explicitness with which propositions have been related to alternate outcomes. In evaluative research, theory must bear upon the relationship between the condition of the population studied and the experimental program to be employed. In other words, the investigator supports a given program and bases his claim that the results will be more favorable than those from no program (or a conventional program) upon a causal relationship between that intervention (the independent variable) and some desired effect (the dependent variable) (Suchman, 1967). The statement should take the form of interrelated, conceptually based propositions explaining the connection between the planned intervention and the desired outcome.

Harold Lewis, in Chapter Five, distinguishes between theory of *what* or *what for*—or knowledge at a low level of organization—and theory on *how to do*. He argues that the latter is the concern of a practical science such as social work, but that the former needs to be related systematically to *how to do* statements. We shall set aside the question of whether knowledge used in the formulation of practice ever attains theory status; professional knowledge can be ordered on a continuum in terms of level of conceptualization, extent of interrelatedness of constructs, and power to explain or predict or both.

Whether sets of propositions guiding social work evaluation research are placed high enough on the continuum to merit the term *theory* is a question of definition. The designation, used here in its broadest sense, indicates the minimal presence of the following conditions: a symbolic construction (Kaplan, 1964) whose component parts (concepts, propositions) are interrelated and permit a specifying of relations among variables for the purpose of explaining a phenomenon (Kerlinger, 1964). Most writers prefer to say theoretical framework or background rather than theory per se. In the following discussion, theory usually means these formulations and occasionally more ambitious ones.

The theoretical content of the thirteen studies was usually the *how to do* type. The level of sophistication of practice theory applied varied considerably from one project to the next, but each research endeavor addressed itself, in one form or another, to the following: the problem and indices of that problem; the method of coping with the problem, either no action or use of conventional techniques; the relationship of the present coping method to the problem, although there was rarely any attempt to relate method to specifics such as incidence and prevalence of the problem; the new experimental program and how it differed from the existing coping methods; and a prediction, with or without formal hypotheses, as to how the experimental program would affect the problem.

While all the evaluation research efforts were addressed to the foregoing issues, some were more explicit than others in reporting the experimental program. The Area Development Project produced the most detailed information, such as separate monographs on planned and on actual service input in the experimental group. Girls at Vocational High furnished descriptions of treatment philosophy and experiences, as did the Neighborhood Improvement Project and Pursuit of Promise. The most systematic data comparing treatment with control groups are given in Serving the Aging and the Casework Methods Project. The Chemung County Study also contrasted treatment and control group services, but only on a limited number of service variables (Brown, 1968). The Midway Project, devoted to improving services by means of innovative organizational processes, furnished comparative data on manpower, staff turnover, absence rate, staff morale, interview counts, and other factors related to the organization and administration of the experimental and conventional programs. The Family Life Improvement Project (Geismar and others, in press) presented detailed information on input in the treatment group only. This study, together with Girls at Vocational High and Pursuit of Promise, reported little on services to their respective control groups as these were designed to be untreated and were assumed to lack any services comparable to those given the experimental group. The remaining research projects described the treatment variable and presented a rationale for its presumed greater effectiveness over other treatment and nontreatment approaches.

Regarding the use of theory of the *what* or *what for* kind in these studies, the researcher was confronted with an issue facing all social work practice, namely, the utilization of theory, covering the behavior of individuals, groups, and organizations, for the development of practice. Kadushin (1959) writes that the knowledge base of social work is mainly borrowed, lacks consistent conceptualization, is not cumulative in nature, and has not been subjected to systematic efforts at validation. Some progress was made on these points during the sixties, but this statement still has to be considered fundamentally correct. Professional knowledge in social work, as in other helping professions, will largely always be borrowed, for it deals with human behavior; numerous academic disciplines have developed expertise and resources for generating knowledge of human behavior which exceed those of the helping professions. Much of this knowledge is poorly suited for practice purposes; thus, social work must promote interdisciplinary efforts to develop the most appropriate body of knowledge. The lack of consistent conceptualization forces social work to select bits and pieces which are relevant to its problem-solving efforts. The studies reviewed here are attempts to develop knowledge beyond the early stage of scientific endeavor characterized by noncumulativeness and lack of validation.

These thirteen projects delineated the nature of the problem but did not so clearly explain its roots, relationship to other variables, change over time, and so forth. Where theory is applied explicitly, it is borrowed from one or more other disciplines; for instance, Pursuit of Promise drew on Heinz Hartman's and Erik H. Erikson's theories of ego development, the Family Center Project utilized deviance theory applied to the family, the Midway Study employed organization theory, and the Family Life Improvement Project used formulations of the developmental approach to family study and structural-functional theory. Other projects drew on conceptual frameworks identified with psychiatry and social work, such as crisis theory in the CSS-DSS Study and psychoanalytic theory in the Casework Methods Project. This latter project was unique in that its experimental program—planned short-term treatment— rested on no theories of personality, change, or intervention different from those in the conventional treatment given to the comparison group (Reid and Shyne, 1969). The investigators in the Girls at Vocational High study approached their experiment in pragmatic terms, employing the treatment philosophy and methods of the agency and postponing consideration of the theoretical relevance of the program until completion of the study. They chose the theoretically most appropriate indices of change by considering a wide range of explicit and implicit outcomes (Meyer and others, 1965).

A coherent theoretical framework is important for interpreting results, adding them to an existing fund of knowledge and providing a basis for various studies to cross-validate each other's findings. However, the use of systematic theory does not guarantee meaningful results unless it can be translated into an adequate research methodology.

Measurement. Evaluation researchers sometimes divide themselves into advocates of objective versus subjective indices of change (Sussman, 1966), also referred to as hard, or tough, versus soft, or tender-minded, data (Kogan and Shyne, 1966). The former means measurements obtained through objectively verifiable methods such as counting phenomena, events, and vital statistics. The latter uses psychosocial tests, which are analyzed for coding. The argument, as Kogan and Shyne point out, can never be resolved in favor of one approach or the other, but has to be dealt with by considering the specific requirements of each study.

By and large, the research projects before us chose the path of diversified measurement—most pronounced in Girls at Vocational High, which, for reasons discussed above, chose a wide selection of change indices ranging from completion of school and out-of-wedlock pregnancies at one end of the objective-subjective continuum to ratings on the CSS Movement Scale and social workers' comments on the client's future adjustment at the other. Almost as wide a variety of objective and subjective measurement was employed in Pursuit of Promise, Serving the Aging, the CSS-DSS Study, and the Comprehensive Program for Multiproblem Families.

No study put all its eggs into one measurement basket, but several selected one instrument as the major dependent change variable for testing the major hypothesis and added other indices, usually of the hard data variety, to test related hypotheses. The major instrument was, in most cases, a scale developed elsewhere and subjected to a fair degree of prior reliability and validity testing. Thus, Serving the Aging and the Experimental Study to Measure the Effectiveness of Casework Service relied mainly on the CSS Movement Scale, whereas the Neighborhood Improvement Project, the Area Development Project, the Family Life Improvement Project, and the Chemung County Study used the St. Paul Scale of Family Functioning. The Chemung County Study also employed the CSS instrument to validate the findings of the St. Paul Scale of Family Functioning. Girls at Vocational High used the CSS Scale as an accessory in the evaluation of change in individuals.

Most of the thirteen research projects engaged in some instrument construction, usually of an uncomplicated nature. The present group of studies, like earlier research endeavors in social work, did not emphasize the systematic study of client attitudes as an index of change. Although clients' views were part of the evaluation, direct measurement of client attitudes was the exception rather than the rule. This stance is rather surprising since practice has become increasingly client centered (Sacks and others, 1970). The CSS-DSS Study, the Casework Methods Project, Serving the Aging, Pursuit of Promise, and Girls at Vocational High went further than the others in making clients' self-evaluation of change a key variable in the assessment of outcome.

The reluctance of some projects to base evaluation on the clients' attitudes about changes resulting from the program does not necessarily point to conservative research methods. There is a general lack of agreement between clients and practitioners in assessing treatment outcome (Ballard and Mudd, 1958; Geismar and others, 1970; Kogan, 1957; Kogan and others, 1953; Sacks and others, 1970; Shyne, 1959; Siegel, 1965). Thus, investigators facing various methodological problems may have decided to resolve this one by eliminating the client as a key indicant of evaluation.

Sample Representativeness. Extending intervention programs to a representative sample of individuals or groups and measuring their progress and that of matched control groups is so expensive that had it been done, most projects could not have been completed. Therefore, even though results from highly selected research subjects are of doubtful value in developing practice theory, it is precisely in sampling that study designers had to compromise most between scientific principle and reality. The major savings device was utilizing subjects already operating within the orbit of an agency or institution. Thus, most of the research programs relied on agency auspices, an arrangement which generally precluded using a genuine control group.

One means to improve sample representativeness is to select cases not from the service agency but from a larger institution, such as a public school or housing office serving nearly everyone within a given area or age group or both. For instance, the Girls at Vocational High and the Pursuit of Promise projects took advantage of public school willingness to cooperate in the research undertaking. Through a random procedure, Girls at Vocational High selected a sample of girls defined as problematic based on criteria developed jointly by the vocational high school and the research team. The Pursuit of Promise tested at nine elementary schools in a socio-economically deprived area to gather a sample of intellectually superior children. In both instances, the sample was more representative of the larger population than were agency clientele because the selection from the universe under consideration was based on objectively defined criteria rather than willingness to accept welfare services and other indeterminate variables.

Two studies went beyond both sampling approaches to increase representativeness. Serving the Aging used a population base of all noninstitutionalized persons sixty years or older living in three New York City boroughs. The experiment utilized random samples of applicants and nonapplicants and extended services to applicants (and a few nonapplicants who could be recruited for service). Though most outcome data came from participants assigned through random procedures to three service programs, the study also furnished comparative data on nonapplicant cases.

The Family Life Improvement Project selected randomly from the Newark Vital Statistics Register young mothers with a first child born in 1964 or the first four months in 1965. Assignments to experimental and control groups were made by using random numbers; thus project clients were recruited for prevention-oriented services regardless of their social situation or degree of problemicity in social functioning. The authors felt that the across-the-board rendering of services could be justified by adapting their nature and intensity—ranging from minimal contact to intensive treatment—to the needs of the client family. The advantage of sample selection from a large and more or less representative urban population was counterbalanced in part by the problem of locating respondents (Geismar and others, 1970; Lagay, 1969/70).

So, while the degree of sample representativeness varies from study to study, all thirteen projects clearly went beyond the techniques—widely employed in practice research—known as convenience or accidental sampling and selected fairly representative study groups.

Nature of Outcome. The subject of outcome forces us to ask how representative these studies are. Clearly, the forms of practice covered are only a fraction of the services offered by social work. The emphasis is on direct services, mainly casework, except for Pursuit of Promise, the Neighborhood Improvement Project, and Girls at Vocational High, where a shift occurred in the course of the study from individual to group treatment; and group work and community organization are accessories. How representative these programs are of their kinds of practice is not known; however, I assume that the programs evaluated are no worse than practice in general and some are probably much better. Research projects offering a comparative design were better able to yield information on this question than was the classical experimental control model. The results of such projects support the assumption that special programs were no worse than conventional ones but do not prove that they are much better.

Thus, despite reservations on the subject of representativeness, the examination of even a few systematic outcome studies is an important beginning in evaluating practice and education. This approach makes outcome crucial because the study results are very important in determining the value of the programs.

Outcome cannot be simply characterized for the research projects as a whole for several reasons. Not all used a pure experimental-control design permitting comparison of treated and untreated cases, although studies using comparison groups instead of control groups may have had more positive results than could be shown. Studies varied widely in the number of hypotheses formulated by the principal investigators, and, in some research projects, hypotheses were more implicit than explicit. The likelihood of supporting a hypothesis—or rejecting the null hypothesis—differed from study to study because of differences in measurement and sample size and also because of variations in confidence limits set by the investigators.

Rather than attempt a complex, multidimensional classification of outcome which would, in any case, be challenged, I differentiate among the studies in terms of how their authors assessed the results. For the projects as a whole, results reveal a range of outcomes the curve of which is skewed at the negative end of the distribution. Four of the projects report almost no significant differences between the experimental and the control group on any of the key measures (Brown, 1968; Marin, 1969; Meyer and others, 1965; Mullen and others, 1970). Two studies report very limited gains— in the first instance, for only one of the subgroups studied (McCabe and others, 1967) and, in the second, for one or the other of the treatment programs on selected variables when treatment cases were compared with control cases (Blenkner and others, 1964). The problematic nature of the treatment group probably weighed this comparison in favor of the control group. The outcomes of the remaining seven projects either support the major research hypotheses or are in line with the desired objectives, although results reported are frequently described as modest by the report writers and lean toward the nonsuccess end of the continuum.

Even if we accept the traditional rules of decision-making used in experimental research, it is still extremely difficult to assess results in terms of their meaning for practice. Statistical decision-making as generally applied helps to weed out cases whose programs are least likely to support an intervention hypothesis but does not reveal much about the effectiveness of a given method. This statement, however, is open to challenge, and it is questionable whether findings based on affirmative, though not quite statistically significant, results of several similar studies are less meaningful than results of a single study which does give statistically significant support to the research hypothesis. Significance even at the 99 per cent confidence level can be attained when the majority of both experimental and control cases do not register any change or when experimental cases show only a slight margin of positive change over the control cases. The attainment of statistical significance is a function of many factors including the test used. Parametric and nonparametric techniques sometimes yield different results (Geismar and others, 1970).

Therefore, positive outcome in these and similar studies should be viewed as a rejection of the null hypothesis of no difference between experimental and control groups and a first step toward conclusive knowledge about the value of a program. Exploring the issue requires replication of the experiment, an exact quantitative appraisal of the net gains from the experimental intervention, an analysis of the human and monetary cost of using the method, and a pilot study dealing with the organizational consequences of using a new approach. Programs reporting degrees of positive outcome have more potential for doing well in such an exploration than do those reporting less favorable results, thereby justifying further research investment, although projects producing unsuccessful outcomes should not be dismissed without careful investigation of the experiment.

If, as stated earlier, evaluative research is so essential to developing sound professional functioning and yet each expensive and time-consuming study fails to provide a conclusive answer to the problems posed, how can social work advance toward science-based practice? Additional large-scale evaluation studies dependent on outside financing are not the answer in a time of scarce research support. A more feasible approach is for the profession itself to build such research into practice.

The findings of the thirteen studies can serve as the point of departure for such a venture, for these results urgently need cross-validation. Social work training centers in academic settings and the large professional agencies must build evaluation into their practice, considering the expense necessary to improve professional functioning. The argument that evaluation comes second to service is unconvincing in the light of the foregoing findings. Since some forms of intervention produce changes in the direction of professional goals while others do not, it is hardly reasonable to continue financing services which contribute little toward the attainment of professional objectives at the expense of evaluation research. Also, evaluation must be ongoing, and the results must be shared through conferences and the professional media.

3

Methodology of Evaluation

Wyatt C. Jones, Edgar F. Borgatta

Howard E. Freeman of Brandeis University and the Russell Sage Foundation investigated the status of evaluation research in federally supported programs. He soon realized that practicality demanded some arbitrary definition of limits to the scope of evaluative research and of critical points on which projects should be assessed. Presumably, we should be able to order the requirements of effective research on the basis of some priorities, but any failure in the design or execution of the research may make it suspect, and many things can be the source of failure.

For many reasons, it is difficult to conceive of a perfect design of evaluation research. The researcher must first ask "What is the purpose of the evaluation research?" The window dressing variety of answer "Well, everybody does evaluative research" is indefensible. Keeping up with the Joneses may be appropriate behavior in some contexts, but there is a difference between determining

whether an agency, a program, or a set of procedures is accomplishing its aims and carrying on evaluative research just because it's
fashionable. Naturally, no one will admit that he does evaluative
research just because it is fashionable, so the question of objectives
and how they might be evaluated must be seen in a reasonable perspective.

If the purpose of evaluation research is the determination
of the accomplishment of program goals, these objectives must be
clearly formulated from the beginning or their measurement is
impossible. Such objectives of broad and diffuse programs are not
necessarily easily stated. The post hoc finding that a program or
agency has many latent functions not stated as the original objectives suggests an incomplete analysis or an unrealistic description.
The situation may be judged even more devastating by some when
the sole finding of an evaluation research reveals that an agency
carries out unmeasured and unspecified latent functions such as
providing employment for qualified personnel and volunteer workers, and that its contribution is important in the fabric of government and the network of welfare services. If this sounds harsh, it
might be well to look into the real meaning of statements like: "It
is difficult to say what the objectives of the agency are, as the
agency provides so many different types of services to so many
different types of clients"; or, "The agency provides vital services,
as one can see by the strong demands on the time of our overworked
staff"; or, "It is difficult to imagine what the community would do
without our agency, as we are unable to satisfy the current demands
for services." None of these declarations provides a meaningful indication of what the agency objectives are. Attempting to pin down
goals in many cases leads to explanations like: "Well, we don't
know exactly what we want to do; that's one of the reasons we
think it is so important to do the evaluation research." All this
brings to mind the acrimonious debate over the supersonic trans-
port (SST) program, which began with the argument that the SST
was needed because the French and British were going to have one
and then shifted to the rationale that the unemployment level in
Seattle might get even worse. Vague descriptions of activities as
carried out are not the same as the statement of the consequences
of these activities, which presumably are related to the implementa-

tion of some policy for the public good. The betterment of individuals and society is the usual justification for the existence of social agencies and their activities and procedures. At some point, objectives should be stated in terms of measurable change in intended directions, and if reasonably identifiable criterion variables are not available, evaluative research is not feasible.

Aside from the need for specification, appeal is often made to the fact that researchers want gross, hard, identifiable criteria, to the neglect of subtle things that are said to be important for the quality of life. Granted that researchers seek the specification of well-identifiable criteria, nonetheless, they must develop measures corresponding to any and all criteria related to the objectives of the program or agency. There are practical limitations, but, assuming relevant knowledge of measurement techniques and the existence of qualified tests, a reasonable set of questions should be achievable for any set of objectives; and, regarding social-psychological qualities, their measurement has to be demonstrable in reliable indicators. These qualities cannot reside in the mind of someone in the agency who knows what he thinks is important but cannot express it because it is too subtle to be communicated or because it is a relationship so fragile that any attempt to measure it would destroy it. Similarly, amelioration is difficult to establish if client contact ends after a brief period but the utility of the contact will not be apparent for a decade—and evaluation has to be completed within the fiscal year. Thus, programs of agencies must have a clear set of objectives for evaluative research to be carried out. Since many agencies and programs have grown like Topsy or have taken over purposes and objectives as good ideas, this focus on their goals may be a salutary exercise; it is not evaluation research.

A perfect design of evaluation research may be difficult to conceive, but the major set of questions lies in the area sometimes called external validity, or dealing with the generality of findings. While there may be local interest in any particular agency or program, the difficulties encountered in setting up an adequate design may raise questions of whether the evaluation research is worth doing at all. Thus, the specified objectives should bear some relationship to a problem considered significant in the society; to do research merely to find out whether Agency X is doing what it thinks it's doing may be a luxury, and, with the shortage of research personnel and skills today, the results may be inadequate. The question must be raised in advance: "If the evaluation research demonstrates the program is effective in its objectives, then what?" Can the findings be generalized to other programs? Therefore, other agencies or programs must consider the objectives desirable, and if so, they are likely to imitate an effective program. The design of evaluation research must get to the specific criteria of the agency or program being studied and place them in a general perspective which might be termed a *replicability criterion.*

If the evaluation research is well conceived, the general perspective impinges upon the research design. How is the effectiveness of the agency or program to be measured except by comparison with some standard, that is, some control group design? At this point some of the serious questions about the purpose of the agency or program run counter to tendencies of self-protection. Appropriate designs for evaluation research consider not merely the agency or program but the whole situation in which these operate. A single agency might be the focus of evaluation research as its own control if there is accurately recorded information about the activities and consequences of interventions through some historical period, but even here evaluation is dependent on knowledge of the general historical changes that have transpired during the period. Ultimately, some reference points must be identified to establish the validity of the assertions of effects, and ordinarily such points must be beyond the scope of the agency itself.

If an agency institutes a new program, how can assertions be made that it is more effective than previous programs? Some criterion measure may show an increase in clients who have been helped. Then come all the hoary questions about explanations other than the program (the manifest procedures) that could account for the findings. Has the client selection been the same? Is the result attributable to more highly motivated or more capable personnel involved in the new program, rather than the procedures themselves? Is this a pioneer set of effects that will not continue and will not carry over to an agency which did not believe the magic formula? The answers to such questions do not come easily, and the questions themselves generate discomfort if one is sponsoring a new program.

Evaluation research is no different from any other scientific enterprise; there is no conclusive proof that a given agency or program is effective. There is, at best, the removal of alternative explanations for a given effect and the consequent growth of confidence in what is being done. This scientific truism is most important in considering evaluation research since agencies and programs subject to scrutiny are so complex that evaluation research boils down to measurement of gross impact because of the inability to specify the objectives relative to any given procedures. Presumably, the impact in a global sense should be evident, and then researchers can pursue questions of what effects are greatest and, hopefully, to what procedures they are related. Evaluation research often proceeds with this progression of refinements in mind but rarely achieves the refinement stage because the overall impact is not found or only a few indicators show change and in an unimpressive way. Confidence in the agency or program may be threatened; and it is common to find researchers (erroneously assuming responsibility for the program itself) embarrassed because they have not been able to demonstrate effects. Equally, it is not uncommon to have the research design and execution branded as inadequate because it did not demonstrate the effectiveness of the program. A program is built upon experience from many sources—ad hoc theory, professional lore, practice wisdom, demands of the clients, expectations of the public, and occasionally scientific evidence. There is here no implied denigration of sources other than the scientific, as human experience (which includes professional experience) generates much wisdom, but it is not a faultless process. So, we need not be surprised and defensive upon finding that programs are ineffective or are no more effective than doing nothing or next to nothing or something else.

The inability to demonstrate effectiveness of programs provokes questions about evaluation research. If the value of a program is so self-evident, why is it that demonstration cannot show that value? Maybe the value of the program is not so obvious after all. Here personnel of the agency evaluated may become defensive, saying, "Well, what was to be expected? Look at the program that was evaluated." Never, apparently, are the *best* programs, those in which the desired changes would have shown up, evaluated.

In order to be done at all, evaluation research depending heavily on external conditions—the cooperation of host agencies, the self-selection of clients, the criteria of eligibility, and so forth—must make some compromises of design and methodology. The thirteen studies surveyed for this book were chosen because they represent the use of experimental design in social work research. Given the exigencies inherent in conducting research in ongoing agencies, the investigators have faced and, for the most part, dealt with many obvious technical problems. The random assignment of subjects to experimental and control groups is the common feature of all the studies. A majority of them also employ a design calling for before-and-after measures, occasionally with the refinement of an after-only control group. Considerable attention is given in several of the studies to the assessment of the validity and reliability of the instruments. Numerous investigators also consider the appropriateness of alternative measures of association and tests of significance. Various statistical procedures are reported as are a number of analytic devices ranging from content analysis of case records to Q-sorts.

We believe that the studies reported here represent a substantial advancement over what might have been expected in the 1950s and certainly over what was the common evaluation study of the 1940s. We no longer find such glaring errors as a presumed or stated randomization that turns out to be the assignment of those who wanted the therapy to the experimental condition and those who did not to the control category. Technical difficulties still exist, however, and where they occur, they encroach on the interpretability of findings. As we noted in the beginning, an evaluation study can falter and become subject to challenge in myriad ways. Intrinsically, whenever an alternative explanation for a set of events can be advanced, the presumed facts of effective intervention are in question. One of the lessons to be taught students, who we must assume are interested in effective intervention, is that the rules of science place the burden of proof on the person who makes the assertion of a relationship, say between an action and a consequence, not upon the person who challenges the assertion. If a student entering the profession accepts the mantle of scholarship and all its mystical truths, he may not be concerned with this scientific rule. If, however, the student is interested in efficacy, as we have suggested, he must be concerned with the canons of science. So, also, must schools of social work make correlative decisions about how they teach their lore and practice.

We are not implying that the curriculum should reflect a judgment that nothing is known, even though, scientifically, we know little except that we do not affect all that we presume to. Any person concerned with support of agencies, education, or other aspects of academic and professional enterprise realizes that such an extreme view, while possibly accurate, undermines the possibility of progress. But we must beware of practice theory based on confidence in the profession rather than on demonstration of program effectiveness through direct evaluation. In examining cases of evaluation research, we must note how difficult it is to make assertions about translating the intentions of workers into meaningful ameliorations for the client. Formulating model experimental designs is one of the best tests—either of the objectives of a program or of those of a student regarding his expectations of social work. Choosing criteria for measuring change in actual cases may open a student's mind to the real objectives of a program or agency. The student sees that there are higher purposes and more mundane purposes. Easy agreement may be achieved when the latter are defined in terms of eliminating extreme social problems. Purposes of an agency couched in higher terms may evoke little consensus and may never get at the reality implicit in a statement like: "So who cares if he's happy as long as he's got a good job." Only when the client's most acute problems are under control can the practitioner concentrate on enriching his life in other ways.

How are we to define the objectives of programs as they impinge on evaluative researches? We should know, for example, that improved family functioning leads to fewer problems before we can be interested in movement on a scale designed to measure such progress. Perhaps the reverse is true—improved functioning may lead to increased deviance or the relationship between family functioning and deviance may be trivial. We must know what we want to eliminate, and this should be the primary criterion for the evaluative research. This is a hard lesson to learn, but a look at the history of social research—even current research—shows us that programs instituted with great professional confidence and community expectation do not necessarily accomplish their stated aims. The second criterion, as to what such projects actually accomplish, may be partly demonstrated in broadly based studies. But, generally, the most conspicuous fact emerging from evaluation is the piecemeal and personalistic ways in which agencies and programs are run. A student learns that the profession and the community are not at a stage which permits the design of programs and researches in ways that answer: "What really works?" Professionals may define their contributions as so vital that they cannot stop to find out whether they are accomplishing anything worthwhile and, at most, make only minimal concession to the fact that this is a viable question to consider. The import of such considerations is not lost on sensitized students or concerned faculty who recognize that there are unresolved problems in the process of specifying the services rendered by social agencies.

In this regard, it is generally accepted that data to evaluate agency services must come from sources other than the social workers involved. The length and intensity of service are recognized as indices of utilization by the client and of cost and effort of the agency personnel, rather than measures of effectiveness. Evaluative research that is to inform social policy must look to ends, rather than means, to outcomes rather than procedures.

Considering the quality and level of services reported by these studies, one realizes that little attempt was made to alter the aspects of attitudes or functioning explicit in the objectives or implicit in the criterion measures. Social-psychological research on attitude and behavior change says success is limited largely to areas in which attitudes have not been formed, behavior habituated, and knowledge crystallized. Thus, clients learn easiest and use best information not previously known. Social intervention does not change existing attitudes as much as it changes the basis of knowledge upon which such attitudes are formed. The potential for change of well-entrenched attitudes is small, given the short-term, minimally involved contacts reported in many of these studies. While this is not, strictly speaking, a methodological issue, it raises questions as to what are the real purposes of a social agency.

The direct implications of these limitations for research design include such considerations as stratifying or classifying clients for purposes of drawing better samples, assigning randomized cases to alternative treatments, and identifying inexpensive controls among nontreated populations. Several of the studies under consideration contrasted new with old programs, single services with multiservices, treatment groups with groups receiving no service, and samples drawn from agency caseloads with those identified in the community at large. The mosaic of services available in the average community makes a complete count of agency contacts difficult to ascertain, much less to measure. An evaluation of what is happening to the client through the program must reckon with these difficulties.

Most researches do not consider or assess the inefficiency occasioned by the competing if not conflicting services available to individuals and families in a community. For example, an observer once identified six overlapping, independent, noncooperating urban improvement programs in one area of Washington, D.C. These were in addition to the normal complement of six uncoordinated public and private services available to the residents. Several of these agencies or their constituent programs were perhaps highly effective, but how could one know? How do these different agencies vie for limited funds, compete for cooperative clients, outbid each other for skilled personnel? And is this confusion what we mean by providing comprehensive services to be evaluated?

The growing interest in evaluations of action programs is based on the idea that research of these interventions can point to underlying cause and effect relationships which are manipulable and amenable to change. The implications of these results for public policy are self-evident. Traditional models of laboratory experiments, pilot tests, or demonstration projects have generally proven to be inadequate or unsuitable for this purpose. The heterogeneity arising from differences in administrative style, operation of programs, and characteristics of clients has plagued most efforts at evaluative research. However, this very diversity makes possible consideration of these differences across a number of situations as a natural experiment as opposed to an intentional experiment. The idea that greatly improved results could be obtained by evaluating social action programs set up as intentional experiments was once entertained by both the Ford Foundation and the Office of Economic Opportunity; and some programs, such as the Gray Areas Projects and the Community Action Programs, were originally conceived to be evaluated in this holistic manner. One problem of the studies we are reviewing is that evaluation is not based on the sample sizes indicated but on a sample of one—the agency being studied. A series of such agencies simultaneously carrying out experimental interventions directed to a common social problem would greatly enhance the analytical powers of our statistical models of evaluation.

Evaluation research, then, in order to reveal more than the mere fact that the agency or program cannot demonstrate its efficacy, must occur in a context which places efficacy of programs on different bases. It will be some time before agencies become the units of observation, but the breadth and scope of some pervasive social problems, as they are defined and responded to in the purview of social welfare, may make such developments possible. We must keep in mind that in order to be viable the design of evaluation research must be built into any innovations. The "self-evident" value of a new program must be treated as what it is—an assumption—and experience shows that such assumptions are usually presumptions. Thus, programs should be introduced into many agencies, and, similarly, many controls should be retained on the grounds that the relative efficacy of the old and the new is not demonstrable in advance. If such programs do not produce demonstrable differences, other types of criteria should be introduced promptly. For example, the huge expense of a sheltered workshop program that is no more effective than a counseling service is hardly justifiable, even if the workshop does keep numerous professionals employed.

Evaluative research has also moved from assessing the success or failure of a given intervention for individuals and families to a broad concern with the effects of large-scale programs on total population groups and their impact on the community. This large interest is not limited to professional social workers but includes legislators and executives concerned with the allocation of public and philanthropic funds. The increase of federal funding in all social welfare programs has made Congress and the Department of Management and Budget particularly sensitive to questions of efficacy and efficiency. This concern is not limited to the effects of a program on its identified target groups but extends to community structure and neighborhood institutions, including political, economic, and social aspects.

Increasingly, evaluations will have to consider the measurement and control of variables relating to community structure and institutional change, even when such are not the goals of the intervention. We need better theories of the effect of community structure and institutional change on individuals and their behavior in order to know what variables should be considered and what data to collect; our colleagues in the social science disciplines must provide us with *grounded theory* upon which to base our interventions and against which we may evaluate their effectiveness.

Evaluation is no longer a luxury to be indulged in by a few well-financed agencies but is increasingly becoming a necessity for any large-scale intervention. The theory of evaluation and the methodological procedures are sufficiently crystalized to permit the development of practical research designs which can be used by many agencies with comparable programs over a wide geographical area. The evaluative findings of such broad-scale research must be presented in ways which facilitate their use and modification in new programs.

The researchers in the thirteen studies reviewed have generally been conscious of the hazards of their methodologies and of the limitations of their studies. They have carefully plotted their research design, specified their inadequacies, and eschewed any unwarranted generalizations. While their modesty is commendable, it should not blind us to the contributions made by their studies in broadening the scope of evaluative research and deepening our knowledge of social work intervention. Within the current framework of scientific investigation and the classical statistical models of evaluation, these studies can be viewed as exemplars of social work research. Their inadequacy, rather than constituting a criticism of the diligence or skill of the investigators, is a commentary on the present shortcomings of theory and methodology in evaluation research.

These studies are built on traditional statistical models which leave the practitioner, and sometimes the researcher, with a feeling of rigidity. Still, the problems generated in trying to satisfy the basic design are not a criticism of the design itself but of the status of the art and the underlying social sciences to which the applications refer. Elementary statistical hypothesis testing is associated with the null hypothesis. An investigator examines the hypothesis that two samples (one experimental, the other control) are drawn from the same population and determines whether the difference between the two is likely or unlikely (using predetermined criteria) to occur by repeated random sampling from the same population. If the hypothesis is rejected, then the observed result is judged unlikely to have occurred by chance, and one of two conditions may prevail. Either the samples are drawn from different populations, or they have not been drawn by random procedures from the same population.

When the two samples are judged different, the statement is translated to an inference that the intervention under study had an effect. To repeat: hypothesis testing in the simplest model of experimental design is oriented to establishing that a difference exists because of the relationship between an intervention and an effect. The failure to reject the hypothesis essentially prohibits inferences of relationship, and thus no additional confidence can be acquired from the hypothesis test. In either case, however, it is a matter of inference and confidence. If the hypothesis test is rejected, confidence accumulates for establishing the relationship, assuming the application of the procedure is defensible on other grounds. If the hypothesis test is not rejected, lack of confidence accumulates for establishing the relationship, unless the lack of confidence can be transferred to other grounds. Such a description as we have here may sound formidable and rigid.

Nevertheless, the simplest model provides a good basis for raising questions about applicability. A statistical test expects to make errors a small percentage of the time; that is, the Error of the First Type (Type I Error) may occur, and the hypothesis may be rejected when it is true. The probability of the Type I Error is controlled directly by the level of significance initially chosen, but the Type I Error cannot be manipulated without giving attention to other considerations. Given a set sample size, the smaller the Type I Error, the greater the difference required between two samples to reject the null hypothesis.

A second type of error (Error of the Second Type, or Type II Error) can occur in hypothesis testing as the failure to reject the hypothesis when it is false. The importance of the Type II Error is apparent when one wants to control both Type I and Type II Errors regarding on alternate hypothesis. In this case, it is necessary to determine in advance that sample sizes are sufficient to make the statistical test possible. Getting such estimates for adequate sample sizes requires little effort, and since sample characteristics become more stable with large samples, the researcher is always encouraged to get sample sizes as large as possible beyond the minimum. The effort to inflate samples has often generated the criticism that small differences may be statistically significant if the sample sizes are large enough. This criticism is occasionally true, but the model of hypothesis testing is designed to establish a relationship, not measure its size, which requires a different test.

This last point gets us to some comments that become relevant to evaluation research. It is not mandatory to use a simple model of hypothesis testing, with the variability of designs possible being limited only by the researcher's ingenuity and knowledge. However, complicated designs may be substantively beyond the researcher. Isn't the prior job to establish that the relationship exists at all? Only practical problems prevent the test of a hypothesis about differences of given sizes. Regarding a disease, for example, if there is 70 per cent spontaneous remission in the general population, how large a percentage of cures would one want to find in the treated experimental group? Unfortunately, here the researcher often encounters vague answers: "Ten per cent would be impressive"; "five per cent would be meaningful"; "one per cent would have an impact if we're dealing with a base of millions of people"; "one human life would be enough!" The rules of the game should be specified in advance; here a substantive as well as a statistical set of criteria are relevant. Once the rules are specified and the sample sizes set, one can determine whether these requirements can be met in the agency or program being studied.

Those who have had considerable exposure to statistics and methodology know that if certain conditions of variable measurement and theory specification exist, many statistical and numerical procedures are applicable in analysis. The next step—an important one—is to move from hypothesis testing to parameter estimation. As variables are defined and enter a system for a content area, various mathematical models can be applied. As the sciences progress in the development of their empirical theories, mathematics seems to keep pace. Indeed, mathematics is often coincident with theory in some areas of physics, and social science has all the mathematics it requires for this century and the next. However, it is not logical to switch emphasis and suggest that in this technology one will find the solution for shortcomings of data collection. But as studies are collected and replicated, we can begin to get an inkling of the sampling distribution and the *power* of the evaluation procedures being carried out.

Many technical developments getting attention in the social sciences will prove useful in the conceptualization of research problems. However, new developments can sometimes provide ways of looking at problems rather than be directly applicable in research. For example, causal inference and *path analysis* in statistical regression models have been emphasized. Their application to evaluation research is small, however, as these models are for the unscrambling of limited range theories and presumably for nonexperimental data. They can be adapted to experimental design, but when so adapted, the inferential procedures constitute a secondary form of data fitting. When variables can be described in a system, many analyses can be made that are imaginative and revealing of the nature of relationships among them, including inferences of causation as defined in some of the current models of analysis. This stage of knowledge goes far beyond merely asking, "Does the treatment make a difference?" Still, knowledge of these developments may instill caution in researchers. For example, how many successful applications of the new causal inference models have had notable success in fitting data in the social sciences? The number of successes is small, and the applications themselves are of very limited scope, usually involving relatively simple models.

Additional new ideas for the methodological orientations of researchers include the introduction of Bayesian analysis, borrowed from economics. In general, the applicability of Bayesian principles is as circumscribed as the classical approaches to regression analysis, for example. The problems of specification of variables are not automatically solved. There is a basic law of conservation of matter, in which matter means sample sizes, reliability and validity of measures, the historical facts of the data collection, and so forth. No statistical or numerical approach, however different, can improve these. However, exposure to Bayesian analysis (and causal inference models, general regression models, analysis of variance models, and others) may whet the appetite for evaluation research designs able to provide interpretable results. Bayesian analysis, for instance, is oriented to historical sequences in the sense that economics must deal with the progression of events. This approach, when applicable, permits statements about the value of the unknown parameter under conditions of uncertainty and about nonrecurring events. Ultimately, because of restrictions on numbers, Bayesian answers must be equivalent to those of more classical approaches; but, in philosophical orientation, the strategy suggested by Bayesian analysis to research design has the advantage that "it provides a clear-cut distinction between creative activity such as hypothesis formulation, which can be performed only by trained and imaginative people, and formal analysis, which is in principle capable of reduction to routine performance by robots" (Cornfield, 1970, p. 39). Still, this has always been the problem. There is nothing magical about computing the "t" test, and all hinges on the original research design.

In the curriculum, the assessment of current evaluation researches and an introduction to the technology of research provide a perspective. Hopefully, these will produce applications, but the lesson taught by scientific interest in social work and its related professions is that evaluation is difficult when possible, and the possibilities are rare today. Social work has always been concerned with ultimate objectives, but there is a difference between a philosophical discussion and moral exhortation and objectively facing specification of operations and intended consequences. Also, the difficulties encountered in such analyses lead to research at other levels. Social system analyses with agencies as elements of analysis are important in developing the perspective of social work, but such descriptive analyses are often limited from the viewpoint of scientific technology. Yet, these analyses may be first in asking questions about the projected impact of an agency or program. For example, from the findings of existing studies, is it possible to know whether a program

would be effective if other agencies and programs of a given type
were eliminated? The reordering and restructuring or elimination of
agencies and programs hardly arise in the concept of evaluation
research as occurs today. Facing up to why it is so difficult to do
evaluation research, to get positive findings, and to accumulate
empirically validated knowledge in the social sciences may force us
to question the operation of the whole system.

4

Theory Development as a Task for the Evaluator

James L. Breedlove

Wyatt Jones and Edgar Borgatta have followed a tradition presuming that better research technology, combined with clarification of social work goals, will improve future evaluative studies. We take the position that, admirable and necessary as those goals are, the solutions for the problems of evaluative research as well as of social work curricula lie in a different direction. The underlying problem for professional practice, curriculum development, as well as evaluative research, is the failure to give serious attention to the development and testing of practice theory. This is not intended to be a criticism of either evaluative research or curricula in schools of social work but, rather, a reflection upon the current state of social work as an emerging profession (Etzioni, 1969). The evaluative studies considered in this book indicate a considerable need for co-operation among theorists, practitioners, and research specialists. If a particular evaluative research project is to achieve its great potential for bringing social work to a scientifically-based professional status, the coordinated contributions of social problem analysts, program specialists, statisticians and others will be required.

The evaluative study is carried out through six interrelated tasks: (1) randomly assigning individuals drawn from an identified population to control and experimental groups; (2) providing an experimental treatment for the experimental group and not for the control group; (3) measuring the results for both groups by clear outcome measures, which are (4) representative of value criteria, and which (5) are measured against relatively stable variables describing the context in which the experiment or evaluative study takes place; and (6) development of a theoretical framework within which all the preceding five tasks can be integrated. These six tasks represent a continuum of progressive utility of the results of evaluative studies. The tasks for evaluative research are the basis for assessing the generality of any particular evaluative study, and the basis for understanding the level of evaluative research contributions to social work practice and education. The quality of a given study's contribution depends on the care with which these six issues have been handled. Depending on how thoroughly it was conducted, the evaluative study may contribute at one of three levels to social work practice: data about a particular service or treatment and its results, that is, the *practice effects;* data about the success of a particular social agency program, that is, *program effectiveness;* and new understanding about a particular practice theory, that is, *professional effectiveness.* Contributions to practice come not from actual results of a study but from theoretical and conceptual analysis developed during the course of research (Millikan, 1959).

Levels of Contribution

Practice Effects. The fundamental contribution the evaluative study makes is the determination of whether and to what extent a particular form of social work intervention has any effect on the client's problem. This determination is the product of an adequate level of response to the first three tasks of evaluative research—

establishing a control group, an experimental treatment, and outcome measurements—which have been recognized as essential by the researcher in the thirteen studies.

Without exception, researchers have acknowledged the first task of setting up identical experimental and control groups from a defined population. The logic of this procedure, the minimum of experimental design, though now apparently universally recognized in social work evaluative research, is difficult to carry out. On occasion, compromises are made with the randomization principle which is intended to take the assignment of the independent or interventional variables out of the researcher's hand. The Neighborhood Improvement Project used a matched neighborhood for the control, making the interpretation of the findings uncertain. Results are particularly difficult to interpret in a neighborhood approach which may be considered a sample of *one* neighborhood, instead of *hundreds* of families. Far more important than matching versus randomization are selection and delineation of the population to be sampled. Unless we take the position that it is unimportant to generalize from the findings, unlikely in view of the cost of evaluative studies, the care in selecting a replicable sample is of fundamental significance.

One important contribution evaluative research can make is the clarification of *diagnostic* categories by identifying the relevant parameters of a problem population. A difficulty not adequately dealt with in these studies is the tendency to identify the clientele of a particular social agency or service with a social problem group. Actually, the client population may be, and probably is, a highly specialized sample which in some ways may not at all represent the larger population of individuals with seemingly similar social problems.

A difficulty of all of these studies, except the Serving the Aging project which relied upon a stratified random sample, is that the population from which the samples were drawn were one-agency clinical populations. Under such circumstances, from which random samples have not been taken, generalizing to other populations, is not possible (Edington, 1966). Although the researcher is more aware of the significance of how the sample is taken than is the practitioner, the neglect of an intensive individual approach in all these studies may indicate that both the researcher and the practitioner are concerned primarily with the statistical inference problems with which sampling theory attempts to deal. The first aim of clinical research, however, is producing meaningful explanations about changes in individual subjects. The *extensive* design employed in these thirteen studies makes it particularly difficult to arrive at such explanations (Yates, 1970). In contrast, "Intensive statistical study of a single case can provide more meaningful and statistically significant information than, say, only end point observations extended over a relatively large number of patients" (Chassan, 1960, p. 179).

The second task of evaluative research, that of specifying the *treatment* or interventional or independent variables, has been handled less thoroughly than the first task. Frequently, a misleading assumption has been made that all social work interventions are homogeneous or essentially equivalent. The very nature of evaluative research, however, requires that the content and characteristics of intervention be approached as an empirical question, not assumed. If the results of an evaluative study are to be generalized to another situation, it is necessary to establish convincingly that the new situation, including the new treatment, is comparable to the one in which the research was conducted. The assurance that the new situation replicates the study situation depends upon the extent to which the treatment or intervention variables can be replicated. Whether this can be done depends on the care with which the variables are identified and measured.

This brings us to another important contribution of evaluative studies to social work practice and social work education. The usual descriptive categories for social work practice have been found wanting in some evaluative studies. For instance, in a recent study of work with the alcoholic's family (Cohen and Krause, 1971), a major classification of treatment procedures (Hollis, 1964) used in casework was found to be irrelevant, at least for differentiating the contrasting treatment modalities in those situations. A negative finding such as the nonutility of categories can stimulate social workers to construct a new and useful conceptualization of practice. Evaluative studies such as those considered here raise the question of a useful definition of social work practice. Global descriptions lacking clear operational referents or procedures for describing specific atomistic techniques of the caseworker will not suffice to specify independent variables in evaluative research. What approach, then, to identifying social work practice will succeed? The answer lies in the intended utilization of the evaluative findings. When we examine the potential utility of the evaluative studies, some basic weaknesses as well as important contributions for social work practice and education become evident. We want to know the effectiveness of a particular practice so that we can improve practice; this is the fundamental rationale for the evaluative study itself and for the specification of intervention variables. However, many of the thirteen studies were apparently undertaken on the assumption that evaluative research is done to determine whether a particular program is effective—a misleading assumption about evaluative research, as we shall see.

This means that social work intervention must be conceptualized and specified as a strategic model for dealing with a particular social problem. These evaluative studies have revealed certain erroneous assumptions underlying the definition of social work. The first assumption, made in teaching materials, is that social work is a global, undifferentiated problem-solving process which can be understood isolated from a given social problem (Perlman, 1957). The second assumption parallels the first: social work practice can be understood as a collection of discrete applications of interviewing techniques (Hollis, 1964) or other *things* done to, for, or with the client. Behavior modification evaluative studies have been criticized for a similar assumption (Yates, 1970). Both assumptions are erroneous and both have posed problems in the interpretation or generalization of the findings of these evaluative studies.

The first assumption, that social work is a global, homogeneous, undifferentiated process, is common. For example, we find such general descriptions as "casework treatment by two experienced M.S.W.s" or "intensive caseload" or "in groups that included immature and impulsive girls, the therapist needed to be directive." In An Experimental Study to Measure the Effectiveness of Casework Service (Behling, 1961), it is assumed that the "amount of contact between client and caseworker is the fundamental element essential to positive change." Not only is it erroneous to assume equivalence among casework and caseworkers, but the consideration that some other variable could be responsible for change is overlooked. For instance, the experimental group received 15 per cent more financial aid than did the control group, a variable which in itself could have been a key factor in producing change. Although this is not the place to critique each study, it is worth noting that the specification of treatment variables was far more neglected than one would have hoped. Even when the treatment variables were operationally specified, there was little conceptual clarification of these variables, and almost no explicit theoretical linkage to the target problem and to outcome measures. In other words, few studies made clear why a particular treatment was expected to bring about a particular outcome.

The second assumption, that social work can be understood as a series of isolated, discrete behaviors on the part of the social workers, is less common. Nevertheless, some of these studies have fallen into this error. This assumption, while providing an empirical approach to the study of social work method, fails to systematize the procedures as a strategic approach for a particular problem. Consequently, the necessary information is not available to answer the question asked of evaluative research: how to choose the most effective treatment for a particular problem.

The studies seldom discuss client problems as unique situations for which individualized solutions are to be found. One may assume that some of the caseworkers believed their clients' problems to be unique and that their approach to helping resolve the problems was based on a clear and explicit understanding of an individual client's needs; however, there is very little evidence in the research design that each client was considered the subject of experimental study on his own terms. One of the more theoretical studies, the Casework Methods Project, although carefully assigning individual subjects to two treatments clearly distinguished from each other, did not ask whether some clients would be more likely to benefit from one treatment as opposed to the other treatment. Not posing such questions is neglecting the purpose of evaluative research— understanding how a particular treatment changes a particular subject in order to improve practice.

The most striking observation to be made about these studies is that they took social work practice as a given entity instead of a problematical subject, needing investigation, specification, and conceptualization. Rhetoric to the contrary, there is no evidence that social work practice is a fully formed, clearly specified, and unified set of procedures. Evaluative studies can succeed in establishing the effectiveness, or lack of it, in a particular situation only to the extent that the method of intervention is both conceptually and operationally defined in a way clearly related to the social problem being treated. Unless this is done, both positive and negative findings are meaningless. We must conclude, then, that the scientific research model which requires the testing of an unexamined hypothesis, for example, treatment x results in outcome y, is inadequate to the needs of the profession. The experimental designs of research into social work practice must be supplemented by attempts at theory building. A notable exception among these thirteen studies in defining the interventional variables is the project Serving the Aging. In this study, care was taken with both the conceptual and operational definitions of the interventional variables, which were delineated in terms of the problems dealt with by the study. Contributing to the coordination between treatment and outcome variables characterizing this outstanding project were the interest and knowledge of the researchers in the social problem, in this instance, aging, under study.

The incomplete specification of treatment variables in evaluative studies has implications for teaching research. One difficulty in studying any therapeutic intervention is the tendency for believers to cling to this or that theory or approach. Surprisingly, there are few descriptive studies of what actually happens in the interaction between the social worker and his client. In an age when even the intimacies of human sexual response have been revealed to the penetrating gaze of researchers (Masters and Johnson, 1966), perhaps that once-inviolable sanctum of social work may also yield up its secrets to science. Certainly, if future evaluative studies are to contribute new knowledge to practice theory, analysis of what actually happens in the social worker's intervention (taking into account such factors as experimenter bias (Rosenthal, 1966) and the placebo effect) must either precede or accompany the evaluative effort. Such analysis can provide new understanding about which aspects of treatment effectively produce change and thus lead to innovations in practice theory. Whatever the approach, the message of these evaluative studies is clear: social work practice must be analyzed through empirical study to penetrate its bias, cults, and mystique before adequate evaluation can be made.

The specification of outcome criteria in operational terms, the third task of evaluative research, contributes greatly to social work education, as the last chapter pointed out. Social workers learn that progress in practice theory depends, in part, upon precise definitions of social problems. Learning how to do social work is only one part of practice; the other part is understanding changes occurring in the client's social problem. The current exclusive emphasis on the process of social work practice to the exclusion of its product is like the sound of one hand clapping. Equal attention must be given to measuring client change, if the social work student is to become fully aware of the meaning of practice.

Program Effectiveness.   Evaluative studies contribute more to social work knowledge than demonstration of specific effects of treatment. A neglected or perhaps unrecognized contribution is clarifying the value position of a particular treatment approach or program—the fourth task of evaluative study. Frequently, the values implicit in a treatment approach or social agency program are confusing or contradictory. An example is the Casework Methods Project which compared brief treatments with extended ones. "Brief" treatment could mean *economizing,* or *concern for the client's need,* or even *anti-introspectiveness,* or a combination of these or none of these. The evaluative researcher must make clear the value position taken in outcome measures, and not mistakenly assume that such measures are value-free. It is precisely in evaluation of practice that the cause and function dilemma in social work outlined by Porter Lee can be resolved. Social work represents both "cause"— dedication to social change—and "function"—the practical procedures for bringing about such changes. The persistent dilemma in social work has been to develop functions which effectively promote a cause. Evaluative research, by demonstrating the connection between a program and its results, is the rational resolution of the cause and function dilemma. Sometimes the task of clarifying values and choosing among competing sets of values is recognized only after completion of the study, when the researcher belatedly attempts to explain confusing or apparently conflicting findings.

The importance of values in scientific work has been seldom recognized and is often considered unrelated to scientific investigation. To correct this, future research courses must acknowledge the critical importance of the researcher's values, not only on what he chooses to investigate, but on the actual results obtained (Rosenthal, 1966). A better integrated approach in research teaching requires examination of the consequences of values held; specifying such values in objective and systematic terms within research courses offers much to the curriculum.

These studies do not seem to clarify their value position, although one can guess the underlying value assumptions of some of them. The early termination of public assistance cases and the saving of taxpayers' money seemed to be a valued outcome in both the CSS-DSS Study and An Experimental Study to Measure the Effectiveness of Casework Service. As Harold Lewis points out in Chapter Five, "The relative influence of agency, profession, and clientele on resource allocation processes determines which of the three—program, problem, process—predominates in shaping service delivery systems" and, he might have added, in designing evaluative research. In these evaluative studies, program and, in some instances, process (that is, administration and practitioners' interests) seemed to determine the evaluative study design, whereas problem understanding (clients' interests) was of far less concern to the researchers.

In the evaluative study, exploration of the relevant context within which social work intervention occurs is the fifth task, one given the least systematic attention in planning the study. Consequently, researchers speculate greatly about the relevant context after the study is completed, when unexpected or puzzling findings must be accounted for. Analysis of attacks on recent evaluative studies shows that much of the criticism is of the circumstances under which services were offered, for example, whether the client was a *voluntary* client, or whether the service offered was based on a diagnosed need, and the like. Also, various client variables, such as the client is not motivated, the treatment does not *fit* the client or his problem, are considered in the interpretation of the findings, again, usually post hoc. All of these are important and relevant criticisms, but one wonders why such questions were not raised while it was possible to build these measurements into the evaluative research design. Evaluative studies can contribute to our understanding of the conditions under which effective intervention takes place, particularly when these variables are included as part of the original planning and design. The generalizability of a study's findings to new situations is determined by the extent to which the surrounding circumstances—not part of the treatment, but directly or indirectly bearing on its effectiveness—are known.

Professional Effectiveness. The third, and most significant, level on which the evaluative study contributes to social work practice and education is in providing information and understanding about the effectiveness of the profession in its approach to social problems. This issue goes beyond testing the effectiveness of a program or of practice, the primary level of contribution addressed by these thirteen studies. The degree to which the *profession* is effective is a strategic issue, a question of the relevance of the profession's practice theory. Should the evaluative study be concerned with theory? There are two answers to this question. The first is economic: there is little use in an expensive and time-consuming program evaluation which does not provide alternative and more promising approaches, and a comparative analysis of approaches demands appropriate conceptualization. The second answer is theoretical, though, nonetheless, practical. As mentioned earlier, the utility of any research effort—and evaluative studies are no exception—lies not so much in the actual results as in the conceptual thought and theory tested (Glaser and Strauss, 1967; Millikan, 1959). Findings are no substitute for a theory, so if the evaluative research design does not reflect a unified theoretical orientation, the findings, no matter how clear-cut, no matter whether positive or negative, have no lasting value.

The development of a theory about the problem and its treatment is, then, the sixth and all-encompassing task for researchers. The adequacy of the theoretical orientation and how the five other tasks—research design, outcome measures, method specification, value explication, and context study—are integrated within that theoretical framework determines the utility of any evaluative study. The danger in evaluative study is that the researcher, as well as the practitioner, may consider the primary goal to be determination of a program's effectiveness—that is, to provide answers— rather than understanding of what happens when the social worker attempts to help the client resolve his problem. However, students and practitioners must learn not answers, but understanding of the principles of effective practice. Among the thirteen studies, the Casework Methods Project most nearly approximates the model of an evaluative study in which treatment variables are conceptually defined within a theoretical framework. To the extent that it does so, it suggests principles of problem management. Curiously enough, the practice principles which stem from this particular study of brief and extended casework have a familiar ring, seeming to echo such prescriptions as *begin where the client is*. We may well ask, parenthetically, what has gone awry in our social agencies that we need a research study to tell us that casework is most effective when the focus is kept on the problem as the client understands it!

Implications

It is said that everyone except the researcher believes the research results, but no one except the researcher believes in the hypothesis. This aphorism catches the twin dilemmas of scientific investigation—the naivete about the tentativeness of factual data, and the all too human need to believe in one's own bias regardless of the *facts*. This implies that a new model for the researcher must be developed if evaluative research is to fulfill its potential contribution to social work. In addition to being technically proficient at experimental design and statistical analysis, the researcher of the future who hopes to contribute to knowledge and practice theory must be familiar with the methods and pitfalls of theory development (Beveridge, 1950; Glaser and Strauss, 1967). The conduct of scientific investigation is not simply a matter of logic, it is a learned skill. We must acknowledge that hypothesis testing is only one phase of the search for understanding—perhaps the least important phase. Far behind it lags hypothesis development, the observation and conceptualization of relationships. No matter how statistically well tested a hypothesis is, if the variables are not adequately defined, the results are meaningless. We must be aware that research requires an attitude of mind different from that required for proof. The researcher's duty, once the hypothesis is under study, is to study what is happening, not whether the hypothesis is true or not. Only with this attitude can experimenter bias be reduced and can understanding emerge through discovery of new findings. This approach to evaluative research employs two valuable principles of experimentation: testing the whole before the part, and eliminating various possibilities systematically. To a considerable extent these thirteen studies utilized neither principle, both because the experimental (treatment) variables were inadequately conceptualized and because the evaluative research was isolated from a larger systematic problem-oriented research program.

There is one example of evaluative research which could well serve as the model for evaluative studies of the future. One of the most sophisticated evaluative studies ever undertaken in social work is described in *Retrieval from Limbo* (Ganter and others, 1967), an investigation of an innovative problem-oriented method for working with a group of disturbed children. The researchers developed a method of treatment derived from field and verbal accessibility theory, yet specifically focused on the problems of their subjects. This study not only evaluates outcome, but because the treatment and outcome variables were carefully constructed and related to each other in order to increase understanding of a specific practice problem, it also makes an outstanding contribution to practice theory.

A great many conclusions may be drawn from the evaluative research carried on so far. For our purposes, only seven conclusions with implications for research teaching will be discussed: (1) understanding the results of treatment is essential for improving treatment effectiveness; (2) understanding the principles of intervention in terms of the client's problem should not be submerged in the effort to determine the effectiveness of a program; (3) evaluative studies must be based on a theoretical framework if they are to have general value; (4) greater emphasis on the art of scientific investigation—the development of hypotheses—is needed; (5) the conflict between the researcher and the practitioner, only rarely explicitly acknowledged in evaluative research, impedes progress; (6) the payoff for social work practice from evaluative research studies is derived from theoretical advances; and (7) existing programs may be extremely difficult if not impossible to evaluate properly.

First, understanding the results of treatment is essential for improving treatment effectiveness. Evaluative research can be immensely useful to the practitioner, for it is indispensable in improving practice; methods teaching and research teaching cannot be separated. Methods teaching must incorporate the scientific position that both the *outcome* of intervention and the *need* of the client must be integrated into teaching about method. A noted educator, Helen Perlman, remarked, "it is possible that contributing to casework failure in treatment has been the maintenance of treatment modes that have not been appropriate to the motivations and capacities of certain client groups. If this is true, then we ought to leave off with both breast beating and evaluative research for a time and work instead on new adaptations of our problem solving process" (1968a, p. 442). This conclusion reveals the misunderstanding prevalent among social work educators about the relationship between treatment process and treatment outcome. It is precisely the light thrown on this relationship by evaluative study which provides the impetus to further refine and improve upon the appropriateness of treatment. We cannot simply *leave off* with evaluative research; it is the essential element without which practice cannot reach a scientific and, thus, a professional level. To leave off with evaluative research returns the practice of social work to the mercy of its historical predicament: the Charybdis of nonsystematic testing of process theory and the Scylla of arbitrary administrative control of the social agency's services. If this predicament prevails, the client's interests are lost. Problem, in Lewis' terminology, will continue to be dominated by program and process.

Second, understanding the principles of intervention in terms of the client's problem should not be submerged in the effort to determine the effectiveness of a program. Some evaluative studies tend to separate technology from values, action from thinking, process from outcome, objective outcome criteria from subjective outcome criteria, when the purpose of the evaluative study is to synthesize all these things and to promote understanding of interventional processes by revealing their effects. The study demonstrating positive results without showing how they were achieved is as useless as the study with negative results which does not explain why the treatment was ineffective. For example, an Experimental Study to Measure the Effectiveness of Casework Service produced positive findings but no explanation for the results. The evaluative study, then, must test theory about a social problem and its treatment, not substitute empirical investigation for theoretical understanding. An important implication of this conclusion is that a social problem orientation for the entire curriculum must be substituted for the present sequence, process, orientation of the curriculum. Practitioners and methods teachers are well advised to insist on intensive individual client studies and to forego the mystique of large sample size. Such an approach is far likelier to provide the kind of information needed to improve practice than does traditional evaluative research. Social workers should beware of mistaking the trappings of scientific investigation—statistics and large sample sizes—for science itself. Science provides understandings, and neither sample size nor statistics can do that, although at times they may be useful in that regard.

Third, evaluative studies must be based on a theoretical framework if they are to have general value. The independent, dependent, and background variables, for example, should be selected and related to each other within a theoretical rationale, which presupposes careful investigations of the social problem itself. Evaluative research, if done properly, is only one component of a total series of studies about social conditions; it cannot be carried out effectively on an ad hoc basis. Thus, schools of social work should develop centers in which evaluative research would be conducted as one aspect of research about social problems. Beveridge (1950, p. 15) attributes a quotation to Hughling Jackson summarizing this position: "The study of the causes of things must be preceded by a study of things caused."

Fourth, greater emphasis on the art of scientific investigation, that is, the development of hypotheses, is needed. The effort expended in hypothesis testing must be balanced by at least an equal effort in hypothesis building. Research teaching must consider some hidden problems in evaluative research, for instance, the researcher, assuming the practitioners' theory and treatment procedures are better developed than they actually are, may begin research before completing the necessary conceptualization of practice. Implications for the curriculum include teachers of both methods and research stressing the inadequate present conceptualization of practice, and stimulating students to creative innovations. Instead of *methods* teaching, we might promote teaching of *methodology*— the science of method—to encourage its development, rather than promoting imitation of the status quo.

Fifth, the conflict between the researcher and the practitioner, only rarely explicitly acknowledged in evaluative research, impedes progress. Hopefully, differences will disappear, when the true purpose of the evaluative study becomes clear to each. Both will gain much from a scientific collaborative effort, not merely to determine the effectiveness of a given program, but to advance knowledge of social problems and their resolutions. When both researchers and practitioners realize that their *mutual* objective is to understand the relationship between the outcome and the treatment method, not to effect a given cure in a given case (desirable as that may be), collaboration will be possible for the advancement of science and practice theory. Surely the schools of social work bear a heavy responsibility for correcting this misunderstanding about evaluative research. The medium is truly the message here. The social work student is all too patently exposed to the wide gap existing between methods and research teachers—a gap frequently cultivated by faculty members striving for their own identity and status. Perhaps the correction of this misconception will only come about when all methods teachers are doing research beyond the master's level as well as doing clinical work. Utopian? Perhaps, but the curriculum is unlikely to improve unless faculty improve first.

Sixth, the payoff for social work practice from evaluative research studies is derived from theoretical advances. The curriculum implication is clear: theory should be the main thrust of teaching. To accomplish this means reorganizing the entire curriculum so that research courses are not isolated from methods courses. If the social work student is to understand the interdependence of research and practice, the content and arrangement of the curriculum must reflect the necessity of both.

Seventh, existing programs may be extremely difficult if not impossible to evaluate properly. For instance, *essential* programs or services, such as ADC or child welfare services, once initiated, cannot for humanitarian reasons be withheld for experimental control. Also, public bureaucracies often defeat evaluative efforts. Thus, evaluation should be mandatory for all newly-initiated programs, for once a program is well established, reconceptualization of the program for the purposes of good evaluative research may prove impossible. The fact that the conceptual work in these thirteen studies was left largely undone clearly indicates that evaluative research is often accomplished for reasons other than improving our understanding of practice.

These thirteen studies demonstrate not only considerable technical progress in the application of evaluative research methodology, but more importantly, their very existence acknowledges that the burden of establishing the effectiveness of practice is upon the practitioner (Eysenck, 1969). Despite the discomfort which some of their findings engender in social workers, and despite their inevitable limitations as studies, the fact that evaluative research occurs at all renews hope of improving social work practice. Now that social work researchers have mastered the theory and, to some extent, the technique of research methodology, they can move ahead to master the art of scientific investigation (Beveridge, 1950). Research may thus contribute to the improvement of treatment methods by replacing evaluations of program effectiveness with evaluations of professional effectiveness. Teachers in both the research and methods sequences in schools of social work have a unique mutual opportunity to bring about this evolution.

5

Developing a Program Responsive to New Knowledge and Values

Harold Lewis

Social work can be an exciting enterprise, reflecting the tensions and temptations associated with shaping the human service environment, capturing the mystery of the linkage of heart and head in human action. Neither a science devoid of values, nor an art stripped of meaning, social work education prepares for a practice. This practice claims for its practitioners a universally appealing purpose: to design an environment of social services in which all people can hope to achieve their maximum self-advantage while furthering society's goals. Although we anticipate an enthusiastic response from the users of our services, and from our students and faculties as to the experience of social work practice and education, too often we hear criticism alerting us to the absence of these qualities.

There is doubt about what we know, or can claim to know, and doubt that we practice what we profess. These doubts gnaw at our insights and drain our convictions, depleting our intellectual and emotional enthusiasms. The reasons for this failing in our practice, our curricula, and our schools can be partly attributed to our epistemologic confusions.

According to our professional literature, what we know should guide our actions and help us attain selected goals. With this epistemological bias, we judge our effectiveness by results of actions which we assume are based on our claimed knowledge and values. We expect evaluations of results of practice to provide evidence of the truth to which we subscribe. The discussions throughout this chapter explore examples of such evidence and suggest ways whereby they can influence the program development efforts of the profession.

Stated simply, if what we do is based on what we claim to know and value and is intended to achieve preferred ends, then the results of our professional actions should test our claims and show us how to improve our efforts. The difficulty, of course, is in achieving consensus on the merits of studies cited as convincing tests. Previous chapters in this book have evaluated the methodological achievements of the studies selected for review. If the results of studies are to be useful for program design and development, additional knowledge is required.

It must be shown that what is being taught is learned and then applied in the practice observed. The constraints of agency and communtiy resources and purposes associated with each practice test must fall within the range of *givens* in what is taught. The results obtained should logically link what is taught to corresponding elements constituting the professional performance. What is taught ought not to be judged in a watered down and dissipated practice version that hardly tests its merits. The consequences of social work activity, distinguished from other activities associated with a program of service, must be observed and judged. Finally, criterion variables relevant to the changes intended to result from social work should be used to evaluate its achievement. Obviously, the study of consequence requires specification of the professional function and purpose and that what is taught be clearly understood.

The argument can be summarized as follows: the structure of social work knowledge and values is typical of professions, serving a purpose different from that served by knowledge derived from the theoretical sciences and values derived from the applied humanities. Program design and development is itself a professional practice, having its own principles, and can only be appropriately applied when the knowledge and values to be communicated in the program are clearly specified and structurally unambiguous. Both conditions are incompletely met in the typical program development processes of social work. Finally, the value context of social work practice and education works against social work goals by persistently subverting its central purposes. This, in turn, makes impossible a convincing test of the consequences of professional activities.

Organizing Rubrics

Program, problem, and process have in different combinations provided the conceptual underpinnings of schemes for categorizing the values, knowledge, and practice of the profession. Each scheme, in turn, stresses one aspect of the threesome constituting the essential elements of practice. Program emphasizes purpose and goal; problem emphasizes knowledge and ways of knowing; and process emphasizes methods, techniques and skills. In terms of the individual social worker, these rubrics suggest the attitude, understanding and behavior elements constituting the substance of his professional identity.

Program. Social workers are employed in a variety of agencies encompassing many programs of services. Each agency requires the social worker to master specific knowledge, so that he will perform appropriately on the job. Agencies sharing program interests are commonly grouped into fields of service, such as child welfare, public assistance, medical, and psychiatric. It is assumed that beyond the specifics to be learned to practice in each agency's program, a body of knowledge is shared by workers in the same field of service. Fields of service may differ substantially in the knowledge they require of the social worker, but they will nevertheless use such workers interchangeably because all social workers are presumed to have the generic knowledge deemed essential to the performance of the social work function, regardless of agency setting or field of service.

The programmatic rubric for depicting the generic and specific in social work practice suggests one possible categorization of the knowledge components of practice. At the agency level, the specifics of practice show how much of what is known is actually applied from day to day. Directives are needed to assure that degree of uniformity in performance necessary for quality control of the service. The body of formulations at this level of program are *rules,* usually codified in agency manuals. At the fields of practice level, common features of agency roles provide generalizations based on a wide range of observations. Such observations suggest *principles* to be applied in practice. Finally, as previously noted, there is the core of knowledge all social workers are assumed to have, which justifies their being considered part of a common personnel pool for all fields of service. It is presumed such knowledge is based on observations of social and individual conditions and behavior under all possible circumstances, not just in one agency or field of social service. These broadly-based observations yield *theories* which systematize the explanations underpinning principles and their methods of application.

Problem Condition. The problem-condition criterion for viewing practice emphasizes the cognitive elements in problem definition and solution. It identifies agencies, programs, and methods with the problem-conditions they are intended to affect, seeking to link these to the interest in causes and prevention evidenced in other disciplines and professions. Societal problems are generated by a range of influences—political, economic, cultural. Their prevention and amelioration may require interventions of many professions and of many interested citizen organizations.

How social work makes its contribution to the prevention and amelioration of these problems generated scholarly and practical interest in the profession throughout its history. In the daily experience of social workers, encounters with personal and societal problems manifest in the lives of clients are commonplace. Thus, considerable information about such problems, descriptions of their genesis and their efforts, have come from the records of social workers. From systematic studies of practice, social work has often provided information dealing with aspects of such problems more interesting to the human sciences and related professions than to social work practice itself. Societal problems, being complex and interdependent, defy simple formulations of their essentials. Many problem-oriented disciplines and professions will try to solve a social problem of long duration, the effects of which are widely felt. Social workers, necessarily, want to use whatever knowledge—beyond that provided by their immediate practice—is developed about the problems they confront and interventive skills of other professions are an important part of the knowledge they need for developing programs and procedures for action.

The social worker seeks established truths which when applied provide predictable results. He studies the body of available knowledge in order to understand significant aspects of the problem which may help solve it and to locate tested solutions and their consequences. He realizes he can learn from past experiences, even if they are not identical to his expectations of the cases at hand. By using analogy and association, exploiting prior experience, and making trial and error efforts, he seeks to place the particular problem he is dealing with in a class of similar problems for which solutions have been found. The specific characteristics of the problem as it confronts him in practice are illuminated as its generic attributes are explained by generalizations from all possible sources. Thus, in seeking to understand the problem, the social worker finds that he is not bound by discipline boundaries.

Once the social worker has mastered what is known about the problem, including the various approaches to its solution and appreciation of their relative merits, he can be expected to evolve appropriate *rules* for performance of required tasks, to identify and develop *principles* to guide practice, and to translate *theoretical* formulations into programs and methods relevant to that aspect of the problem to be solved. Social agency services at best contribute only partial solutions and their programs must be evaluated within the framework of an overview of the problem. Thus, a sound and sufficient knowledge of the problem is primary since on this depends skills in methods of intervention and program development.

Process. The process rubric for viewing practice emphasizes skills evidenced in social work methods. Casework, social group work, and community organization have traditionally been considered the primary methods of social work, but, now, social policy and planning, social administration, research, consultation and supervision are emerging as methods of practice. Changing programs of service, client involvement, and new conceptions of problematic conditions have produced methods tailored to the tasks and roles they entail and these methods have combined to form new ones, directed toward fresh conceptions of client systems. This frees the social worker to employ whatever processes are necessary to achieve service goals.

Focusing on how a process is to be affected and what *materials* are involved in that process, this approach to practice categorizes what is to be known (Studt, 1968) in accordance with the processes of interaction to be influenced and the pertinent characteristics of the client system and social workers in the process.

All three of the traditional methods need to know about human growth, social development and interpersonal behavior, yet each emphasizes special interests in arriving at the basic knowledge required for practice. Current developments have modified practice in these three methods such that a reformulation of methods based on new combinations of roles and tasks can be expected to alter the knowledge required for practice.

This conception of practice requires specific knowledge for target client-systems, including tasks to be performed and roles to be enacted relative to such targets. The building block distinguishing client-systems is the individual, who is seen in his personal, group, intergroup and community functions. Knowledge in all areas of the client's social experience contributes to social work practice at whatever point service affects changes in the client-system. Similarly some commonly shared competence in task and role performance will be required of all practitioners regardless of method. These shared competencies constitute the generic base of practice knowledge. Work on tasks in this scheme requires *rules* to direct action; role performance necessitates *principles* to guide practice within a purpose-oriented context; and target client systems and social processes to be influenced need *theories* of personal, social, organizational, and societal development which justify the methods employed in practice.

Schematism.   Factors other than the natural course of events account for organizational patterns that structure the form, content, and methods of providing service. The relative influence of agency, profession, and clientele on resource allocation processes determines which of the three—program, problem, process—predominates in shaping service delivery systems, educational curricula, and recipient involvement. Agencies sense the challenge to their existence in programmatic change; the profession's relevance may be questioned when problems are differently defined; where process is altered, the client's involvement and impact on service may be threatened. Thus, the interacting power interests of agencies, profession and client play some part in the choice of organizing rubrics.

The societal context of practice also affects such choices. In periods of social unrest, when ideological conflicts are frequent, goals and purposes are likely to be reexamined, and programs questioned. In periods of liberalization, when new resources are mobilized to deal with problem conditions, problems will also be differently perceived. In periods in which entrenched interests strongly defend the status quo, and *what is* is taken as a given, efficiency of methods and the processes they entail are subject to scrutiny.

These speculative observations caution us against a narrow, static view of organizing rubrics. It is beyond the scope of this chapter to pursue these interesting observations further; nevertheless, it may prove helpful to depict their relationships as in Table 1.

Table 1

	Values (Ideology)	Knowledge (Power)	Practice (Work)
Program	Goal and Purpose (Policy Procedure)	Theory	Tasks
Problem	Problem Condition (Target)	Propositions (How)	Roles
Process	Imperatives, Commendations, Commands	Methods (Techniques and Skills)	Activities (Relationships)

This analysis of organizing rubrics suggests the following cautions for curriculum designs. First, the governing rubric of a school's curriculum ought never be taken as a given. Viewed as one plausible response to the societal stresses that shape the service preferences of agency, profession and clientele, the school's curriculum should be approached as being in the process of developing. Second, conclusions based on findings of practice evaluations are likely to influence the curriculum of a school if their implementation for program, problem and process is formulated in terms of the rules, principles and theoretical frameworks common to all such organizing rubrics. This degree of specificity provides the school's faculty with concrete directives, appreciated because the changes recommended anticipate the school's operational limits. It is noteworthy that this analysis suggests that in all three rubrics, rules, principles and theories formally structure the knowledge of the profession. Each incorporates terminal and instrumental values in its action directives. If the intention is to influence curriculum, then the input of the new and the different and the rejection of the false and irrelevant must dovetail with the elements of that rubric which provides the framework for a particular school's curriculum design.

Structure of Knowledge and Values in Professional Practice

Competence in practice requires an integrated application of knowledge and values in the performance of tasks. The relationship of knowledge and values to practice, however, is not direct; there is an intermediate structure of rules, principles, and theory which link knowledge and values to practice (Wilson, D., 1969).

Knowledge. Substantive knowledge is organized in theoretical models. Principles incorporate empirically testable propositions in their formulations, and rules prescribe the action to be taken. Rules provide concise directives for practice and, typically, are codified in agency manuals. Principles, incorporating imperatives and causal assumptions, generate rules appropriate for specific settings and circumstances. Theories justify methods, providing explanations connecting the causal assumptions underpinning principles.

Rules define a practice, and tell the social worker how to engage in it (Rawls, 1955). A social worker, starting in an agency, quickly learns to follow the rules, as given. He may be held responsible for failing to follow them and may argue that the rule encompasses various possible activities, but as long as he accepts the agency practice, the rules are the test of his adherence to the practice requirements. To challenge the rules is to question the practice itself, and the challenge should be to the principles on which the rules are based, not the practice. Such rules offer no guidance for decisions in uncertain situations and allow no exceptions. Thus, each case must be made to fit the rule, or the rule must be qualified in such a way as to provide for the unanticipated elements introduced by each case. Obviously, rules justifying discretion on the part of the social worker are needed. This is particularly true when, absent relevant rules, unanticipated occurrences must be acted on. Where such discretion is not allowed, the social worker who finds the prevalent rules inappropriate must appeal to the practice principles.

Rarely do rules make an explicit claim to knowledge or belief, nor do they make reference to goals and purposes. They merely spell out how the worker is expected to initiate, sustain and terminate his practice. It is sometimes assumed that rules put into practice the values and theory justifying the agency's goals and program. Whether this is so, and whether workers are able and willing to implement these rules must be determined empirically. The dissatisfaction of persons served and contributors with the services of agencies frequently shows that rules do not implement either values or theory, for a social worker may carry out the requirements of rules, yet fail to achieve their real purpose. From the wording of a particular rule one cannot determine the principle justifying its application in a particular instance. This is understandable, since rules taken separately are commands; and commands are to be followed, not justified. From a set of rules, however, one can deduce what result their sequential or simultaneous application should impart. Thus, the social worker in each instance of task performance must be aware of the principles informing his practice; otherwise, he may apply the rules in an unjustifiable manner or as a habitual response to situations no longer calling for their use.

A principle is reflected in an opinion, attitude or belief which influences behavior. Principles are more than the sum of experience, since they represent generalizations from particular cases; principles justify practice, in contrast to rules which justify a particular action of practice (Rawls, 1955). A principle involves certain implicit or explicit imperatives and incorporates causal assumptions in its formulations (Guzzetta, 1966). Principles, in order to have a bearing on practice, must be elaborated in rules which direct and assure some regularity in the prescribed behavior. The order appearing in the structure and form of the social work practice directed by such rules represents the guiding principle in its production. In other words, for a principle to be observed in practice, it must appear as a structure in the product. The individual style of the worker and the unique attributes of the client manifest themselves as distinctive features of the product, but will not qualitatively alter the principle-determined structure manifest in the product.

Principles of practice, as well as the rules they generate, contain constraints expressed in such terms as *will, shall,* and the like, which constraints prescribe the limits of choice of action open to the social worker. In contrast to rules, principles avoid specifying tasks to be performed, providing instead elements to be considered in role enactment. Considerable leeway is assured the social worker, who must find his own way to apply these principles in practice. Propositions and commendations are incorporated into social work practice principles. The propositional element assumes that in order to achieve the purposes and goals of practice, such and such must be done (Simon, 1957). If the "will," "shall," and the like commendation is removed from the principle statement, no intention is implied, leaving only propositional formulations that may be proven true or false.

Research intended to test such propositions would be expected to provide for requirements associated with the agency context of practice and worker activities, if the findings are intended to illuminate social work practice. Outcomes of service and resources provided in response to client requests may be studied without consideration of these requirements. Where this is the case, knowledge derived from the research is not immediately usable in practice, but contributes to what Simon calls the theoretical sciences. Generalizations derived from studies that do not take these requirements into account contribute to a practice science of social work. A practice science incorporates the confirmed propositions derived from causal assumptions imbedded in practice principles. Its propositions include in their formulations these requirements, which may be viewed as contingent or intervening variables evidenced in the context and activities of practice (Simon, 1957).

Practice principles use knowledge from the human sciences and related professions for their propositional formulations. Implicit in these formulations are characterizations of organizations, persons, professions, services, and tasks utilizing theories about man and society developed outside the agency and social work activities. Mastery of social work practice science is essential to professional intervention; only selective knowledge from the human sciences and related professions, varying by program, process and problem, is necessary for such practice.

Theory in social work is intended to explain the phenomena of practice, that is, why the phenomena behave the way they do and are what they are. Rules and principles tell the social worker what to do, but only the theories justifying such rules and principles explain why he does it. Theories provide understanding but they do not impose conditions on the use of that understanding, nor do they give specifics such as time and place, both essentials of rules and principles.

A theory may be taken to mean more than the generalization it embodies. In social work literature, it often provides a model of what the generalizations describe, having heuristic function as well as aiding understanding (Wartofsky, 1968). No systematic theoretical model attempting to explain all social work practice has thus far been proposed, though many ad hoc models of a limited nature have been entertained. Social work has also utilized nontheoretical models to depict the drama of practice. These models order their components so as to suggest their roles and place in practice, but do not offer explanations of either. They are not to be confused with theoretical models, which are stated in such a way that they suggest propositions to be tested.

The human sciences partition knowledge about man and the environment with which he interacts. For social work, such partitioning merely fragments the orienting knowledge needed for practice. Knowledge of man, his biopsychosocial functioning, and the societal context in which he experiences his time in the cosmos needs to be synthesized to be greatly useful to social work professions. Characteristically, such knowledge refers to *what* and *what for,* not to *how to do,* which is the main concern of social work practice science. A practice science utilizes the *what* and *what for* type of knowledge, but systematically relates such knowledge to *know-how* statements derived from observations of practice, or analogous to practice, in order to explain such practice. However, principles of practice are the most probable source of know-how generalization of a practice science. All professions depend on *know-how* theories which explain the helping process, aid in decision-making, facilitate choosing among alternatives, and provide guidelines for identifying alternatives and for suggesting organizational patterns of work to improve choices (Simon, 1957).

In addition to knowledge organized by rules, principles and theories, there is self-awareness upon which every social worker depends for sensitivity and style in practice. Self-awareness, a form of personal knowledge (Polyanyi, 1958), is composed of both convictions and evaluative statements which can be confirmed by their consequences. The latter form of personal knowledge shapes practice, providing its satisfactions and infusing the social worker with empathy giving the helping relationship its humane qualities. Personal knowledge is also important to a theory of practice; Mary Richmond's comment that "in the last analysis, the practitioner of an art must discover the heart of the whole matter for himself" (Richmond, 1917) suggests the need for synthesis rather than analysis in attempting to understand the personal dimensions of practice. We must recognize the importance of personal knowledge in practice and realize that it is knowable as fact whenever it enters to affect the helping relationship. We need not relegate the *art* of practice to a realm beyond knowing explanations, although we may not know how the aesthetic originates in a person.

We can now depict the hierarchical structure of professional social work knowledge, having briefly described the categories— rules, principles, theories—constituting the structure. Each category interacts with its adjacent categories, while maintaining a degree of autonomy and stability that permits intracategory interactions which accounts for the events and patterns occurring in that category.

Categories support each other, but do not control each other. Each has room for innovation, which can occur without affecting another category. Each category incorporates content from adjacent categories, bringing forth new components and reordering existing components; thus every category includes components that have preceded others in time. The exchange among categories is not uniform or inevitable and always partial. Reordering of components within any one category, resulting from internal changes, can produce innovations in category characteristics and influence adjacent categories. These processes of interaction are responsible for changes in knowledge which are utilized in practice (Bunge, 1969; Mesarovic and Macko, 1969).

Values. Values traverse a set of ordered levels through which they are transformed from beliefs to practice guides in professional activities. These levels are conveniently labeled in terms of what they require from the social worker who seeks to implement them. The level furthest from action is the set of *values* themselves, which designate a moral perspective. A step closer to action are the *ethical imperatives* formulating behavioral requirements through which the values may be realized. Still closer to action are *commendations,* incorporated in principles, which specify how imperatives are to be applied. Finally, closest to action are *commands,* codified into rules which are based on principles.

Previously, we noted that rules viewed as commands may not, when applied, carry out the values and theory justifying an agency program. This can happen if the social worker implements the formal requirements of rules, but fails to accomplish their real aim. Failure to achieve desired results after following a command effectively discourages adherence to that command. Such failures are caused by many factors, including inadequate resources, limited talent, unfavorable circumstances. But, supposedly, commands are formulated in anticipation of such factors and will safeguard practice from such unfortunate influences. In a conflict between command and result, result prevails; the command must yield to the corrective pressure of unrealized intention. Initially, attempts are made to modify, add or drop tasks required by the rule, in the hope that deficiencies will be overcome. If, with these changes, commands still produce poor results, justifying propositions or commendations or both will be challenged. One can deal with such challenges at the rule level, as long as rule-modification and rule-exception offer directives appropriate to the lessons gleaned from disappointing results.

Increasing modification of commands weakens their influence, and, in time, they must appeal to a higher authority to retain their force. Thus, at the level of practice principle, where commendations and propositions blend theory and values into professional guidelines, the critical struggle between behavioral norms and professed ethical imperatives will take place (Toren, 1969).

Commendations to act in certain ways are empirically justified by tested hypotheses, the predictions of which are confirmed. At the level of principle, such commendations are further justified by ethical imperatives suggesting models of behavior. Imperatives thus harden the social worker's attachments to commendations in a manner that is not characteristic of his attachments to explanatory propositions. The model of ethical social work conveyed by imperatives prescribes the characteristics of good practice. At the level of principle, imperative statements cement commendations strongly together, embodying deep convictions. For this reason, a challenge to a commendation threatens not merely the rules it alters or the program it overturns, but casts doubt upon beliefs that have justified fields of service. Discarding propositions, in comparison to overturning commendations, appears far less divisive; typically, such changes affect methods and problem formulations, not purpose. Science assumes knowledge to be both tentative and partial, and rules for rejection of knowledge claims are fairly well-established. Thus, when propositions are dropped after being proved false, science is served. In fact, one of the goals of empirical research is the toppling of propositions.

Rules for rejecting commendations are not so well-established; a rejection of a commendation threatens the ethic itself. Therefore, one expects commendations to change more slowly than propositions, ethical imperatives more slowly than theories, and values far more slowly than knowledge. While it is not uncommon for different, and sometimes contradictory, theories to be used concurrently to justify propositions and the methods they prescribe, it is far less probable that different codes of ethics, particularly contradictory ones, will be concurrently used to justify similar commendations and commands. In general, a profession can tolerate far more challenges to its means than to its ends. Nevertheless, in the social work profession means and ends are joined in statements of principles, and changes in one cannot easily be insulated from changes in the other.

At the level of value designations, where ideology is formulated, one finds justification for ethical imperatives. Values that justify professional goals are themselves influenced by prevailing norms. When the norms influencing agency, professional and personal social work practitioner values are at variance with each other and with their imperatives lead to conflicting commendations and commands, the shortcomings of the program are obvious, both to the clients and the practitioners.

We can now summarize the hierarchical structure of social work values. The relationship between commands, commendations, ethical imperatives, and values is influenced by their intended use as guides to action. Each level is rooted in the next, in descending order from value designations to rule commands, and the pattern of justification follows this arrangement (Bunge, 1969). The value of designation level generates the goals of action and describes the purposes of the structure; the imperative level generates modes of behavior and describes how values are recognizable in the actions of the social workers. The commendation level generates guidelines for behavior prescribed by ethical imperatives. Finally, commands generate actions which show that professional performance conforms to the justifying values. There is a dominant-subordinate relationship between levels, although each level is not completely determined by the level from which it derives its immediate justification. One cannot significantly alter the substance of one level without concurrently upsetting its cohesion to adjacent levels. Norms identify the disparities between expected and actual adherence to commands, commendations, imperatives, and designations.

The context of practice helps shape behavioral norms; personal, professional and agency beliefs influence value designations. Thus belief and practice contexts affect the substance and form of designations and actions. It is apparent that commands go unheeded when their consequences contradict purpose. If justified by normative requirements in performance, such failure to observe rules points to the necessity of changes in other levels. Within any one level, requirements may vary from person to person, from agency to agency, and from one area of professional practice to another, as long as contradictory prescriptions are avoided and justification in relation to the dominant value is maintained. Each level organizes its directives independent of other levels and must be understood in terms of its particular mode of expression.

Implications

The structure of knowledge and values have been carefully examined to emphasize the distinction to be made between theoretical and practice sciences, as each influences professional practice. Theoretical sciences serve an orienting function, locating the practitioner in time and place and pointing him in relevant directions. They suggest natural and societal constraints to be heeded, lest energies be wasted in trying to change what will not or ought not be changed. Practice sciences, in contrast, are concerned with the *how* of practice, prescribing purposeful actions. The professional worker must know more about practice science than theoretical sciences. In social work, the differences in roles and tasks in a given practice call for different theoretical inputs, while sharing a wide range of practice science principles. A sound professional curriculum includes both types of knowledge and is sensitive to critiques of both. Nevertheless, unless an evaluation of practice reveals what knowledge—theoretical or practice—needs reformulation, it is not likely that a significant modification will occur.

Further, if findings challenge purpose, without designating the level of specification—imperative, commendation or command —the reexamination necessary for an incorporation of value changes into curriculum is stymied. Values yield slowly to change, in contrast to empirically derived knowledge. An undifferentiated challenge directed against purpose questions the hierarchical structure, and the findings may be viewed as a threat, rather than as a welcome contribution. From the above, we can draw the following implications for curriculum design and development.

First, conceptualizations of levels of skill and degrees of educational preparation should reflect the differential nature of the structure of knowledge and values, if justifications for new patterns

of preparation and new careers are to prove more than oppor-
tunistic responses to the changing manpower market. For example,
educational curricula training staff to follow rules, under the generating principles justifying an agency's program, are more appropriate for in-service training efforts than for university sponsored
education. Associate degree programs, four-year undergraduate degree programs, the master's and doctoral programs similarly need
to be justified in relation to the level of competence to be achieved.
Organizing rubrics may also vary according to level of educational
achievement intended.

Second, skill, a measure of competence in the application of
knowledge and values, must be distinguished from style which characterizes a performance. At any level of practice, beautiful style
may be evident and should be awarded appropriately. Work requiring minimal skills may be done with a style which shows its
practitioner to be gifted, and work requiring considerable skill may
be performed in a clumsy manner. Nevertheless, the gifted practitioner with limited skill may be unable to perform in a job requiring the mastery of knowledge and values for which he is educationally unprepared.

Third, orienting knowledge (in contrast to practical knowledge) is more crucial to program and problem than to process. The
profession has experienced the negative consequences of misdirected
efforts and unjustified claims. We learned long ago not to see set-
tlement house work and scouting as solutions to the problems of
juvenile delinquency. We have known for some time that contra-
ception and abortion are more potent techniques than psychological
counseling in reducing illegitimate or unwanted births. As long as
problem formulations and programs are the targets of evaluation
studies, and processes continue to receive limited attention, the human sciences and applied humanities content of curricula, not the
practice sciences, will benefit most from these studies.

Principles of Design and Development

Assuming that the implications drawn from this analysis are
worthwhile, it is questionable whether schools and agencies would
effectively incorporate them into their curricula. The program
design and development process must be based on principled pro-

cedures governed by principles, if they are to be effectively responsive to new intellectual sources. The program development process resembles other professional processes in that it seeks to implement a design. As a practice, it formulates its understanding in principles which justify its behavior. Consider the following four curriculum development practice principles. First, professional curricula should anticipate the needs of the society for which future social workers will be responsible, and, second, should prepare the student to cope with those anticipated needs. Third, the design and maintenance of a professional curriculum should be a dynamic, continuing process. Fourth, professional disciplines should be integrated into the curriculum so that the student can easily use them in practice.

These principles, though derived from the husbanded wisdom of curriculum builders, are beliefs, not statements of truths, since their propositional assumptions have not been established in accordance with procedures meeting minimum standards for obtaining evidence. However, some rules are justified by one or more of these principles. For example, the professional societies and agencies institute regular surveys to determine national and regional societal needs to be satisfied by the professions and requirements for professionals as to type, quantity and educational level. Also, surveys of practicing professionals are regularly conducted on a national and regional basis to furnish career profiles of professionals and to correlate the career profiles of an institution's graduates with the effectiveness of past curricula. These rules, with minor modifications, and the principles cited, are taken from Rosenstein's (1968) study of engineering curricula. Whether adherence to these action guidelines and commands can yield a curriculum responsive to new knowledge and changing values will be determined only after observation and evaluation of their application. Viewed as an attempt to determine the consequences of a particular educational preparation, findings of evaluative studies of social work practice can be analyzed to identify curriculum deficiencies and to suggest ways to overcome such deficiencies. Viewed as evaluations of practice, the findings can be incorporated into courses concerned with the nature, scope and effectiveness of practice, and courses teaching how to evaluate practice. In neither application will the findings contribute to our knowledge of the curriculum or program development process as a practice science; thus there is critical need for evaluative research on the curriculum and program development process itself.

In this chapter, we have reviewed the epistemologic stumbling blocks to the efficient use of new knowledge and values in professional programs, and we must conclude that we can trace many difficulties to the shortcomings in our society which defeat our practice intentions at every turn. Our society has not developed systems of awards and denials based on principles of distributive justice; as long as we allocate our intellectual and financial resources to further benefit the advantaged, often adding to the burden of the disadvantaged, we will have little opportunity to apply what we claim to know and value under conditions conducive to the achievement of our purposes. Small successes in delivering social services are less than satisfactory if they are achieved at the price of a general worsening of conditions of the most disadvantaged needing service. In these circumstances the results obtained will necessarily have to be limited, as will our practice science whose generalizations are strongly conditioned by societal constraints. In what circumstance, if any, would our work be truly tested on its merit? Should we seek such circumstances, or should we be satisfied to accomplish what we can, adjusting our means to our ends?

6

Utilizing
Research Findings for
Macrosystem Intervention

Walter L. Walker

Examining the relationship between evaluative research findings and the professional social work practice of policy development, welfare planning, and administration on the macrosystem level highlights the importance of research activities in ongoing social welfare activities at the macrosystem level. Discussing the integration of research findings into the conceptual tools that the macrosystem practitioner must learn to utilize raises the question: "How can he be taught to evaluate research findings in policy terms as they become available?" The following are working definitions of various terms utilized in this chapter. Definitions of these terms are in such a state of flux that those we present represent concepts specifically related to this chapter.

Planning seeks to facilitate decision-making via identification, quantification and/or qualification of relevant factors relating to the decision. Planners attempt to predict the consequences of future acts. We should remember Martin Rein's (1970) statement that rational planning is a myth when the value consensus on which it depends is illusory and the technology for eliminating arbitrary decisions is not available. Lacking value consensus and technology, planning is simply an extension of political conflict in which power, guile, and sometimes good fortune determine the course of future events.

Policy is a method of action selected from alternatives to guide and determine present and future decisions. In order to have impact, policy must be based on an agreement guaranteeing compliance of those governed by the policy; once again a value consensus is necessary for policy to become operative.

Administration is the coordination and supervision of actions designed to implement policy efficiently. In this chapter costs as well as benefits are considered an integral part of the concept of efficiency.

Macrosystem refers to a large-scale complex social system. Use of the term here refers to system-wide interventions affecting a large, geographically scattered population. We should remember that macro is simply a level on a continuum and that the distinction between large, intermediate, and small-scale systems is not amenable to precise definition.

Curriculum is a set of experiences and opportunities which provide a student with a framework for attaining specified academic goals. A curriculum should help the student organize his search for knowledge so that his energies and talent are directed to maximum achievement. The goal of the relationship between these activities is the efficient resolution of and prevention of problems. While the state of the art in these two activities is such that the accomplishment of the goal seems far off, establishment of the goal prevents the development of plans, programs, procedures, or practices counterproductive to its attainment. To establish a goal requires organizing activities which demands a substantive commitment to the goal;

this commitment means that the goal and the wisdom to reach it come before tradition, pride, biases, and other narrow interests.

However, the choices are never so clear-cut, since distinctions between alternatives are not always obvious. Ideally, the disciplined practice of evaluative research, planning, policy development, and administration facilitates choosing at various levels of specificity within an organized effort to reach the goal. In reality, there is much to discover and create in formulating policy and planning disciplined activity. Administration is an old process, a watchword of modern society, and, as a science, has been hardened by theoretical and empirical inquiries, as well as conventional trial and error. Pure research is further advanced than evaluative research. Thus, ideologies and tradition still provide answers to problems that are becoming more severe. Instead of identifying the nature, incidence, and scope of the problems so that relevant solutions can be identified, planned, organized, administered and evaluated, our profession tends to cling to methods, measures, and rationales believed effective. Further, the profession has not faced the implications of its failure to deal effectively with many problems over which it claims jurisdiction.

Evaluation research basically attempts to help society understand the full impact of its efforts to achieve specific goals. In the context of this chapter those efforts involve solving or ameliorating social problems. Impact evaluation should enable us to answer various questions. What are the goals of the program? Are these goals stated in terms that are both measurable and related to the target population? What is the specific program design, and to what extent is it followed by those operating the program? To what degree does the program reach its goals? To what extent do unintended side effects result from the operation of the program? What per cent of the target population would have realized the program's goals, if the program had not been implemented? None of these questions is easily answered in even simplest programs of social intervention. Answering them in more complex circumstances requires talent, money, clear thinking, effective communication, commitment and good fortune. Impact evaluation is a primitive art form which has great potential as a valuable weapon in our society's efforts to solve its social problems. This development will not happen automatically or without much trial and error, but it must happen.

The popularity of the evaluation symbol largely results from its ambiguity; as a term, it can be widely shared. Trouble starts when believers in ambiguous symbols try to impose their definitions on others. Hence, the term, as used in this chapter, has not been conclusively defined, and variations in points of view are encouraged. We accept the terms *evaluation, knowledge,* and *action* as given, making possible the examination of Lewis' (1947) proposition about the relationship of these terms: "Knowledge, action, and evaluation are essentially connected. The primary and pervasive significance of knowledge lies in its guidance of action: knowing is for the sake of doing. And action, obviously, is rooted in evaluation. For a being which did not assign comparative values, deliberate action would be pointless; and for one which did not know, it would be impossible" (p. 3). In the professions, value is placed on deliberate action. What converts a search for knowledge into an evaluation project is that the knowledge sought is to be used to guide practical action.

The impact evaluations discussed in the following pages describe the efforts of large, formal organizations to resolve various problems. Parsons (1951) and other social scientists have postulated that any organization is influenced by two competitive drives—stability and survival: short-term stability requires routine and long-range survival requires change. The selection of an intra-organizational evaluation method depends on whether short-term stability or long-term survival is more highly valued. An organization valuing short-run stability typically tolerates a ritualistic form of evaluation; it acts positively only on those study recommendations that will not disturb it. Conversely, an organization placing high value on change for the sake of survival leans toward those methods of evaluation which facilitate an optimum adjustment between the organization and its environment.

In the ritualistic model, a range of norms are expressed as numerical units, which meaure what should be influenced by the activities of the organization. This method concentrates on the activities of the organization with respect to its clientele; statistics reflecting services rendered, instead of success or failure, are typical of this evaluation method. The series of studies by Helen Jeter (1960, 1962, 1963) on Child Welfare Services in the United States is an example of ritualistic thinking in which one tends to evaluate service in terms of volume, rather than effectiveness. Ritualistic evaluation assures the organization that changes are not necessary, if the problem is demonstrated to result from contingencies external to it. This method assumes that the organization can cope with the growing problem by growing itself! A rapidly expanding problem provokes only the old, routine methods of solution, rather than an appraisal of those methods in terms of their appropriateness and effectiveness. A graphic example of this phenomenon was the escalation of the Vietnam war by the United States. Our belief in our armed forces as an instrument of foreign policy resulted in the safety of our armed forces in the combat zone being used to justify our foreign policy. Ritualistic evaluations are useful for focusing on the extent of problems, but they are unable to stimulate critical examination of the organizational intervention supposed to cope with the problem.

The United States Department of Defense has used an alternative method of evaluation in recent years. Organizational needs for stability are given low priority as are a few factors important to organizational survival, whereas, efficiency is a prime value. Alternative combinations of manpower, technology, materials, place, and time are examined to identify maximum yields per unit of costs. The examination of results and the projection of anticipated results against a preconceived scheme of technical values is not without its hazards. The operational method is precise, but fails to account for all the conditions under which an organization must function. Considering technical efficiency the only value can lead to seriously defective evaluation studies. A history of the Atlantic slave trade underscores this pitfall (Mannix and Cowley, 1962). Transporting marketable flesh to Atlantic seaports was the objective of this trade, and it could be measured in terms of hundred-weight delivered per dollar expended. The principal cost, transportation, was fixed; the variable was the number of individuals transported per square foot of cargo space. Constraints were the mortality rates from communicable diseases, the speed at which the vessel could move to elude coastal patrols, and other factors—all a function of the load size. The managerial staff debated whether to ship the cargo standing room only or with reclining space. Modern operations-research techniques would have resolved this problem with precision by constructing a mathematical model accommodating the significant variables. However, these calculations would be based on the cargo's unquestioning obedience to orders as any deviation of the cargo from these orders would result in unanticipated costs. In social welfare administration we like to think that the clients are not cargo, and the assumption of obedience to preemptory orders is not valid.

In the social welfare field, we must go beyond ritualistic evaluation and look at programs in their totality regarding service statistics, behavioral imperatives, and service effectiveness in either absolute or relative terms. An eighteen-month evaluation of the New York State program for the rehabilitation of crippled children did not accept at face value the legislative and programmatic statements of purpose for the program (Fleck, 1966). The field survey interviewed all significant participants, and a tentative statement of program purpose was inferred from observations of the participants. Next came a review of all documents describing the relationship of the state to the physically handicapped in the nineteenth and twentieth centuries. Finally came an analysis of the caseload, the cost, and the revenue sources. The basic discovery was that collective behavior was directed toward attaining social insurance to supplement private resources for payment of the children's medical care. This goal conflicted with the stated purpose of rehabilitation of selected cases, enabling them to achieve economic and social self-sufficiency as adults. Within four months after circulating the first draft of the study, top management recommended that the governor's office take steps to implement the report's suggestions. Concomitantly, twelve meetings were held with the program operators to reach agreement on the content and format of the final report, which was issued ten months after the release of the first draft. At that point the governor announced the master plan looking toward a broad program of medical aid for the children of the state. The evaluation revealed the discrepancy between the original program design and the activities of the staff. The identification of this deviation resulted in the design of a program for deliberate action which was implemented.

There are obstacles to valid impact evaluation; despite increased demands for it, impact evaluation has taken place in social welfare programs. Many people argue that money spent on evaluation is better spent in helping more people (Sherwood, 1967); they are not impressed with the results of past evaluative efforts, and are not willing to throw good money after bad. Another obstacle is the shortage of social scientists capable of competent evaluative research. Universities and colleges have just begun to address themselves to the issue of impact evaluation. For the most part, social work institutes and centers within institutions of higher learning tend to emphasize problem identification, search for causation, and design of intervention programs. The next logical step is a growing emphasis on program evaluation.

When competent researchers *are* funded to undertake evaluation, other problems can develop. First, there is the basic commitment of the social workers to the program in which they are participating; they know the program is good and they wish the research people would let them get on with it. The practitioners tend to view researchers as evaluators of their professional competence, and consider the researcher's potentially corrective role a threat to their professional self-image (Rodman and Kolody, 1965). Operational staff are often preoccupied with program components without reference to program objectives or to the relationship between components and specific kinds of change the program seeks to produce (Aronson and Sherwood, 1967). Thus the staff are unable to specify goals or theoretical links between the program inputs and desired outcomes, which creates problems for researchers who evaluate a program of intervention in terms of its components and their relationship to outcome (Levine, 1967).

Determining the extent to which the target population would have realized the program's goals if the program had not been implemented often requires establishing a control group. Practitioners are loath to refuse service to people they feel they can help. When the reason for refusal is a research design, this feeling is particularly strong, provoking remarks such as "When are you going to stop experimenting with people and let us start to help them?" (Aronson and Sherwood, 1967) The issues of confidentiality and invasion of privacy are often raised by practitioners and clients. The President's panel on "Privacy and Behavioral Research" in 1966 maintained that behavioral scientists must obtain subjects' consent (Davis, 1966). Thus, the researcher must be willing to convince practitioner and client of the value of the research when their cooperation is required. A basic professional rule forbids collecting data about the client which is irrelevant to the helping process (Aronson and Sherwood, 1967). Therefore, the researcher must demonstrate the relevance of the data he seeks, and hope that this demonstration will not prejudice his findings.

Industry has long practiced quality control, an organizational attempt to ensure that the factory is turning out products which meet prescribed standards. As industry is concerned with failure of some components of an assembly line, so impact researchers should be concerned with evaluating the impact of the program actually delivered. The program design must establish a range of acceptable behavior for practitioners who are providing client services, and the administration and the researcher must establish a means for determining when a practitioner is functioning outside the range of acceptable behavior. Practitioners often respond to client needs with actions outside the range of acceptable behavior; if this deviation is not noted, then outcome evaluation will be based on the planned program instead of the service actually delivered. In some cases, therefore, the planned program is credited for an outcome caused by an alteration in that program. In those instances where the change is appropriate, modification of the program to include the new procedure allows all the practitioners, not just one or two innovative ones, to give better service. Still, as reasonable as quality control sounds, the notion is bound to be seen by many practitioners as a personal threat to their status as professionals (Aronson and Sherwood, 1967).

Many of the programs designed to cope with social problems are based on solutions consistent with the ideology of those who don't have the problem (Davis, 1966). Those who advocate education as opposed to strong antidiscrimination laws as a means of obtaining racial or religious justice are following opinions which have prevailed in this country for years. Yet, those who argue that you can't legislate morality regarding racial justice are among the strongest advocates of legislation to prevent street crime by applying massive force. Impact evaluation threatens this stereotyped thinking which forms the basis of many programs. So, the developers of such programs protest "I know I'm right, don't confuse me with the facts."

The organizational commitment required for valid impact evaluation is staggering. Professional resistance, the issue of confidentiality, the implementation of quality control measures, the control group issue, and the requirement for specific program goals demand an intensive effort of both researcher and practitioner to establish an evaluation program acceptable to everyone. This effort takes time and, in an organizational sense, time is money. The issue becomes whether practitioner and researcher are willing to expend resources for evaluative research. The final decision rests with those who are the source of funds and depends on how much they value evaluative research.

Review of Evaluations

Twelve of the thirteen projects discussed previously (the CSS-DSS Study was not available for review when this chapter was initially prepared) were evaluated for impact. The data resulting from each project were collected under the limitations and constraints built into impact evaluation efforts. Each research team sought to minimize the effect of identified obstacles. The persistence of these obstacles in each project indicates the state of the art of impact evaluation. The project findings, however, have begun a posing of questions of immediate concern to the social welfare planner, administrator, or policy-maker.

Serving the Aging was an experiment to determine the effectiveness of three alternative service patterns in resolving problems of an independent population all over sixty years old (Blenkner and others, 1964). A pattern of effectiveness having been established, results were reexamined in terms of their relative costs. Effectiveness was measured in terms of amount of problems and level of adjustment at the time of follow-up. Costs were measured in terms of intensity of service rendered until the follow-up six months after the original assignment. Older persons were randomly assigned to three service programs, implemented so their relative effectiveness could be tested. One segment received regular family agency services. Another received combined social casework and health services provided by public health professionals and social caseworkers. A third segment received a short-term serivce designed to provide maximum input over a short time span. The evaluators found that the ordinary program of the agency was at least as effective as the collaborative program or the short-term treatment, and the ordinary program was the least costly. The short-term service was also effective and much cheaper than the collaborative service. Referral to services outside the agency was an important feature in each of the service programs.

These findings question the notion that interdisciplinary collaboration on an ongoing basis provides the best service for the client. The findings were much less clear on the issue of regular service versus short-term service. From cost perspective, the regular service, as effective as short-term treatment, was less expensive; on the other hand, short-term service could serve more clients in a given period of time. The findings identify three dimensions crucial to planning, policy, and administration on the macrosystem level. Effectiveness, including time and cost per unit of service, is the bread and butter of those concerned with the development of service delivery systems.

The Area Development Project (United Community Services of the Greater Vancouver Area, 1968–1969) was based on two familiar assumptions. First, the concept of integrated services: It was assumed that a family benefitted more from the focused efforts of one worker than from services of various agencies. Second, it was assumed that changing the neighborhood conditions, presumably affecting family functioning, would improve the family functioning of the neighborhood residents. Identified for measurement were two levels of variables: dependent, assessed in terms of the hardest data available, that is, the recorded behavior of clients; and intermediate, such as feelings, attitudes, and interpersonal adjustment.

The families selected for treatment had many characteristics common to multiproblem families. They were in the caseload of at least one participating agency; were known to at least two other agencies; and had established a pattern of continuous agency contacts over a period of at least three years prior to the study. Regarding services to families, the project produced findings with implications for the development and management of service delivery systems. Modifications in family functioning were not associated with either the volume of service (with the exception of the care and training of children, in which a significant negative correlation was established) or the duration of treatment. The extent of the social worker's adherence to practice ideals tended to correlate with the improvement of family functioning. The implications of these two findings seemed to identify a significant factor for those concerned with the development and management of service delivery systems. The question of quality control previously discussed has obvious implications for the training and supervision of operatives within social service delivery systems.

The second assumption of the Area Development Project dealt with the supposed positive impact to be derived from improving neighborhood conditions. The program saw neighborhood development in three dimensions: first, citizen involvement in the community's problems was a goal in itself; second, institutional changes were needed to produce effective extension and coordination of services to the community; third, developing new programs to meet unmet community needs was considered valuable in the environmental approach to improve family functioning.

Evaluating this aspect of the Area Development program produced the following: neighborhood groups, formed as a result of community organization activities, were not self-sufficient and, without professional services, tended to weaken; community organization activities originated a dialogue between citizens and agencies resulting in constructive action on the part of agencies; citizens learned the rudiments of the community decision-making process; and the positive impact of this activity had expressive as well as instrumental value to the client system.

The overall impact of this last finding is difficult to measure in a form which could guide those interested in macrosystem intervention. It has not been demonstrated that the expressive values maximized via macrosystem intervention are comparable to the instrumental values resulting from a massive improvement in community resources without a significant amount of citizen participation. It is equally unclear that the weakening of community organization resulting from reduction in professional services would have occurred if a longer period of development with professional help had been possible.

The Casework Methods Project (Reid and Shyne, 1969) was a four-year study to investigate effectiveness of short-term treatment for middle-class clientele with self-perceived marital or parent/child problems. While the researchers admit they cannot necessarily generalize beyond their sample of clients and practitioners, their findings have posed a question needing further investigation. Reid and Shyne found that short-term treatment yielded more durable progress in problem resolution than long-term service. They hypothesized that the difference arose from short-term treatment being goal-directed, producing in the client an expectation of progress, in contrast to the process-oriented diffuse character of extended treatment. For those practitioners interested in intervention at the macrosystem level, Reid and Shyne emphasize the importance of two planning dimensions—costs, and characteristics of the planned-for client population. It is interesting that questions were also raised about the efficacy of long-term treatment in Serving the Aging (Blenkner and others, 1964).

A Comprehensive Program for Multiproblem Families (Marin, 1969) tested the effectiveness of family-centered social services. Two experimental groups and two control groups were selected from active cases receiving continued child welfare services for at least five years in the metropolitan area of San Juan, Puerto Rico. Family-centered social services consisted of social casework, social group work, and social work in the community used in a cumulative pattern and focused on the family as a whole. The family-centered social services were dispensed by the Division of Public Welfare; the control groups continued to receive the standard services of the Department. The results of the project showed that the experimental groups did not produce a significantly higher number of successful case closings than did the control groups.

However, the apparent failure of the experimental treatment should not preclude further consideration of this concept by practitioners at the macrosystem level. One obvious explanation for the lack of significant difference between the control and experimental groups is the possibility that the experimental approach is inappropriate for people with a five-year history of receiving agency services. Experimental intervention might be significantly more productive if accomplished before clients develop a *response style* to the agency. Thus, planners, administrators, and policy-makers cannot take research results at face value, but must use various theoretical frameworks to explain reality, and be alert to the possibility that an intervention might prove effective with a slightly different target population.

The Pursuit of Promise (McCabe and others, 1967), a three-year experimental program to enhance the self-image, aspirations, and verbal skills of intellectually superior children in the slums, pointed out the importance of the cultural context within which programs are implemented. The program attempted to intervene early in the child's school career in order to combat the deleterious effects of his environment. Control and experimental groups were selected from a population of Black and Puerto Rican children who had demonstrated relatively high achievement on performance tests. The hypothesis was that the functioning of the control groups would go down, while that of the experimental groups would maintain itself at a relatively high level.

The data indicate that many more Puerto Rican experimental group members improved their functioning than did Puerto Rican controls. The Black controls, however, improved as much or more than the Black experimental groups. While the program found its hypothesis tenable in the Puerto Rican context, the performance of the Black controls and experimental groups casts doubt on the basic assumptions of the program. While this was not a reading program, it was found that both the Black and Puerto Rican experimental groups did better in reading than did their respective control groups. Development of coping skills, self-image and the capacity to influence one's environment is obviously related to the child's cultural background. Thus, the variable of cultural background must be considered by those operating on a macrosystem level.

The Familycenter Project (Kühl, 1969) raises a question for

macrosystem practitioners: To what extent is the social worker-client relationship influenced by the legal and institutional constraints on benefits? The Danish experiment provided multiproblem families with a social worker who had three principal tasks: coordination of benefits from various agencies, providing advice on pressing problems without offering therapy, and relating each problem to the family situation as a whole. The experimental group improved in family functioning; the control group, receiving standard social welfare services, also improved in family functioning, although an a smaller scale.

The experimental group social workers identified the danger of the clients' expectations being raised by virtue of a change in the organization of services available to them; they, then, became hostile when increased attention from the family social worker did not bring them more benefits. It is not clear what produced the hostility—the frustrations of the workers faced with problems on a more concentrated and comprehensive level or the client's own perception of the helping relationship. Thus, practitioners at the macrosystem level must consider the nature of the helping transactions and its impact on both practitioner and client.

An Experimental Study to Measure the Effectiveness of Casework Service (Behling, 1961), addressed itself to the question: Can chronic relief dependency best be prevented and reduced through the intensive use of casework? Behling describes an experiment in which matched families were divided into one group that continued to receive routine services in caseloads of seventy-five to two hundred and fifty, and another group that received intensive service, that is, it was served by caseworkers responsible for less than seventy-five cases. The social workers involved were matched in terms of education and experience. Over the term of the experiment, the experimental group received intensive service in the form of a significantly greater amount of casework time. At the end of the experiment, the progress of these control and experimental groups was measured on the CSS Movement Scale. The experimental groups showed significantly greater progress from beginning to end of the project than did the control group. The data further suggested that smaller caseloads were instrumental in successful resolution of difficult cases. From the perspective of macrosystem intervention, the study suggests that caseloads be determined by the nature, severity and scope of the problem than by other administrative criteria.

Girls at Vocational High (Meyer and others, 1965) concluded that casework services and group counseling had little positive impact on the academic careers and out-of-school behavior of various vocational high school girls identified as potential delinquents. Control groups, experimental groups, faculty ratings of behavior in and out of school, and personality tests combined to affirm that the described intervention made no difference.

This study resulted in a heated controversy within the social work profession, since the concepts of casework and treatment were seriously threatened by the findings. The controversy was never resolved because the parties to it had no power to change the theoretical articles of faith, professional practices, or blind prejudices of those who disagreed with them. The data did sharpen the issue for planners and others at the macrosystem level. The issue is not whether treatment is the answer; rather, one must have an open mind in defining the question. If the coping skills, personality traits, and emotional characteristics of the girls were the dominant factors determining their success or failure in a high school context, then the study intervention addressed itself to the right problem. If the life situations of the girls, structure and purpose of the educational institution, or realities of the job market were the determining factors in the girls' experiences at vocational high, then the interventions described may have been the right answer to the wrong question.

In 1961, Winifred Bell, then a faculty member at Columbia University, argued that "substantial savings to the taxpayer could be secured by reducing caseloads of public assistance workers, so that they would have more time to counsel recipients in order to increase 'the clients' chances toward self-sufficiency" (Wallace, 1967). This declaration of faith was put to the test in the Chemung County Study (Brown, 1968). In the Chemung County Study, fifty multiproblem families were treated by M.S.W.s in reduced caseloads, whereas a control group of fifty families received the normal services of the County Welfare Department. Both groups were rated at the beginning and end of the experiment on family relationship and unity, individual behavior and adjustment, child-rearing, money management, household practices, and family social life. While the group served by the M.S.W.s received more service time than the control group, the quality of service for both groups was rated by supervisors as average. The group served by M.S.W.s did not make a significant improvement over the group receiving normal services.

The findings in this study reinforce the proposition that alternative means and resources must be used to help multiproblem families. However, the assumption that improved functioning along specified dimensions is amenable to casework intervention is dubious in the case of multiproblem families. And when the assumption includes the notion that improved functioning along these dimensions reduces dependency, one ignores the external factors contributing to dependency. If improved functioning is thought likely when the family is treated under special conditions by specially trained people, one risks concluding that experimental intervention failures means that the specially trained people have no legitimate claim to jurisdiction over this problem. In reality, however, the specially trained practitioners may simply be a right answer to the wrong question. A physician can hardly be expected to save a poisoned person unless he can cut off the supply of poison at the same time he administers the antidote. From a policy, planning, and administrative point of view, the potential benefits of the casework relationship have to be seen in a realistic light.

Ludwig Geismar investigated the problem of family functioning from a slightly different point of view (Geismar and Krisberg, 1967; Geismar and others, 1970). He acknowledged the theoretical proposition that certain functional requirements must be satisfied if a social system, in this case the family, is to survive at any given level. In both the Family Life Improvement Project and the Neighborhood Improvement Project, Geismar noted that a workable philosophy of intervention should stress the reciprocal relationship between behavior and functioning of systems in which behavior occurs.

In the Neighborhood Improvement Project, the experimental intervention was tested on forty-five of the most disorganized families in one housing project. These families received casework and group work and, at the same time, efforts to stretch the policies and resources of the agencies serving them were carried on as a result of community organization input. Control group families, matched along significant dimensions, received no special input. The experimental group showed much greater progress during the project, but Geismar was unable to determine what each service element contributed to the success of the treatment families. Similar progress was noted in the experimental group of the Family Life Improvement Project. The main difference between the two experiments was that the Neighborhood Improvement Project cases were selected on the basis of their long-term resistance to orthodox treatment and the Family Life Improvement Project cases were a random sample of the community. Practitioners on the macrosystem level should note that these experiments demonstrated that families could be helped, but that the researcher could not specify which experiment element was crucial to its success. Thus, until the crucial element is identified, a comprehensive program offers the greatest chance for progress.

The Midway Project (Schwartz, 1966; Schwartz and Sample, 1967) tested two dimensions of the public welfare system in terms of client outcomes. Both the caseload size of public assistance workers and the supervisory-discretionary continuum under which social workers' tasks were organized were systematically varied in this study. The results of these experimental innovations were evaluated primarily as to improvement of client functioning, staff attitudes about their work, and productivity and efficiency of the work arrangement. The clients served by teams in which M.S.W. supervisors retained direct responsibility for all the cases assigned to the team and in which the supervisor delegated to his workers specific tasks in relationship to these cases showed greater positive change at the end of the project, regardless of caseload assigned to the team. However, improvement was greatest in clients served by teams with a caseload under forty-five. Obviously, the team approach produces more progress than simply reducing the caseload without altering the traditional work pattern. These insights into the impact of organization on the effectiveness of service are valuable for macrosystem practitioners.

Implications for Education

The task of those destined to serve at a macrosystem level is formidable indeed, and educating students for that task is no less difficult. While some insist that experience and training as a direct service practitioner is a prerequisite for macrosystem intervention, others claim that such preparation produces a trained incapacity to function on the macrosystem level. We should keep the opposing sides of this dilemma in mind as we focus on the dimensions to be understood and utilized by the macrosystem practitioner. Whether individual schools offer educational experiences that analyze these dimensions is a question each can answer for himself. Further, each dimension discussed here must be considered within various political contexts. We will not, despite the temptation to do so, discuss macrosystem politics here, however, the reader should realize how much political context influences decisions made within it. Cost is an important element in the development of plans, policies, or administrative guidelines, and can be considered under three crucial aspects: money, time, and other forms of institutional commitment. A related aspect of cost is a thorough understanding of the ramifications, in terms of costs, of alternative sources of resources. Understanding the fundamentals of public finance, cost benefit analysis, and various forms of voluntary financing are essential for the macrosystem practitioner.

Those proposing to act on the macrosystem level must recognize the importance of the relationships between the etiology of a problem and the characteristics of the intervention to solve the problem. The *right* answer to the *wrong* question is an exercise in futility, and a trap easily fallen into as a relatively young profession seeks to establish jurisdiction over particular problems. Students familiar with a wide range of theoretical explanations of the causation of problems are best able to recognize the characteristics of this trap. Macrosystem practitioners who cling to one theoretical framework, forcing a relationship between theory and reality, are doomed to repeat past failures. The macrosystem practitioner must thoroughly understand the cultural context of those to be served, and how the cultural orientation of those providing the service affects the service transaction. The quantitative and qualitative impacts of the helping transaction are what our profession is all about. To fail to understand and control the potential counter-productive aspects of these transactions is the height of professional folly at the micro-, mezzo-, and macrosystem levels.

Utilization of research data is very important for social work practice and the social welfare practitioner; to effectively utilize research data at the macrosystem level requires responsible criticism of research design and conclusions, presupposing a thorough understanding of the problems of forming research questions, collecting data and developing conclusions. Thus, the practitioner must acknowledge the importance of the ongoing search for answers respecting the theoretical and empirical basis for social welfare interventions as a vital part of planning, policy, development, and administration at the macrosystem level. Organizations as instrumentalities of service demand the attention of the macrosystem practitioner. A thorough understanding of the behavior of organizations is essential if these organizations are to continue to be the means through which social work and social welfare services are delivered. The practitioner must also understand how having to negotiate on a short-term or extended basis with relatively complex organizations affects the client. In addition, macrosystem practitioners should be familiar with the interaction of representatives of various disciplines and the levels of authority within helping organizations.

How can the student be exposed to these areas given the current master's degree curricula in most schools of social work? The answer to this question depends on the extent to which schools of social work have been teaching tradition-based dogma. In such cases, training macrosystem practitioners to cope with the dimensions described will be difficult indeed. If, on the other hand, schools have been centers of inquiry, rather than transmitters of tradition, they are probably teaching their students along lines previously suggested. Social work will probably always be an eclectic profession because of the complexity of the problems with which it attempts to cope. Practice at the macrosystem level is no exception to this generalization. Training for macrosystem practice requires massive inputs of useful products of a wide variety of disciplines and viewpoints. These inputs must be assimilated into a usable repertoire of concepts and techniques which lend themselves to analysis and solution of social welfare problems. The problem is: how do schools of social work make these inputs available in usable form to their students? Each school, in the context of its institution, should consider these three models.

First, many schools of social work have added representatives of related disciplines to their faculties. These representatives from different conceptual frameworks have broadened the base of social work education for the students. This approach, however, has some built-in difficulties. Seriously questioned is the ability of these representatives to retain the best contributions to knowledge of their own discipline or to keep up with the discovery of new concepts in their own discipline once they have become acculturated by the school of social work. The scope of inputs available to students is also reduced by the limits of the school budget and the availability of academicians and professionals willing to join the faculty.

Second, some schools of social work have taken advantage of the universities within which they exist by encouraging students to register for courses in other academic units that would expose them to other viewpoints and methodologies. This step away from parochialism broadens students' perspectives considerably and highlights the problem of our profession's developing capacity to make use of new theoretical frameworks. The students generally struggle alone to develop a meaningful relationship between practice and theory. One of the major difficulties associated with this procedure is that many social work students are forced to pick courses corresponding to the times when they are on campus rather than courses which fit their interests and level of preparation. Under these circumstances, field work begins to constitute a part time job that limits the range of courses available.

A third and not so popular model must be thoroughly tested by a number of schools located in universities with rich graduate offerings. The faculty should audit in other departments courses which give promise of providing creative input to social work education and social work practice. The faculty could then teach students those elements of other disciplines having direct relevance to social work practice and social welfare problems. Thus, the student would not be forced to integrate input from these extra social work sources into his own practice without the active assistance of a social work faculty member. While this process will pay off more slowly than the first and second models, it is conceivable that the payoff will be qualitatively and quantitatively more useful to students in the master's degree programs and to the faculty as well. If this proposal is acted on and the result is more effective social work practice, it will be well worth the effort required for social work faculty members to go back to school.

7

Rethinking Macrosystem Intervention

Gene E. Webb

Although the research reviewed in this book consists of evaluations of discrete agency programs carried out in local communities, several of these programs have macrosystem reference points in the form of various national planning, policy, and administrative inputs. And all the programs have some relevance as either inputs or feedback for future macrosystem activity in the field of the delivery of social services. Social work manpower traditionally, and in the present, has been concentrated in local social service. The professional minority working at the macrosystem practice level seems to allocate the major portion of its activity to planning, policy, and administrative tasks related to social services. From a macrosystem perspective, the research is also of interest because of the focus of the programs studied on social problems such as employment, health

111

care and education which cut across individual and local community situations. The studies provide information useful in the ongoing assessment of the role direct services can play in interventions to resolve social problems.

In the preceding chapter, Walter Walker discusses the studies and deals with issues in evaluative research referring to the relationship of planning, policy development and administration in the macrosystem practice arena. He focuses on what can be learned from the programmatic experience reported in the research studies that is useful for effective planning, policy development and administration in social welfare. He finds the studies yield few concrete guidelines for restructuring the delivery of the social services examined. In fact, most of the research reports describe individualized, group and community services including in their basic components familiar and long used social service concepts. Yet, when experimental research designs, including the use of control groups and reasonably well-developed evaluation measures, tested the effectiveness of the social service programs, most could not demonstrate the occurrence of significant planned change in target populations.

In a few instances where positive results were obtained, it is difficult to interpret results credited to programs because of the multidimensional nature of interventions which included combinations of counseling, neighborhood organization and community work. Thus, it is not known whether results were produced by the total package, or if some components were more influential than others. Further, making generalizations from these and similar studies about the effectiveness of social services requires specification of the operating conditions under which experiments were conducted. Organizational, staff, client and community characteristics must be known and assessed in order to adapt the programs for further testing in other settings.

Walker makes a major theoretical critique: in several of the programs studied, there are discrepancies between the *real* problem scale and the nature and level of the intervention. These discrepancies are most apparent in studies relating to multiproblem families and public assistance clienteles, and least apparent in studies describing programs aimed at circumscribed problems. Experience suggests that most practitioners are reasonably well reality-oriented in their day-to-day work of setting objectives and problem-solving with or on behalf of clients. But when practitioners' activities are generalized into a model or plan for an intervention program aimed at a specific target population, there is a tendency for problems to be scaled outward and upward and for goals to become inflated, without concomitant changes in intervention activities. As an example, the Chemung County Study, while rigorous in its research design, suffers from the weak programmatic input relative to the identified problems of the public assistance population serviced.

Recent reconceptualization of social services as *service delivery systems* has provided in many instances a broadening and expansion of services and altered static ideas about service utilization and client population characteristics. Target client populations are more likely to be reached out for, rather than waited for, and motivational incentives can be designed into programs as well as rest with clients. Environmental as well as psychological adjustment problems can be dealt with in service programs. However, expectations for the accomplishments of expanded and redesigned social services may have been so overstated that programs lack an adequate theoretical base for explaining change and directing planned change activities.

The studies considered are reasonably representative of the rather large volume of social service research conducted over the past decade. The stimulus for much of this programmatic experimentation and the accompanying evaluative research came from federal grant programs which encouraged innovation in services and service delivery and required some kind of research monitoring. It should be noted here that the federal grant programs, along with similar ventures by large private foundations, are examples of action emanating from macrosystem arenas or, more precisely, the articulation of macrosystem planning and local operations. The evaluative research record probably tells us more about happenings at macrosystem action levels than it does about results of direct practice with social service clients. Since a considerable part of the evidence regarding the social service experimentation of the 1960s is available, macrosystem practitioners have substantial feedback for evaluating policies and plans promulgated earlier and still largely in use.

If we focus on the policies and plans behind the programs

evaluated, then questions about the effectiveness of casework, group work, community organization or other professional methodologies are much less relevant. It is one thing to consider the effectiveness of a particular agency activity with its clientele; it is another to consider the impact of a dozen or more similar programs directly and indirectly reflecting major ideas supported by professional associations, educational bodies, government policy and public philanthropy.

Walker refers to some major ideas for social service reform which have been recommended at the national level by social welfare spokesmen. Reduced caseloads. M.S.W.-trained personnel, interagency cooperation, and better coordination of existing community resources are examples of popular ideas influencing recent experimentations with the delivery of social services. From the macrosystem perspective, we are interested in the nature of feedback information provided by evaluative research about such ideas. This moves us a step ahead of the more passive role of consumer of research results to a role in which we assume some responsibility and accountability for what occurs when plans and policies recommended or supported at the macrosystem level are tested in specific intervention projects.

If we consider changes in the problems of client populations before and after the provision of social services to be important in service delivery policy and planning, we must account for many negative results. The evaluative research record indicates policy and planning errors have been made and we must ask why. We could argue that the research record is incomplete, and that more and better studies must be made of social service programs. The programs might benefit from larger staffs with higher qualifications, and since saturation programs appear to show some results, the addition of more resources might be necessary. In some cases, research designs might profit by alterations. Some of the recently developed counseling and group methodologies might be used in place of conventional treatment approaches.

While social service research is still in an exploratory stage, even where experimental designs have been used, the research record provides sufficient information to consider new policies for dealing with the societal aspects of the problems of social service client groups. For example, Walker contends that the research record indicates many of the generalized problems of client populations are not amenable to social service intervention and further research and experimentation along these lines is unlikely to be fruitful.

Notwithstanding the negative results from many social service programs, we have learned much from evaluative research which is useful in social planning and in formulating social policy. Granting there have been improvements in the substance and delivery of social services, the next important step is distinguishing objectives consonant with individualized service programs from those most appropriately sought through other intervention models and professional activities. Walker suggests that the insufficient effectiveness of social services may result from some right solutions being used for the wrong problems. It may be completely unrealistic to expect that problems which individuals experience by virtue of their *positions* in society can be substantially resolved by direct social services. There now seems to be general recognition of this point, although it appears to be forgotten or ignored in the plannnig (macro- and mezzo-) of some intervention programs.

The source of difficulty may not be the mutual exclusiveness of social service intervention problems and social change intervention problems, but rather in distinguishing aspects of problems common to both interventions which are better resolved by one approach than another. There are problematic aspects of the social structure which if altered by policy change may not directly affect specific individuals or particular local dimensions of a problem. But policy changes at the macrosystem level may substantially alter problems for a population aggregate as well as the conditions for individual or local community problem-solving. Consequences of these policy changes and the adaptations they require stimulate the need for social services and local community activity which can deal with the problems of specific individuals and families or particular local dimensions of problems. Macrosystem practice needs to be addressed to structural and policy change which can directly affect resolutions of social problems. This practice must also include concern for the delivery of social services which can be responsive to the unique ways in which individuals and local communities react both to social problems and to policy and structural changes aimed at resolving social problems. Appropriate selections and matchings of problem scales and intervention levels require refinements of theories about various problems to understand the ways in which problems are manifested in different social units from the individual to society. This would facilitate goal specification in interventions and the translation of change theory into intervention models. In addition to their theoretical problems, the health and welfare professions must consider recent social pressures on them to deal more directly with social problems. These pressures have stimulated quests for *relevance* and *innovation* by planning organizations and social service agencies, which in some cases may have led to oversights of basic intervention characteristics. Also, macrosystem practice by more than a handful of health and welfare professionals is relatively new; thus, developing this kind of practice may produce new possibilities for intervention at the macrosystem level.

Problems, Practice, and Roles

To further develop a macro perspective regarding the profession's recent attempts to deal with social problems, some characteristics of macrosystem problems and practice will be considered below. Walker described macrosystem practice as encompassing roles and tasks in the areas of social planning, social policy development and administration. Within a macrosystem context, these roles and tasks are usually distinguished from role-task sets in other system contexts by the large scale and complex problems addressed and the problem-solving interventions. The macrosystem, in Walker's terms, refers to a large scale complex system as a whole, and to system-wide interventions affecting a large geographically scattered population. This definition may be useful in establishing the theoretical parameters of macrosystem practice, although some operationalization of its major concepts is necessary to use them in considering practice frameworks.

Macrosystem problems include poverty, racial and social class discriminations, substandard housing, drug abuse, mental illness and similarly conceptualized problems not lending themselves well to analysis within the concrete frameworks typically used to organize the human experience—the individual personality, a dyadic relationship, a family, a neighborhood, or a local community. That is, these problems break through or slip through conventional analytic problem-solving frameworks and seem to disappear into abstractions which are difficult to get hold of. Generally, we do not deal with any particular natural system as a whole, but rather with parts of a system, or parts of several systems. Therefore, the construction of problem-solving systems is often the chief task of the macrosystem practitioner. The target or risk populations making up the client groups of many of the intervention programs reviewed are small-scale examples of attempts to define subsystems for intervention purposes. Risk characteristics were used to form experimental program clienteles who would receive direct services but, apparently, were not used in substantial ways to determine the nature of intervention—perhaps because significant problematic factors were recognized to reside in systems outside social service control, toward the macrosystem.

Planning in social systems or subsystems to which we assign boundaries, such as national society, the state, and the local community, has become increasingly difficult because of the complexity and the interdependencies of social units; and, recently, we have become sensitive to metropolitan and regional problems. Problems examined within these kinds of systems, however complex, are still based on the principle of territorial boundaries. However, the physical and social spaces which formerly buffered separate social units have given way to strong and complex interdependencies: economy, resources, education, communications, housing, and social problems intertwine in metropolitan and regional areas and with other social or physical sectors of the total society. Communications developments have produced subsystems which are not dependent upon continuous boundaries; examples of national phenomena which cut across miles of geographical territory are the youth culture and the civil rights movement.

Identifying health and medical care problems of the American people and considering a health and medical care program similar to those in Britain or the Soviet Union is an example of planning which stretches the boundaries of Walker's definitions for macrosystem problems and intervention. Occasionally, such large-scale plans are drawn, although, as experience shows, such plans serve more of a directional than a working function. Usually, however, problems are identified which relate to particular population aggregates, such as health care for the aged, and problem-solving boundaries are drawn narrowly, including at one time or another an aggregate identified with the problem, target systems who must sanction an intervention or representatives and parts of social institutions identified with the resolution of the problem. In either situation, planning for the total population or planning for a particular population aggregate, the system is large and complex and intervention relates to large, geographically scattered populations. Planning for the total population, however, relates to a *natural* system, the total society of the United States. In the case of a national health plan, while the target is medical care arrangements, the interdependencies involve the total population as recipients of medical care, as well as affect, in various ways, all other social institutions. Smaller scale planning for a particular aggregate identified with a problem frequently involves the construction of a problem-solving system since many problems and their resolutions may not rest neatly in natural social systems. If, for example, the objective were alteration of medical care arrangements for the aged, the direct focus of the intervention would not be systemwide, although there is an interdependence between such medical care, other medical care arrangements, aggregates other than the aged, and parts of various social institutions.

Macrosystem practice takes place in large organizations in which the targets are various intersecting points between population aggregates and the social situations in which they function. The intersection points of most interest are those adjudged by some criteria to be problematic or potentially problematic. Macrosystem practitioners initiate and respond to problem-solving stimuli; and planners are increasingly sensitive to problem indicators which provide information for initiating planning, policy and administrative action. Planners are also responsive to leaders of aggregates with grievances and to representatives of groups concerned not with their poverty, their lack of housing, or their children's education, but with the impact of problem aggregates upon specific communities or society as a whole. The case of public assistance, to which several studies relate, is an example of the value conflicts characteristic of macrosystem practice. Advocates of the poor lobby for larger grants with fewer restrictions; other groups seek to reduce grants and impose restrictions upon eligibility.

The idea of problem and intervention scaling provides us with some clues about the nature of problem-solving at the macrosystem level. For example, it appears in demonstration projects with groups such as public assistance populations that we are concerned with the relationships between an aggregate and some larger, defined systems, such as sectors of the national society or some other groups. When as a matter of social policy, a problem is defined as one affecting the whole society, such as costs of public assistance, life styles of low-income people, and so forth, then we are dealing with a matter of social control. Such control can be attempted through measures such as counseling and neighborhood organization which seek the cooperation of members of aggregates or through more forceful measures such as grant penalties and incentives. However, social workers have usually opted in favor of benign controls, that is, social control through voluntary measures. To the extent that other sectors of society become concerned about a population group, the task of benign social control is more difficult, and social workers often try to intercede in the conflict between a group and other sectors of society. Thus, social workers attempt to defer or buffer punitive or law and order approaches to social problem-solving. The profession balances social tendencies which are detrimental to specific population groups as well as to the total society. Examining some common large-scale problems expressed in communities across the country forces us to look at some of the factors leading to their development. These factors are often of a nature difficult to control—for example, the movement of people into urbanized areas during the last decades. Other factors are the movement of black people into southern and northern urban areas and the movement of poor white populations out of depressed economic regions into urbanized work centers. Social problems produce these movements which represent adaptation on the part of the population groups, but the movements themselves shift all or part of these problems elsewhere. Industrial change, such as the textile movement out of New England, produces problems for that region but relieves difficulties in parts of the South where industry relocates. The civil rights movement solves one problem by providing new opportunities for some blacks, but it creates other problems—interracial competition, unrest, rising expectations where the movement is not fulfilled or where change is not fast enough.

At the macrosystem level, we see that if we aim to prevent such problems or to resolve them in substantial ways, then we need social welfare programs which relate to these factors. If we define professional tasks as easement of these conditions, such as softening the shocks of dislocations, then service programs to individuals and identified groups may be in order, and the test of their effectiveness is the extent to which the groups experience such easement. It seems that many of the programs considered in this book should have been evaluated along these lines.

The CSS-DSS Study, for example, seems to have aimed at preventing dependence in terms of keeping the use of public assistance from becoming permanent; economic dependence, not social-psychological dependence was the major concern here. Had social-psychological dependence been the major concern, the results might not have been substantially better, for the ongoing transactions between the recipients and DSS may be more relevant to social-psychological dependence than the relationship between CSS and the recipients. Possibly CSS services were useful in handling the crisis aspects of persons becoming public assistance recipients, if and where crisis was operating. We must know to what extent use of public assistance was part of the group's expectations or to what extent it conflicted with other group expectations. For some group members, public assistance was no more of a crisis than many other situations facing such a group. Thus, we can think of a program designed to prevent social-psychological dependence as geared to alleviating the negative consequences of becoming a public assistance recipient in a society which stresses economic independence or in public assistance organizations which dehumanize their clientele. Those familiar with the New York City scene should determine the extent to which the organization exacerbates the problems of its clientele. Given a service program focus, perhaps only some of these things can be accomplished.

Let us assume for a moment that the factors maintaining various poverty life styles are beyond the control of the individuals who make up poverty aggregates. Thus, the assumption is that for the aggregate to alter its position (re-form, become a part of another aggregate, reduce in size, disappear as an identifiable aggregate, and the like), a set of external social factors must be altered. Members of the aggregate may view interventions aimed at changing them, rather than the forces maintaining the aggregate as is, as harassment. Only recently have possible negative effects of interventions come to light or been considered. Questions have been raised about interventions in various problem areas where goals are not reached, unanticipated negative consequences are observed, or intervention benefits subsequently are shown to be short lived. For example, some social welfare professionals have begun to question and study the effects upon the unemployed of short-lived job placements. What are the effects of continued counseling of parents about education when there is no resulting improvement in children's learning or school adjustment? What are the motivational effects upon the unemployed of having service populations deal with what are perceived as social role failures and personality/behavioral inadequacies when nothing changes? What are the effects of organizing neighborhood groups when measurable results do not accrue, when some groups discover what they assumed all along—their powerlessness to control their environments? What is the impact of encouraging use of community resources, which already are overcrowded, overused, and often inadequate?

Stimulating interest in intervention outcomes through impact evaluations is one of the most important contributions of evaluative research. Goal development, companion to outcome evaluation, would profit by greater specificity as opposed to open-ended goals and searches for change. Problems formulated at the macrosystem level can be stated in progressive goal achievement terms; for some problems, only modest goals would be planned, whereas for others, greater expectations would be considered. Also, formulating different goals is highly compatible with a cost-benefits approach in considering alternative interventions.

Macrosystem practice, whether through direct social action or arrangements for delivering local services, has an ultimate aim— the change of the quality of social life. Macrosystem practitioners define their professional competence in terms of their position in the social welfare system for examining and intervening in problems. This position is at a distance from the social interactions in which social welfare problems are acted out. These problems are viewed in aggregate terms through research reports and sampling of issues. The disadvantage of this position is that distance also distorts; a change may not produce anticipated consequences, and a recommended program may not be what is really needed at a local level or in a specific organization. The quality of life may be differently experienced by planner and social workers; "The Helping Hand Strikes Again," a game developed at the University of Michigan, vividly demonstrates the problems encountered by supervisory personnel who try from a distance to advise practitioners as to appropriate courses of action with clients. The subversion of macrosystem-planned programs by local organizations and practitioners is not sabotage but may reflect real differences in perspective. Direct service practitioners are not always wrong and macrosystem practitioners are not always right.

A recent significant complication in social welfare is the articulation of social policy and social planning among many different levels of systems. Community mental health programs, poverty programs and others demonstrate the difficulties in making a national policy which fits different situations and in transmitting information correctly when it does.

We must distinguish between macrosystem practice and the practitioner working in macrosystem settings. It is erroneous to think of a macrosystem policy developer, planner, or administrator as a person who is highly influential and looks at only grand design problems. There are notables in the profession who resemble such giants and the more we have the better. However, the typical practitioner—and the role for which we can train more occupants—is the practitioner behind the scenes whose collaboration with colleagues and others produces much of the work. Some of these practitioners may have less responsibility for decisions than administrators and planners working at the local level, but the decisions to which they contribute may relate to larger and more complex interventions. Thus, we are concerned about the nature of practice knowledge these practitioners bring to bear on problems, which are complex since we assume that social workers in macrosystem settings perform more than routine, technical functions.

Macrosystem practice, like other types of social work practice, is not an object of discovery but rather of development, which must be related to the practice realities of various macrosystem action arenas. We can assume that many variations of this practice either have been or will be developed and that macrosystem practice will change over time. While social workers have historically played significant roles regarding macrosystem problems, specificity in identifying and formulating macrosystem practice and the development of professional training for it is relatively new. Thus, this practice is becoming less a matter of an event or accident in career development, and is now the object of training and employment opportunities.

Problems of Evaluative Research

Walker has commented extensively upon problems encountered in the conduct of evaluative research. While there are some significant problems, it is somewhat of a luxury to have problems to complain about, given the paucity of evaluative research in the past. The following are some problems which appear to be under the control of macrosystem practitioners.

(1) Organizations may set unrealistic goals and engage in superficial evaluation; at the same time, planning and funding centers—likely to be influenced by, if not under, the control of macrosystem practitioners—are equally unrealistic in the standards applied to grant applications.

(2) Organizations may resist evaluative research when negative findings are used to publicly indict the organization or the profession, rather than merely to point out an unsuccessful attempt to deal with what may be a complex problem.

(3) Evaluative research may be resisted or carried out haphazardly when it is handled as an activity external to the organization and solely for the consumption of superordinate bodies.

(4) Evaluative research may be poorly carried out when the time period for feedback to the organization is too distant in the future.

(5) Evaluative research may suffer from the impatience of its practitioners to gain quick results, which are then generalized indiscriminately. Few issues are settled by one piece of research, and careful replications of experimental programs which produce new evidence about intervention are necessary. The Casework Methods Project is an example of a piece of research so excellent that it deserves careful replication in similar settings.

(6) In the conduct of evaluative research, issues must be sifted to determine which ones are theoretically significant to the achievement of intervention goals and which ones reflect social and political realities.

(7) Evaluative research may be difficult to carry out when its requirements intrude into the natural human rhythms of social interaction. Elaborate forms and equipment may lead to a breakdown in the evaluation system.

(8) Service evaluations, in particular, would profit from consumer evaluations, since the problems resolved through social services are most likely to be observed by the consumers.

(9) More exploratory evaluative research appears to be desirable before commitments are made to long-term and expensive evaluation programs, as a moderate amount of explanation might discredit them.

(10) Practitioners at the macrosystem level should devote more attention to developing simple evaluation procedures which could be built into ongoing intervention programs not necessarily under the control of experiments. It is odd that so much action is engaged in without serious attention to outcome expectations or measurement, for it is a loss to be unable to collect information about the activities engaged in by many organizations and practitioners.

(11) Particularly at the macrosystem level, more sophisticated evaluative information regarding organizational and interorganizational interventions is needed, as evaluation of planning methodologies and social action strategies lags far behind service evaluative research. Many concepts such as coordination and integration are still handled in oversimplified terms and would profit from careful research operationalization and evaluation.

(12) The profession should design and support the role of

experimental practitioner, one who is trained to engage or lead in new interventions for emerging problems, and skilled in their evaluation.

Evaluation of any kind is a sensitive area around which tension, anxiety, defensiveness, and resistance are to be expected. Walker describes evaluative research as providing society with information regarding the impact of social welfare programs. Social work has apparently accepted to a large measure that continued support and credibility depend upon its acceptance of responsibility for evaluation and demonstration of results with problems. Avoiding evaluative research because it is difficult or seemingly unfruitful is a major tactical error which could have many undesirable consequences given the increasing visibility of and interest in social welfare activities. Assuming that continued investment in evaluative research will begin providing evidence regarding problems with which social work is particularly effective, there will be new opportunities to influence social policy for resources needed for social welfare operations. The technical-political tension in social welfare decisionmaking may be a healthy one, but the technical input could be substantially increased to provide information for sounder social policy decisions in the political process.

Education for Practice

Social work education for this kind of practice is included in some doctoral study programs and, increasingly, in the specialized master's programs of selected schools of social work. Social work education taken as a whole can be seen as an actor in the macrosystem arena, because it delivers professional manpower to staff planning, policy, administrative, and direct service positions. Educators' participation in the effort represented by this book illustrates a consumer role of intervention and its implications, which have macrosystem implications. That is, there is interest in influencing future changes in social welfare programs and social work practice. The evaluative research considered is also feedback to social work education, which can be used in selected ways to influence this change. Some of the main theoretical ideas and intervention strategies described and reflected in the programs evaluated have been part of the educational offerings of the profession over the past decade. For a profession which must rely upon field testing of its theoretical propositions, the body of evaluative research sampled here represents the most substantial organized information available.

This book and the rethinking it represents are perhaps significant bench marks in the maturity of the profession, in its recognition of the potential contribution of research to social work knowledge. We know that there have been extensive changes in social work education during the past few years. These changes have occurred less in response to information obtained through research than to professional assessments of changes needed and reactions to stimuli from external groups, such as government and client and consumer populations. A significant problem using education to affect practice is the long time lag between the appearance of curriculum changes and its impact in practice. Greater use of research as a practice focus and methodology may help reduce this time lag, but programs related to macrosystem practice are relatively new and will take time to develop. There are still problems of moving recently trained professionals with special qualifications into positions traditionally reserved for experienced persons. It is possible that knowledge related to large systems in which social workers practice may be more relevant to practice effectiveness than years of experience in practice not directly related to macrosystem problems.

Macrosystem practice emphasizes the interdisciplinary nature of this practice arena, and the need for social work students to study economics, political science and other social science disciplines. The macrosystem practice arena requires that social work practitioners be conversant with the methods and cultures of other groups, as well as with information and theory directly relevant to social work practice. Stimulation by social work educators of interdisciplinary interaction is not solely to have students learn what other disciplines offer, but also to assist them in developing interdisciplinary interactional skills.

The macrosystem practitioner needs special personal characteristics, such as flexibility, adaptability, autonomy, habits of inquiry, tolerance for frustration and ambiguity, and leadership. These characteristics are important for all social workers, but are considered essential for the macrosystem practitioner who usually works without the immediate supports available to social workers practicing in highly structured social welfare organizations. While these characteristics may be relevant to admissions criteria of schools of social work, their development should be fostered in those schools by considering the nature of social environments of educational settings.

Increasing rates of change in postindustrial society have special implications for macrosystem practitioners whose practice is necessarily oriented toward setting future conditions for social policy and social work intervention. Macrosystem curriculum programs can prepare practitioners to deal with change by emphasizing learning how to learn, rather than by presenting terminal packages of knowledge which may relate more to the past and the present than to the future.

Professional socialization of the macrosystem practitioner was stressed because there is something unique to be gained from applying the social work perspective to macrosystem problems. This point of view challenges the notion that professional preparation for macrosystem practice should include only training for highly specialized role functions. Policy, planning, research, and administration are highly complex subjects which can be the object of study in their own right; yet, there may be dysfunctions in the isolated study of these areas, including the possibility of their becoming ends in themselves. In short, macrosystem practice needs to be tempered by the value perspectives of the profession, including its social responsibilities. This brings up the old social work problem of specialization versus general training, which has been dealt with before and will have to be continually dealt with as the profession expands its education and practice into new areas. Few argue or conceptualize any longer a profession as a holistic system, with all of its parts tied tightly together. Professions, including social work, are increasingly seen as loose social organizational units held together more by common value orientations than by common methodologies.

Walker's significant point is in his critique of the discrepancy between professional means and ends, which he discusses within the framework of the association between social welfare problems and social work interventions. His review of evaluative research suggests that many of the experimenal programs fail to demonstrate intervention effectiveness because of the mismatches between problem formulations and program designs. In this examination of the research and Walker's commentary, the recently accumulated body of evaluative research is seen as feedback to macrosystem planning, policy and administration, rather than as measures of the effectiveness of potential practice methodologies.

8

Forgotten: Mezzosystem Intervention

John B. Turner

By now, most social work educators have heard the terms *macro* and *micro;* however, less attention has been paid to the in-between of these social work intervention terminals, that is, to mezzosystem intervention and behavior. Social work practice at the mezzosystem level refers to efforts to initiate, design, create, influence, manage, and evaluate programs and policies affecting people locally. Such social work deals primarily with institutions and their subunits on behalf of individuals, families, and groups.

Because authority and resources, as well as forces, positive or negative or both, which influence human well-being, are increasingly located beyond local, state, regional, and national levels, mezzosystem practice seeks to influence these components in terms of local perspective, no matter how defined. Mezzosystem practice also seeks to control or serve as the structure through which manpower, resources, and facilities can be procured, organized, and implemented locally into program and policy. Its activities take place along both vertical and horizontal lines of community structural lines of community structure processes and interaction; thus, individuals and groups having an interest in mezzosystem decisions are found on all geopolitical levels. Mezzosystem activity at times overlaps micro and, at other times, macro and, at times, appears to be indistinguishable from these two polar levels of activity.

Aspects of Practice

One way to approach the implications of these studies for mezzosystem interventions is by looking at the kind of decisions which are the focus of much activity in mezzosystem practice. Among these decision-making areas are the following: (1) the definition and documentation of human needs and social problems; (2) the articulation of goals related to human well-being; (3) the establishment of priorities; (4) specification of service outcomes; (5) accountability of services at the local level; and (6) management of the service agencies. While other areas can be listed, a brief discussion of these points up their lack of focus in formulating the variables to be manipulated and the design of evaluation.

One area for decision-making is documentation of local social needs, that is, studying, maintaining, analyzing and appropriately utilizing information about characteristic conditions and problems of the local community. Hence, it is necessary to have a standardized unit of data collection such as the household, which is a key element because it is the smallest social unit of communication, social control, power distribution, and socialization readily accessible; within it income is distributed, housing is shared, and children are reared. Documentation requires establishing sources of data and a plan for ordering and analyzing the data as well as interpreting and utilizing it.

A related task is discovering unmet needs of individuals due to lack of contact with existing appropriate services, lack of an appropriate service, and lack of utilization of service. A screening device must be established which counts and identifies people from these three areas. Local persons and organizations who are knowledgeable about welfare agency dropouts must be involved, which requires a communications network of formal and informal leaders. Then, there is the related process of matching persons in need with the appropriate service, if available, or, if not, trying to make such service available.

Another aspect of documentation involves monitoring trends of large-scale social and economic development. Who, within the community, is to be responsible and how is information about the scope of needs and the local expression of needs and social problems to be collected, interpreted, and reported? How is such information to be secured by the various decision-making centers in health, welfare, education, manpower, and economic development? And, how can it best be interpreted and utilized in terms of local conditions?

A second area for decision-making is articulation of local community goals related to the well-being of its citizenry. Perhaps the most direct and meaningful way social work practice intervenes in shaping human goals is projecting and predicting consequences to individual and communal life of social behavior and institutional policies which either threaten or promote life and humanitarian values. Such consequences may develop from the intentional or unintentional neglect by the community of cases of individual and social dysfunction; or from a projected community policy and practice. The major questions confronting social work practice in this area are: How is social work practice to come by such wisdom? Upon what does it base its claim to speak and be heard? Performance in this area requires at least the ability to assert an association between a given social practice and social and human outcomes considered to be harmful or threatening, and the responsibility to prescribe a remedy.

A third area for decision-making is the establishment of priorities. When decisions are being made to expand, discontinue, continue as is, or reduce a community service, regardless of the means employed, a service priority is being expressed. Indirectly, social problem priorities are also being expressed. Welfare planning groups, governmental and voluntary, have faced such choices all their organizational lives. Some organizations probably first face such decisions consciously under crisis conditions: when this year's money runs short of last year's allocation, what is to be deleted—

a particular service, a category of services, or part of all services? In spite of the availability of additional funds, other organizations face such decisions because these funds prove inadequate to finance all asked-for expansions or new services. Perhaps a few must make priority choices when evaluating existing services and money and when searching for more effective ways of reducing or preventing social problems.

It should be noted that not everyone in a community agrees that a centralized priority determination process is desirable. Many people strongly believe that individuals and organizations should have the right to initiate and pursue problems and programs according to their own interests and capabilities—which right, they insist, represents a fundamental strength of the American way of doing things. Others, who may consider rational, centralized priority decisions desirable, question the possibility of carrying out such decisions; they maintain that the vested interest of individuals and groups are such that they must be dealt with not rationally but in the arena of power struggle and survival.

How is the process of rational decision-making about the relative importance or urgency, or both, of community needs and resources to be carried out? Where and how can facts be introduced to produce more rational decisions? Where do value premises become the overriding consideration? To what extent should the possibility and feasibility of implementation enter into the decision-making? How is the importance of a community problem, need, or service to be ascertained? When effectiveness of service is not clear, what weight should be attached to this condition in the priority process? What is the most effective way of guiding priority decisions? How should old services be evaluated? How is the gap between those making priority decisions about needs and those making priority decisions about resources to be bridged? Is the priority determination process under public auspices similar to or different from such a process under voluntary auspices? When responsibility for making need and resource priorities is shared with more than one geographical level of organization, how are differences in perception and authority to be managed? How is conflict between equally legitimate ends and competing interests to be resolved?

A fourth area for decision-making is specification of local

agency service outcomes. The importance of efforts to improve agency specifications of outcomes can be illustrated by asking what solutions meeting the expectations of consumers, sponsors, and social workers can we offer to single parents, to families with dependent children headed by females, to pregnant teen-age girls, to angry and volatile youth? What solutions can we promise for the socially and economically deteriorating neighborhood? What can social workers offer low-income parents of mentally retarded children; children who are being undereducated for future adult roles; unskilled young adults; people suffering from poor housing, debts, and illness; and families of those who are sometimes in jail? While it is not the conscious intent of social workers, some solutions offered result in making clients even more dependent, more resistant to being helped, or openly hostile toward the profession.

To effectively unite knowledge about problems and service outcomes with interventive methods and strategies requires the social worker to keep an eye on both the individual and the risk population groups from which he comes, while taking into account the social systems context in which the individual moves. How does the social worker and, in particular, the management of his agency change in order to integrate agency policy and practice as they relate to outcomes for the consumer? How can agency policy and procedures be established and implemented to make it clear whether the consumer's expectations as well as the worker's have been met, thus establishing an additional criterion for workers' satisfaction—success and rewards?

A fifth area of decision-making involves helping agencies to modify, extend, and curtail services in line with local conditions. On the local level, plans must be developed wherein agency accountability for its claimed impact upon social problems and conditions may be evaluated periodically. While this approach may limit the number of service needs to which agency resources can be put at any one time, it does promise greater accountability, which over a period of time provides more quality control of social services. That is, the flow of human services to risk populations as well as geographical areas should be functionally related to demand and impact. Such a plan of accountability should be worked out for all agencies and should include not only operations involving social problems or social welfare agencies but impact and demand involving desirable social conditions.

In professional literature and in conferences, references are often made to the need to achieve better coordination and integration of services at the client level. The need for open intake and service mechanisms and for task specialization is now being recognized. The job of mezzosystem planning and action is to facilitate the horizontal as well as vertical communication of agencies in the interest of better services to clients, but this is difficult when institutional barriers prevent communication and power changes.

A sixth area for decision-making is management of local organizations. There are presently a number of old and new demands challenging routine and traditional agency management habits and procedures, such as the notion that consumers of human services should have an equal voice in the planning and administration of services and perhaps a majority voice about some aspects of service. It is also necessary to relate planning and delivery of social work services to nonsocial work programs like employment and education; for agencies to set new priorities without being able to substantially increase their present resources; to provide more and better information for planning, program design, and achievement of quality control of services; to use differentially several levels of professional and nonprofessional personnel; to revise and change the mission of the social work agency; to organize service delivery on a larger scale and at the same time decentralize many service units; to find more effective ways of relating voluntary and public resources; and to become involved in, rather than avoid or modify, issues that have a high component of controversy and conflict.

Study Findings

The thirteen evaluations of social work interventions have tested the impact of at least nine variations in social work delivery patterns upon practice outcomes, singularly and in combination. The chief variations are increasing the potential for better service by reducing the caseloads of social workers; changing the service target from the individual to the family system; enlarging the social worker's control over the number and kinds of resources available to clients; utilizing planned short-term treatment in lieu of open-ended treatment; collaborating with a second related professional discipline rather than making a single discipline responsible; integrating group work, casework, and community organization; using personnel with less than graduate training in lieu of and in combination with graduate social workers; using staff team practice in lieu of conventional practice; and using more intensive treatment versus institutional care.

Some of these studies deal with only one experimental variable while others combine two or more. A similar spread in characteristics of the study populations makes it difficult to draw implications from the thirteen studies. For example, there are variations in social class, ethnicity (majority or minority status), and categories of problems—clients with multiple problems (including economic dependence); clients with a monolithic structure of problems including economic dependence, age, family, and other interpersonal problems; and clients whose problems are severe, are repetitive, or vary in chronicity.

In general, these thirteen studies are of interest to mezzosystem interventions, but it is apparent that they were designed mainly from the orientation of microsystem practice. While these studies have been reviewed in previous chapters, they can profitably be reexamined here from a mezzosystem viewpoint.

The Area Development Project tested the effect of an integrated service model in delivering services to multiproblem families; the project operated on the assumption that one worker coordinating services from a number of agencies could provide great impact upon the family system. The report concluded that integrated service in and of itself did not result in greater effectiveness although it did prove more effective than uncoordinated multiple services.

The pattern proposed for achieving integration at the worker level raises a question about the possibility of developing truly effective interagency collaboration on any extensive basis. A number of administrative problems interfered with its operation—lack of financial commitment to guarantee necessary manpower; difficulties with selection, turnover and termination of workers; differentials in workers' experience and position within the collaborating agencies; difficulty in sharing administrative responsibility for project outcomes. Although the success of this part of the project rested on the notion that service integration could be better accomplished at the individual worker level, the project did not raise, as a part of the design, questions about organizational conditions which needed to be established in order to sustain the workers' efforts. Precisely these organizational constraints make the project outcomes appear less conclusive.

The second part of the Area Development Project concerned efforts to strengthen and improve a somewhat deprived neighborhood through social development. Although this part of the project was not a controlled evaluative study, the project did produce some short-term changes: new groups in the neighborhood with a special interest and a somewhat representative view of the community were established, although the stability of such groups was considered doubtful; citizens working together for changes established procedures and experiences, although the project did not make a basic change in the status of the neighborhood; and while there was an increase in community services, the *amount* of community services and the precipitating factors remain unknown. Thus, the importance, as well as the durability, of the changes in citizen response to planning services are doubtful. The issue raised by this part of the study points to the need for critical assessment of the dimensions of the critical mass of power and influence required to produce and maintain change. Neighborhood power, while a necessary condition, appears not to be a sufficient one for the scope of changes sought in the second part of the Area Development Project.

The Casework Methods Project reports an experiment which varied the length of casework treatment provided to middle-income, self-motivated families. It was hypothesized that short-term planned treatment would prove better than open-ended treatment for marital or parent-child relationship problems. Reid and Shyne report that the short-term treatment resulted in generally superior outcomes. They also point out that some continuing services were being carried beyond the point of diminishing returns. This study, along with Serving the Aging, demonstrates the need to carefully examine the usefulness of a short-term plan utilizing problem classification and related circumstances with alternative outcomes. If such findings hold up, they promise important gains in manpower utilization, cost reduction, and service to consumers. Thus the findings illustrate the importance of two major concerns of mezzointervention: specialization of outcomes and accountability mechanisms.

The Chemung County Study contrasts intensive casework provided to multiproblem families with a control group which received regular agency services. The conclusion reached was that casework alone, of the quality in this experiment and under the study conditions, was insufficient to produce significant changes in family functioning. The study was unable to account for these negative results. As in the Area Development Study, the question of under what conditions intensive casework can produce a positive and sufficient change in functioning of multiproblem families suggests almost immediately the need for interventions in the social environment. The omission of this orientation from the study while revealing the impotence of casework does not provide clues about other possible approaches.

The CSS-DSS Study sought, through intensive casework by M.S.W. workers in a voluntary agency in collaboration with public welfare, to bring about more improvement in the economic and psychological functioning of the experimental families in contrast to a control group. While the results tended to support the major hypothesis, the difference was not significant. Here, as noted in the Area Development Project and the Neighborhood Improvement Project, the collaborative aspects of the planned interventions were not implemented, pointing once again to the difficulties of ad hoc interorganizational efforts which lack sufficient autonomy and resources to carry out necessary activities. A further observation was the incomplete data regarding input of social workers and the specifics of client problems and attendant conditions; this observation appears to apply to most of the studies under consideration here.

A Comprehensive Program for Multiproblem Families is a study of the effects of a multi method, family-centered approach to rehabilitation of multiproblem families. The findings failed to show that experimental group families receiving special services fared better than control families receiving regular services. This study, however, did seek to distinguish outcomes in terms of objective and subjective categories, although the differences between categories were not significant. Regrettably, the relation of specific social work interventions to the outcomes sought was not discussed in this report.

An Experimental Study to Measure the Effectiveness of Casework Service sought to demonstrate that a small caseload of persons considered potentially economically dependent would show greater social and psychological tendencies toward self-sufficiency over a fifteen-month period than persons in a group of regular-size caseloads. While Behling reports that the major hypotheses were supported, it is not clear how this resulted. One interesting finding reported that the experimental group received significantly more money durnig this period than the control group; certainly this is of interest to mezzosystem interventions. While no conclusions are reached as to how this finding relates to the outcome, certainly major questions for macro- as well as mezzosystem practice concern providing an amount of money necessary to move people toward economic self-sufficiency and the conditions under which this best occurs outside of the normal pursuits of work.

The Familycenter Project reports on an experimental program of special aid to multiproblem families in a low-income area of Copenhagen. The basic finding is that persons who received the special aid showed modest improvement in almost all respects. The experiment, by tackling subjective issues first and then moving to objective ones, seems to be at odds with the idea that tangible objectives such as housing and income must be dealt with first. However, Kühl points out that the latter type of objectives cannot be overlooked and must be dealt with effectively. For example, the report cites an association between improvement in areas such as housing and income and in areas such as the physical and psychological state of families and the relationship between adults and children, but draws no causal inference. He reports a systematic relation between the activity intensity level of the social workers and the amount of change in all functioning fields of the family. These findings require more investigation as they are, at points, at odds with other studies. Yet, some evidence suggests that the lower the socioeconomic class of the consumer, the more intensive the activity from the worker in order to help. This report also calls attention to the favorable economic climate which made economic gains possible. It would be of great interest to test these findings with other populations and other social workers in another setting.

Girls at Vocational High is a study of efforts to promote better school achievement in adolescent girls in a vocational high school. The assumption tested is that casework and group work interventions have a positive impact on school achievement. However, the findings do not confirm the major hypothesis. It does seem that traditional case and group work services might not, in and of themselves, bring about significant changes in school performance pending the analysis as to the probable causes of such inferior performance. One could profitably ask what influences in the social environment should be mobilized to assist in achieving the desired result. Subsequent studies in this area should include this dimension as a part of the design.

The Midway Project pursued the question: Can available personnel be more effectively utilized in providing public assistance services than they are at present? To answer this question the design called for testing the usual pattern of manpower utilizations against a team form of organization which sought to increase specialization opportunities, while providing built-in coordination through middle range management, planning, and control. Involved in this arrangement were case classification as a basis for assignment, differential use of skills and expertise, and breaking down traditional responsibilities into tasks and assigning them to members of the team. It was hypothesized that clients receiving services from staff members of experimental teams would show greater improvement or less deterioration than clients receiving staff services from the conventional group. The design called for variation in size of group loads. The major findings were that reduction in caseload proved significant in producing client change; the team approach, while effective, was most dramatic in its impact under conditions of reduced loads; and short-term treatment was quite effective in the conventional high caseload groups. Application of these results could lead to a radically new pattern in social work manpower utilization. Therefore replication of the study under similar as well as different conditions is important.

In the Neighborhood Improvement Project, the observations made about the disappearance of the agency alliance are of special interest to mezzosystem practitioners. The report presents an interesting account of the dynamics of agency collaboration as it occurred in this project; of the six agencies involved at the beginning, only one remained after four years. While no objective evaluation exists for this phase of the project, the account is quite significant since one of the action-research goals of the project—and of most service-oriented research—was to carry out the research so that its positive findings would be incorporated into present agency operations, bringing about changes in service techniques and in portions of service delivery. Although the reasons for the disengagement of the five agencies are not known, the investigators concluded that differences among the agencies respecting service priorities and orientations eventually led to the breakup of the agency alliance and to the gradual emergence of a centrally and unilaterally administered project. Further, when the project director and the re-formed staff no longer had to check with six agencies, they were able to collaborate more effectively and to modify approaches more easily.

Social work literature and conference discussions in recent years have reflected great concern for the action evaluation projects conducted, more or less, outside of the existing network of services. The most frequent criticism being the question of what happens when the special project is over. Experience indicates that many special projects, in spite of their positive findings, when conducted solely within one agency are not continued after the project period. How is change to occur if existing agencies change slowly or not at all and new ones, after an initial period, soon behave like the others? Certainly one mezzosystem practice difficulty is the inability to create and sustain adequate rewards, encouragement, and support for change and developmental behavior of organizations.

The Pursuit of Promise sought to test the power of a group service program to maintain and enhance the functioning of intellectually superior children living in a socially deprived area. Commonly held myths about people indigenous to deprived urban areas such as their difficulty in engaging in programs and with instrumental behavior (frequently attributed to psychological pathology and to a low level of organized family life) were contradicted by the study findings. These findings although incidental and inconclusive to the main thrust of the study should not be overlooked. They are supported by other studies dealing with the life-styles of the poor and by the words of the poor and urban inner-city minority residents themselves. The implication here is the need for greater flexibility in format and objectives of programs designed to help the poor.

The experimental groups showed inconclusive evidence that they benefited over the control groups (except for an improvement in reading skills which is in itself an accomplishment) which suggests that efforts to enhance the functioning of individuals living in deprived surroundings without influencing that environment may not yield an appreciable effect. It would be useful if future experiments could attempt a saturation approach simultaneously bringing about related interventions in relevant systems. The finding that improvement among Blacks occurred in both the experimental and control groups should be pursued since it raises the possibility of forces at work for change on a much broader level.

Serving the Aging reports work with a largely white population sixty years of age and older, economically dependent and with other problems. The study sought to determine the effectiveness of three modes of service provision. The findings of this study are of interest in several decision-making areas; for example, the most common problems for which older persons seek help from a voluntary family health and welfare agency are those involving housing and living arrangements or health; the least common are those involving interpersonal relations. If most family service agencies are primarily geared to providing help with interpersonal problems and if among the elderly seeking help the most frequent problems involve housing and health, it is not difficult to understand why the elderly do not come to family service agencies and why if they do come once, they may not return.

Keeping in mind the particular characteristics of the study population, questions are raised as to the mixture of services which can be obtained in one location at the retail level, and the extent to which social workers view the mobilization of material resources and the promotion of direct utilization as central to the responsibility of the social worker. If similar information could be secured from agencies regarding various service populations and their social class, age, and nature of dependence, such information could prove useful in arriving at a more objectively rational distribution of services. Regarding utilization and cost of service, the finding is that short-term service is as effective and less expensive than open-ended service, and the effectiveness of more intensive collaborative service involving a second profession—such as health or housing experts— is of interest. If these findings hold when tested with other populations, they offer some potential for reducing the cost of services. Of particular interest is the finding of a negative association between applicant survival and the amount and length of service, coupled with a positive association between amount and length of service and placement in protective settings. This finding, now supported by other studies, points out the need to examine community goals regarding the removal of certain people from their homes for institutional placement.

Implications for Practice

It is quite apparent that these studies represent an enormous commitment of talent, time, effort, and interest by the researchers, social workers, clients, and agencies involved. Yet the reader who reviews the research is likely to feel discouraged at the inconclusiveness presented by the findings. The review, however, may be very instructive, particularly if one steps back some distance from the details of any one study and reacts to the gestalt. Perhaps most significant are either things which appear to have been omitted from the design of the investigations or things which proved somewhat problematic.

Those programs requiring interorganizational collaboration seemed to encounter resistance which, while not so intended, appeared strongly subversive regarding project goals, raising a fundamental question for administrators, program designers, and educators. When financial, facility, and manpower resources of two or more organizations are required to achieve programmatic outcomes, how can the continuing commitment of these separate organizations be concerted and maintained even when this commitment may be in conflict with their other priorities and interests? Called into question here is the nature of the power relations of service delivery systems, their utilities and limitations, their uses and misuses.

Although in only two of the investigations was the question of the relationship between the social development of the community and the servicing of individual and family needs formally addressed, the issue seems to lie just below the surface of each study. How is the organization to behave when sufficient citizen responsibility is not taken for their institutions, or when social conditions exist which negate their efforts, or when higher geopolitical allocation centers are not responsive to local needs? Just how is the agency —not just the social workers—to systematically respond to forces in the environment which may negatively affect the outcomes they seek with or on behalf of their consumers?

From the perspective of the mezzosystem practitioner, the investigations point to some serious defects in present agency operations: descriptions of target populations appear too general to help in determining significant variations in service techniques and service delivery patterns; the rules for determining the dosage of social work interventions seem underdeveloped (this dimension was taken into account in very limited ways in most of the studies considered here); and the description of services is so general, which makes it very difficult to compare services and results with any degree of confidence.

These defects, to the extent they exist, contribute to two problems plaguing the investigations: how to avoid equating methods of intervention with the full parameters of service; and how to avoid defining practice outcomes in terms related more to methodological considerations as opposed to terms which reflect changes in the status or relationship of the consumer, or target of intervention.

Useful as a first step in making a more basic classification of service-outcomes is a listing of service functions, that is, design and implementation of activities and resources which will meet needs of consumers by linking the consumer with need-satisfying systems, change or modify those characteristics of a system which negatively influence the social competence of its members or others, and increase or restore the social competence of individuals and small groups to function within other systems.

While professions understandably define outcomes in terms of technique and method, service-oriented organizations must define outcomes primarily in terms of their meaning to users and sponsors. And, where these two outcomes conflict, professional ethics dictate that the practitioner opt for outcomes that meet the need of the consumers based on the values of the profession.

It is difficult not to feel that some investigations presume our knowledge is more advanced than it is. At this stage of professional development would it not be useful to discover what is involved in success with one of each type of case, systematically varying related conditions and variables? Such a step may be a prerequisite to better classification of service objectives and outcomes.

The research and evaluation seem to be very much the product of ad hoc ventures conducted in part by people outside the ongoing decision-making machinery of agencies and communities. Only in the Midway Project does the evaluation appear to evolve from an ongoing commitment to research and development. To devote the attention and gather the knowledge required for the study of such complex problems as dealt with in these thirteen studies, research and evaluation must be made an integral part of service design and delivery. The agency must become the chief sponsor of such research as opposed to outside auspices. Is it feasible that significant advancement in the state of our practice can come without a great commitment from policy boards, staff, and other collaborators to develop ongoing investigations as a part of business as usual? One way to facilitate such commitment would be for universities to develop greater technical assistance and evaluative or developmental research capabilities in conjunction with agencies. Certainly greater teamwork between university and agency is called for instead of the parallel play which all too frequently characterizes university-agency relationships.

Implications for Education

The findings from these studies selectively support the variety of changes currently under way or being considered by schools of social work; two ideas supported by the gestalt can be identified. First, emphasis upon research must be increased in schools of social work but along a somewhat different path than that traditionally followed. Research should become an integrated component of all classroom and field instruction; accomplishing this requires satisfying two important conditions: retraining faculties for teaching research as a tool, in analysis and in practice; and developing field teaching centers in which both students and faculty can participate in ongoing research.

Second, present practice developments suggest a continued need for more and better trained personnel at the mezzosystem level. With developments in undergraduate education in general and in undergraduate social work education, it seems reasonable to expect that many M.S.W. programs will assume a large responsibility for training students for entry jobs into middle management, planning and program analysis, program design and evaluative responsibilities. Nearly all schools electing to go this route must thoroughly examine the utility of making room in present programs for additional knowledge developed in related disciplines of management, economics, political science, and anthropology. Here, too, faculty development needs strong support. Also, the need for manpower may give many schools the opportunity to develop specialized programs in continuing education to prepare people for practice opportunities in this area of social work intervention.

The needs for research, for better and more effective evaluative studies, and for better and more effective manpower are so great that if not supplied by social work education, they are likely to be met by educational programs in related and even nonrelated disciplines.

9

Mezzosystem Intervention as a Link Between Individual and Collective Development

Simon Slavin

Two difficulties present themselves in addressing mezzosystem intervention as a link between the individual and the collective. Few of the studies examined deal with social work practice at this level. While two or three studies seem so oriented—the Midway Project, the Neighborhood Improvement Project, and the Area Development Project, looking as they did at problems of interorganizational exchange and the reorganization of some aspects of social service delivery—most of them examined the effectiveness of microsystem intervention with defined population groups.

A second difficulty deals with the conceptualization of mezzosystem intervention as a useful analytical tool. This question is not merely semantic, but deals with the reality of practice and the orderly pursuit of useful distinctions. John Turner suggests that there is, on occasion, overlap between mezzosystem activity and both microsystem and macrosystem practice, but, at other times, no discernible difference can be found, presumably depending on scope, time and context. Overlap and identity, even if occasional, are poor conditions for differentiating discrete phenomena, bringing into question the trilevel model of social work practice assumed in this book.

There may, however, be heuristic value in this kind of analysis since it tends to underscore the connection between the two polar patterns of professional activity. The studies and Turner's comments pose major questions which deal with the intricate and inevitable relationship between micro and macro aspects of social work practice. Intervention in a microsystem always takes place in a specific agency and community, and is defined by policies built into planning and administration. Thus, by implication, all micro services have macro relevance and all macro pursuits deal with micro services. Microsystem activity provides data and insight into policy development which, in turn, gives direction to micro practice as it fashions and delivers social services. To be sure, policies and services meet on the local level, and are the essential ingredient of social agency administration. One view of social administration is seeing it as that function in social organization which links, organizes, and monitors social policies and social services. In this sense, administration belongs as much to micro as to macro activity.

Mezzo and microsystems have size and locality relevance, but do not provide good handles for pursuing system concerns. For example, agency administration does not yield easily to size or place variables, though scale does have significant bearing on certain elements of analysis. Large-scale administration is found locally, and small-scale administration regionally and nationally. The categories reviewed earlier by Harold Lewis—rules, principles, and theories—

do not, similarly, lend themselves to differentiation according to these artificial constructs.

Local issues, practices, and organizations have broad and narrow undertones and should not be singled out for either unique practice characteristics or training requirements. It seems that we are dealing here with the relationship between problems of social service delivery and planning, administration, and policy development, wherever such problems are found and whatever their boundaries and domains.

Turner points to competing interests in practice and to potential confusion in relating methods of intervention to service outcomes. He speculates about the perceptions and expectations of consumers, sponsors, and social workers who meet in the agency as it organizes its unique service system. The studies under review focused on the relationship of consumer and worker and sought to determine the effectiveness of that social transaction. Yet all these elements are inevitably involved in what happens when services are provided and used. Service outcomes depend on numerous variables, only one of which is the particular method employed in the relation between worker and client. Factors that bear on effectiveness include at least the following: the client constellation and needs; the nature and definitions of the client's problems; the policy, orientation, and resources of the agency; the distinctive competence and skill of the practitioner; the time dimensions of the service—time of onset, duration, and intensity; environmental externalities, that is, job opportunities, training resources, income supplements, and so forth; the state of knowledge; and the comprehensiveness of the service.

Service goals such as client independence and self-direction are easily attained when the job market is open, when training opportunities are available and accessible, when experience and knowledge are sufficiently advanced to guide practice, when agencies can make available comprehensive service, and when other essential services, such as health care and financial assistance, are at hand. Research on social work effectiveness is especially difficult precisely because it is not easy to hold all but one factor constant for impact evaluation.

The diverse interests, needs, and predispositions of consumers, sponsors, and workers present another issue for service delivery and for education for practice. This threefold classification is similar to that of Lewis' specification of relationships between problem, program, and process. Each has its own dynamic, and the juxtaposition, as Turner suggests, presents some real questions concerning the effective delivery of service. Service outcomes are best achieved when these elements interact congruently. Often there tends to be strain between them, essentially because they package their elements differently, and locate their distinctive rewards according to idiosyncratic considerations. Agencies establish services in a field of practice and try to address the demands of specific social problems; practitioners are trained in methods of intervention established according to professional norms; clients, in contradistinction, come to the agency with problems that are dictated by human vulnerability to environmental and institutional circumstances. How this strain is reduced or resolved is an important issue for social work practice and for institutional change.

Essentially the strain between the three universal elements of practice—agency, practitioner, and consumer—is relieved by compelling compliance to one or another of these elements. Significant consequences follow on this choice. When agencies compel practice adaptations, practitioners respond by subordinating professional perspectives to organizational demands and predispositions. Thus, for example, Maas (1964), Briar (1964), and Billingsley (1965) found that workers' judgments were fashioned more in accord with the ideology of their employing agency than with professional norms. When client need does not fit the distinctive pattern of agency service, characteristically service is withheld or the client referred to other agencies. Practitioners and consumers, the dependent variables, are pressured to change, while the organization remains the constant. Professional norms, when made transcendent, influence both organization and consumer to change, a circumstance characteristic of efforts to professionalize agency services. When this leads to fee payments of one sort or another or to particular brands of therapeutic intervention, the nature of the clientele inevitably undergoes change.

Turner points out that in case of conflict between users and sponsors in service-oriented organizations, ethics require opting for outcomes that meet consumer need. He clearly implies that client perspectives ought to define both organizational and professional adaptation and that change strategies should be directed at modifying agency orientation, policy, or structure, and at packaging practitioner skill, so that imperatives of client service goals can be met. This calls for a degree of professional flexibility and adaptability to both practice and training and suggests a significant agenda for administrative planning and social work education. It seems the latter has never focused in sufficient depth and detail on organizational and institutional dynamics.

Much of what is problematic in the research under review reflects this conventional preoccupation of the profession. The client-worker transaction always takes place in an organizational context which affects process and conditions outcomes. This context is as much foreground as background and, frequently, quite determining of practitioner role and performance. If organizational context is important to practice, then it should be important to training and to research. As Carol Meyer suggests in the following chapter, the institution must be seen as part of the case, and evaluation accordingly oriented. Indeed, Girls at Vocational High speculates in its conclusion about the need for research on social serving institutions and the structure of services. To the extent that this perspective is omitted, effectiveness research is flawed.

Aside from these differences in perspectives, divergences in interest and in power tend to shape the behavior of organizations, of consumers, and of practitioners. Agencies tend to be mindful of organizational rewards as well as service outcomes, and naturally so; the dictates of organizational survival and strength are very compelling. Those at the organizational helm focus on such things as prestige, organizational growth, financial strength and stability, community roots, and so forth. Programmatic and consumer considerations are often subordinated to these demands. This is most clearly seen when agencies become involved in controversial issues; pressure to eschew service goals in favor of agency needs for financial resources or community acceptance are palpably present in times of national conservatism but potentially present at all times as a natural part of the organizational environment.

Conflict between the interests of consumer and those of both agency and practitioner has been sharply visible in recent years, and is largely responsible for the demand for community control and consumer participation. The most glaring conflicts are seen in emergency and out-patient facilities of inner-city general hospitals, in community mental health programs, in public welfare programs, and in universities and schools of social work. Diverse and conflicting interests distort service delivery processes and service goals and testify to the power struggle of the constituencies related to social services.

The studies point to an increasingly significant aspect of contemporary social work practice—problems of interorganizational exchange and collaboration. While only two of the studies deal specifically with attempts at concerting interorganization energies, all implicitly suggest the power of organizational environments in enhancing or limiting the ability of practitioners and agencies to achieve stated goals. Turner's comments on the presence of forces in the environment negatively affecting outcomes suggest an important strategic consideration for social work intervention; for example, helping clients avoid dependency may be more affected by job market conditions than by interviews with social workers. In other words, practitioner attempts to enhance employment or training resources may be more effective in dealing with client vulnerability than direct work with the client. Taking another example, intervention in a school system through relevant transactions with teaching, administrative, and guidance personnel may be more potent in handling personality distortions of a child than individual or family treatment.

All this suggests the importance of the reciprocal and sequential relationships of organizations and institutions as they bear on the effectiveness of any single aspect of social practice. Research on intraagency worker inputs ignores these relationships and, consequently, distorts the reality of interorganizational influences that either retard or enhance such effort; this is as true of longitudinal as of existential service considerations. The reinforcement of community supportive services as clients experience social reentry more often determines social work effectiveness than does the most skilled and appropriate treatment provided by the social agency. This is especially true of work in the total institution. Research on recidivism rates points sharply to the strategic significance of postinstitutional care that is consistently accessible and available. Experience with the additions similarly underscores the importance of long periods of social reintegrative services—perhaps years of reinforcing social mechanisms.

Organizational environments have become very significant as modern industrial-technological societies mature. This is, in part, a consequence of pressure for greater organizational and professional specialization as knowledge accumulates and skills proliferate. Much planning effort has gone into devising structures for the effective consolidation and integration of knowledge and skill; examples are child and youth programs, O.E.O. comprehensive health centers, and Community Mental Health Centers. Current experience suggests that the local community and even the neighborhood may be the most viable setting for consolidated planning. These developments demonstrate the importance of insight into questions concerning the mix between centralization and decentralization and the place of consumer feedback and participation in agency program development.

The major point in this discussion is that social workers must be increasingly concerned with the system relationships within which they function. Client service is enhanced through interacting relationships between functionaries within a single social agency and between various social agencies. Relationships within the social welfare system have been systematically explored by the profession for years. Information, referral and brokerage activity, caseworkgroup integration, interdisciplinary experiences of one kind or another including teamwork patterns in rehabilitation and orthopsychiatric programs, interagency case conferences, and joint agency programs all move in this direction.

What is now surely as imperative as the relationship with the the social welfare system is the interdependency of divergent institutional systems. Failure in one system predisposes failures in related systems; for example, inadequate schools make residential stability difficult to achieve, and debilitating housing facilities make educational adequacy problematic; economic insufficiency counters social work effort at achieving self-realization in clients. Research on the effectiveness of microsystem intervention must recognize the power of macrosystem characteristics, and conclusions about practitioner effectiveness must be tempered by consideration of the externalities which impinge on helping processes.

Most of the studies ostensibly sought to assess the effectiveness of microsystem practice, yet it is not clear what was actually evaluated. Because the research took place in single agencies—thus making comparative study impossible—and involved, in each case, limited numbers of practitioners, the conclusions are merely suggestive, if not thoroughly questionable. For example, it is hard to know whether the object of investigation was the method used in the transactions under review or the quality of social workers providing the services. If the quality of social workers was being investigated, it is difficult to know whether that quality reflects his training or his theory of practice, or the quality and influence of his teachers and supervisors. Again, the critical variable may be neither of these but the agency itself, its orientation and ideology, its pattern and organization of service, and the resources it makes available to social worker and client as they cooperate in dealing with the social problems that brought them together.

The ambiguity of the critical inputs in the experiments studied makes it difficult to derive significant lessons for practice. The studies do point to pervasive issues and trends confronting the profession on both theoretical and empirical dimensions. Turner has summarized them well, but some considerations can be added to his list. Too little was said in the studies about value assumptions underlying the goals which guided the social work practice. For example, an important objective of several studies concerned reducing client dependence. While this seems unexceptionable, the overriding virtues of such motivation are questionable. For many who seek service this is a most appropriate goal; for others, the reverse may be posited. Income supports over time seemingly reinforce dependency, yet providing adequate levels of cash income even for long periods might well guide agency policies in the face of institutional failure. The current debate concerning supporting mothers with dependent children so that they can remain at home rather than enter the labor market suggests the importance of differentiating service goals according to individual preferences and value choices.

One is constrained to view the reported professional behavior and its related research in light of an implicit model of organizational effectiveness and evaluation. Goal models force researchers to focus on specific outcomes and ask whether stated goals were achieved. Thus, measures of dependence reduction are logically applied to the experimental outcomes. If one is guided by a systems model, different questions are put to the researcher. In this illustration, important and useful aspects of practice are demonstrated if clients' lives are made comfortable, even if dependence is not materially reduced or unit costs are not lowered. Taking another example, residential treatment centers may vary in professional inputs but not in recidivism rates, yet humanizing the social environments of total institutions constitutes a valued consequence even if the ostensible goals of these services inputs are not achieved.

A pervasive and important implication in the studies deals with the diffusion of practice innovations and the development of strategies of organizational change. The studies suggest little about the technology of changing but point to the significance of insight into change processes. It is one thing to demonstrate the superiority of one approach to service delivery, and quite another to build new insights and skills into functioning organizations, each with its distinctive history, tradition, interests, and natural resistance to anything that might upset stabilized equilibria.

Professional behavior is intimately linked to service provision, which, in turn, is always part of a system of services. Service systems of agencies are, in turn, integral units of community service systems, both affecting and affected by them. Spotlighting microsystem intervention inevitably leads to examination of systems of service delivery and their associated operations concerning organization, development, and system change. The studies suggest the importance of conceptualizing these relationships and developing conscious linkages between them in practice. Social work education, similarly, must adapt such learnings to curriculum design and to practice theory development. Micro and macro practice are mutually determininative. Practice experience suggests system modification, planning imperatives, and social policy development. These in turn yield professional practice guides as to service delivery patterns and role repertoire delineation. Research on case work effectiveness should lead to policies, procedures, and administrative decision-making. The studies say little about these dimensions, but prepare the basis for a useful agenda for continuing study.

Turner's review of evaluative research on the local level leads naturally to implications for social work education. His suggestion that research should be taught as an integral part of all classroom and field instruction seems wise, as the field might be a more congenial setting for such integration than the classroom is. In any event, such effort should be encouraged, perhaps using research consultation for agencies interested in experimenting with research-oriented field learning experiences. Field teaching centers, as Turner suggests, provide a natural medium for this, as would a consortium of agency interests, particularly in a defined field of practice. Research teaching personnel might be more effective with students' field experiences and with individual student consultation than in didactic class instruction.

Research relevance in social work practice varies between microsystem and macrosystem intervention. In the latter, research on the nature, extent, and intensity of selected social problems is frequently a prerequisite for effective social planning and, in this sense, is an integral part of professional function. Courses on social policy and planning inevitably introduce aspects of social research, a pattern that could well be further developed and adapted in some ways to education for the delivery of social services to individuals and families. Much the same is true of evaluative research.

Evaluative research naturally suggests evaluation of the effectiveness of research teaching. In light of known data on how little quantitative subject matter is retained, one anticipates a permanent residue of insight into the nature and process of research through realistic adaptation of research to natural learning situations. One has the impression that students retain little from research courses after they enter the professional work force. Modifying patterns of teaching and studying the effectiveness of alternative models would advance research teaching objectives.

A further word might be said about the content of research courses. Objectives which guide research teaching should stress the development of orderly thinking and the canons of logical inquiry, with focus on rules of evidence and the rigor required in inductive and deductive reasoning. Technical competence in research practice is better reserved for those few students who can be stimulated to pursue refined paths of inquiry or who wish to major in research.

Turner points to the need for more and better trained personnel at the mezzosystem level. While this is undoubtedly true, it is no more so there than at other levels of practice. If the comment is intended to suggest that education be especially directed to this aspect of practice, then it is debatable. The local community as a setting for intervention does not require distinctive skills and knowledge, though, as suggested earlier, there is much about the context of such practice that is necessary for competent performance. Training in the delivery of social services, and in planning, policy development, community organization, and administration should prepare practitioners to deal with social work tasks at all levels. One ought not confuse setting and skill, and while graduate education programs increasingly stress supervision, middle management, consultation, training, program development, and policy-planning, these functions and skills are attached to professional practice in a variety of settings and levels. Organizing curricula according to the demands of service delivery and system development approaches the requirements of education for practice.

The new tasks awaiting graduate students require, as Turner hints, great inputs from the social and behavioral sciences. How to provide these inputs presents serious dilemmas to educators. The characteristic pattern of teaching about human growth and the social environment has led to more frustration than satisfaction. Social scientists have not always been happy in the social work setting, and too few social workers are equipped as social scientists. What to select from the vast array of social disciplines has always presented knotty problems; even more difficult has been the search for relevance to practice and to practice theory. The competition for additional room in the curriculum has also tended to delimit the amount of social and behavioral material that could be made available to students.

In any case, segregating social science knowledge in the curriculum is not the preferred way to reach course objectives. We must find ways to build such teaching into regular practice sequences so that social science evidence and insight can be brought to social work skill. In this way, the integration of social theory and social practice could be achieved in the very process of discovery, without the necessity of putting together diverse strands separately woven. One way to do this is through team teaching; another is to use social and behavioral scientists as trainers of and consultants to faculty. Social work teachers should expect students to be competent in the cognate sciences. Ultimately, social work educators must have a broad range of social knowledge; doctoral programs in the social sciences are primary sources of such knowledge. And at least one school is experimenting in the master's program with an integral sequence in social science theory and social work practice.

Finally, we are dealing in this book with two essential cultures of social work, which reflect society's concern for the microsocial unit and the potential enhancement of the quality of life, and the macrosocial unit, the social environment and its related institutional systems—the individual, the family, and the primary group; the aggregate, the class of individuals, and the social compact. Social work as a whole deals with both individual and collective destiny; it attempts social repair of those who are most vulnerable to the disabling aspects of social organization, but it also strives to create social conditions which encourage man's capacities for growth and fulfillment. These two foci can never properly be rent asunder; each is a condition for the attainment of the other. How to link the technologies that address individual and collective tasks and to provide effective and responsive social services and the policies and strategies that make them possible presents social work with a formidable future agenda. The reviewed studies and the discussion throughout this volume point to some promising directions in this quest.

10

Practice on Microsystem Level

Carol H. Meyer

This chapter focuses on microsystem practice and education for microsystem intervention. Microsystem, a pretentious term at best, as compared with mezzo- and macrosystem, means small system; in social work, the units of attention involved are the individual, the family, and small group, each viewed systematically and transactionally. As *cases* become viewed in systems terms, it becomes necessary to differentiate among systems levels with new concepts and not just new terminology. The implications of systems thinking is the substance of this analysis. Wherever our deliberations take us, our starting point in microsystem intervention is a commitment to individualizing services. What form these services take, who provides them, and who receives them must be debated seriously in the field, but attention to the individual, as himself, in his family, his group, and his community, is the organizing principle.

Fields of Attention

This chapter examines the thirteen reviewed studies from various perspectives. According to a very rough scheme, the studies can be placed in three groups according to field of attention. First, five of the thirteen studies focused entirely on *worker-client interactions;* they did not meaningfully consider the interlocking environmental aspects of the clients' world, including the organizational life of the agencies in which the practice took place. Included in this group were The Chemung County Study, the CSS-DSS Study, A Comprehensive Program for Muliproblem Families, An Experimental Study to Measure the Effectiveness of Casework Service, and Girls at Vocational High.

Four of the remaining eight studies addressed *the client field or surrounding systems,* although they actually focused their research on the worker-client transactions through one-to-one modes or through group services. Included in this group were The Family Life Improvement Project, The Familycenter Project, The Neighborhood Improvement Project, and The Pursuit of Promise. The remaining four studies demonstrated and evaluated *new practice modes.* While not all addressed the client's field, all did try to invent some new kinds of practice which then served as the experimental variable. Included in this group were The Area Development Project, The Casework Methods Project, The Midway Study, and Serving the Aging.

The first group included the studies that evaluated casework practice as it is, taking as givens traditional definitions, goals, and units of attention. The second group of studies reflected an effort to account for influences upon the client's well-being that were larger, insofar as the unit of attention was concerned, than the worker-client transaction. The third group of studies attempted to redefine methods and goals of practice, although in this group, too, decidedly little attention was paid to the sources of environmental strain.

Research Questions and Casework Ideology

The studies raise some hard questions about casework practice, and while it is tempting to criticize the research methodology alone, one must face the fact that there was a strong association between the way the research was done and the way casework presented itself to the researchers. The research studies under examination are prototypical of the traditional casework method, demonstrating some of the strengths of the model and succumbing to some of the pitfalls for which it has been lately criticized. The reason for associating the research approach of some of the studies with the practice of casework is that in the case of the second grouping, for example, those researchers who addressed the client's field or environment through collecting and assessing demographic and other data relating to housing, school, health care, and the like, didn't seem to know how to use it as the focus of their experiments and evaluations and finally wound up studying the client-worker or group-worker transactions. According to this observation, a caseworker may be cognizant of environmental influences, may collect data on the significant aspects of the client's surroundings, and will likely include his developing understanding of the environmental strains in his psychosocial assessment or diagnosis of the client; but when it comes to action, intervention, or treatment, the social worker often falls back upon what he knows best—the interview, the relationship, and the interactions between him and his client.

This is not due to mischief or narrow-mindedness. Nor is it as true as it once was that caseworkers have eyes only for the psyche. It is more likely that behavioral theory—it is not necessary to specify which kind—tends to be more unified and functional for practice than sociological theory. For one Freudian theoretical framework which explains the force of the unconscious in a person's actual behavior, the practitioner must draw upon several sociological theories, each self-contained, to interpret a complex phenomenon occurring in the person's environment. For instance, one might have to draw upon organizational theory, theories of cultural relativity, theories of deviance in the opportunity system, and so on. Social role theory has not even been as productive an integrating concept as we had hoped; Eriksonian formulations are only beginning to take hold as bridging concepts; and general systems theory turns out to be not a theory but a framework for viewing interrelated phenomena. It is small wonder that the casework practitioner has, in a sense, "stayed with the guy who brought her," for applying updated views of Freudian theory was and is very useful. Freudian theory is parsimonious, consistent, and coherent, is applicable through a professional relationship, and explains behavior. However, it does not explain society, and there is no single sociological theory that does or that provides the practitioner of any discipline with intellectual tools to work with society.

An illustration from one of the studies may clarify the research and the casework problem just described. The Pursuit of Promise recognized that a pathological environment had a deleterious effect upon children's ego functioning; the study described the environmental situation in which the children lived, albeit it did not include data about the workings of their school. Despite their obvious environmental deprivation, the children and their parents received service in the form of activities designed to improve their ego functioning and to stimulate the intellectual pursuits of their families.

The point is, then, that admirable as the underlying theoretical assumptions were, and as carefully as data were collected about the pathological slum neighborhood, these findings served only as background of the experimental service program which was primarily about group services. The minimum differences noted in the findings between control and experimental groups of children may be explained by the fact that no direct intervention was attempted into their environment. For example, if the school is thought to be giving shoddy education, improvement of ego functioning through group or one-to-one or family treatment service programs will never affect that shoddy school program; the school organization itself must be an object of change. Such research, like such a direct service program, is almost doomed to failure or to middle-range success, for its parameters of study are too narrow. The study designed a large, interlocking jigsaw puzzle but only put together the easy pieces; left out was the "large blue sky" that everyone wants to avoid because it is formless, nonconceptualized, and so hard to work with.

This problem will appear in different guise as we examine other studies, but for now let us ask "Can casework or group methods ever be sufficient as modes of service unless they include clients' impinging environment?" Asking this unleashes a world of questions, some of which are derived from viewing other studies under examination here. This question is difficult and concerns reconceptualizing some favored definitions, reassessing some goals, and readjusting our view of exactly what ought to be the unit of attention of the direct service practitioner. It is going to take more than our agreement to put the *social* back into social casework to do that successfully.

The more one thinks about these studies, the more evident it is that the researchers, in most instances, got their cues from casework practitioners. We are familiar with the criticisms of some studies which permitted ambiguous input and then applied rigorous, objective measurements at the outcome. For example, both Girls at Vocational High and the Chemung County Study described the casework process (input) in vague and global terms; yet the final evaluation used objective tests, in the first instance, and a structured scale of family functioning, in the second instance. Thus, as long as the casework process was erroneously viewed as being precise, the outcome would be viewed as precise in its assessment of incapacity. Even if the studies produced positive findings, and results showed client groups functioning better, nonspecified casework intervention could not explain the positive movement any more than it explained the negative movement.

Whether the researchers were aware of what they were doing is beside the point. In both studies researchers refer to the fact that they consulted with caseworkers prior to the studies in order to understand the thing they were evaluating, that is, the casework process. Unfortunately, they received the impression that casework was a coherent system of operations and that it was recognizable without reference to the case situation. In effect, they assumed that casework as an object was whatever the practitioners said it was, and not that it was essentially an individualizing process. Even before we consider the definitions of casework, another question for discussion all but thrusts itself upon us. Casework is no longer confined to internal professional consumption, since research instruments demand clarity of concepts and the growing use of paraprofessionals demands articulation of concepts so that elements of the process can be communicated; thus it is relevant to ask "To what degree is it possible to teach students to specify what casework is?"

It is no longer sufficient for teachers and supervisors to know how to conceptualize the process. Practitioners, beginning with the graduating student, must have access to their intellectualization of practice. It is not enough for the practitioner to do well: he must know and be able to articulate what he is doing and why he is doing it. In the Area Development Project, as in other studies, it was found that practitioners themselves did not represent a uniform input, that their individual styles of social work practice were powerful variables in determining outcome. This might have been expected since casework is, in some measure, an art; but when individual style seems to account for *good* or *bad* practice, social work education is mocked. If quality of practice depends on style, then why not seek nonprofessional workers to practice all casework, as long as their style is consonant with the case situation with which they are working? The quality of professional practice depends on access to knowledge, and this means developing practitioners who are intellectually as well as emotionally aware of what they are doing in their work. The fact that the two workers in the Chemung County Study did not reflect a high level of practice, although it was expected that they would be average caseworkers, should be an embarrassment to the entire field of social work. Another question must be asked: "How can we hold graduates accountable for knowledge and skills on which is based individual artfulness?"

Again, this is not a question easily answered since it involves familiar dilemmas. Among these are the seemingly polar ideas that the higher goal for practitioners is to do and feel, rather than to think and intellectualize. These are not antithetical goals but actually complement each other. Another dilemma is that practitioners can be accountable for only so much, usually their own caseloads, versus the idea that professional practitioners are in short supply and will have to raise their level of responsibility a few notches to attend to concerns larger than an individual caseload, while nonprofessional practitioners attend to more tasks and functions in the cases themselves. Yet, whatever direction the practitioner's role takes him, it is reasonable to expect him to be knowledgeable and accountable for the work he does.

The research done in these studies reflected in important ways the state of the art of social casework. Before moving on, we must say a few words about the state of the art of research methodology. We can pose two serious questions about research, at least in groups one and two reviewed earlier. First, there were more important things to study in this complex world of social work than the effectiveness of casework practice. Second, two basic assumptions underlying the research were wrong—that casework could be evaluated without reference to what else was going on in the clients' lives, and that the process was so clearly articulated it could be evaluated through objective tests of measurement.

In some instances there was a preoccupation with a rigorous design, assuming detachment from the problems and the findings, and assuming that such rigor was possible in the field of social work. As David Wallace, the research director of the Chemung County Study said, the translation of statistical measurements from the scientific laboratory to human problems can surely be questioned as to its appropriateness. It is one thing to assume a finite number of variables in a test tube, but it is quite another thing to assume a similar research stance about urban family life or casework practice, when we have not yet determined the number or kinds of variables existing. Granting the necessity to quantify data in order to study them through statistical manipulation, we must ask: why rely on statistical judgments in the first place?

Recognizing that we all work with soft data, one cannot help wondering how valid even complicated statistical findings are, when they are derived from qualities which defy numerical measurement. Statistical methods in evaluative research are unquestioned in those areas where qualities can be numerically measured, for example, demographic and descriptive characteristics. However, these are not the same qualities as attitudes, feelings and functioning as seen by clients, workers, or organizations. The place of statistics in evaluative research on practice is still questionable, and sometimes one gets the impression that the research methodology is an end in itself. One of the basic questions being raised from the cumulative findings about casework is that it appears to be an end in itself when it does not affect family functioning. The researcher may suffer the same criticism when he makes his arithmetic so complicated it turns in on itself.

Studies

Group I: Worker-Client Interactions. The studies in Group I have several qualities in common. First, they dealt with seriously deprived families, in many instances in situations so deteriorated that intervention through any professional discipline would have been too little and too late to be helpful. Second, the studies were carried out in settings which gave evidence of dysfunction insofar as the organization's programs did not do their required part even to their own goals. Third, researchers assumed that casework was a specific action undertaken to treat a known condition and aimed to arrive at a definable cure. Thus, pursuing this medical model, they evaluated the effectiveness of treatment, usually by studying an experimental group that got treatment, and a control group that did not. The findings were negative, in that desired results were not found to be demonstrably or statistically more evident at the outcome, in the experimental over the control groups. Fourth, the parameters of the cases studied were limited to behavioral, attitudinal, affectional, and functional characteristics of the families, without reference to the environmental strains and the paucity of real socioeconomic, health, and educational resources available to the families, and without precise connections to the arena or systems in which behavior, attitude, affection, and functioning would take place. Fifth, the goals of casework service in each of the studies were not clear and provided mixed messages to social workers and to clients.

Girls at Vocational High (Meyer and others, 1965) examined girls known to have school problems; probably, most of the girls were in a nonacademic high school because somewhere in the school system it was thought they would be more adaptable to that setting. Knowing what we do about large city school systems, and particularly those in New York City where this study took place, we can assume that some of the girls were there because they were poor and preoccupied with needs more basic than education or because some of them spoke Spanish and there was an industry in the city that could provide jobs for them, or because some of them had exhibited unrestrained (nonacademic?) behavior and were not thought to be acculturated enough for another kind of school. Despite the research design, this was not an ordinary school situation in which so-called typical girls were represented. Yet, the school setting was accepted by researchers as well as caseworkers as a given, giving one the impression that the girls were deviant. Thus, no questions were raised about the school's criteria for appropriate behavior, and it was assumed that each successive grade completed meant that much more education. It is a large and unwarranted assumption that a vocational school in New York City provides an atmosphere enabling teenagers of varying life styles to learn and be comfortable learning. Much that happened and that was studied was based on this assumption, and the report noted that the only role caseworkers played in the school which their adolescent clients attended was *to gain cooperation* so that the study would run smoothly.

This could hardly be called intervention in the client's field of significant systems. As we do not know the school's role in the deviance of the children, we cannot tell from this study whether there was an attempt to make the girls' lives a little more bearable at school, whether the teachers were understanding, whether the surroundings were conducive to learning and to recreation, whether the atmosphere was welcoming or inhibiting, if not threatening. But we do know that an experimental group was provided with nonspecific, intensive casework treatment and later with group treatment outside the school auspices, just as if the girls had come into the agency's program off the street. Can casework do as much for a truant girl as can a school which provides inducements so that she will want to attend school? Is the school, then, part of the girl's case, to which the caseworker should address his practice?

The researchers raised questions about the caseworkers' emphasis on the clients' change of feeling rather than on explicit school functioning. Perhaps they had in mind some thoughts about behavioral modification, but it is not at all antithetical to the diagnostic casework practiced in this agency that a caseworker could emphasize a client's feeling about explicit school behavior and functioning. There is no dilemma here: feelings are as legitimate as behaviors, but they must be linked in both the caseworkers' and the clients' minds. Can the caseworker's attention to how the client feels be carried on in a vacuum and be unconnected with how the client feels about what?

The relevant *what* in this study was often the school, and often the family or the boyfriend. The research, of course, was concerned with improved school behavior, but this may not have always been the prominent concern of either the worker or the client. What are appropriate goals for direct service practice in social work? Who determines them—the agency, the worker, the client? Is client need necessarily correctly assessed by the community? Only as we grapple with the question of goals will we achieve clarity in our specification of casework practice.

An Experimental Study to Measure the Effectiveness of Casework Service (Behling, 1961) asked: "Can chronic relief dependence best be prevented and reduced through intensive services equated with small caseloads or through routine services equated with large caseloads?" At the beginning of his study, the researcher comments that the solution to the problem of reducing relief chronicity requires that employment be available and that individuals have the physical and psychological well-being to take advantage of employment. Unfortunately, the researcher does not state as clearly the disproportionately tiny share of relief cases that are at all employable; nor does the study say anything about the labor market and the availability of jobs, or how available jobs suit the capacities of clients who are on relief because they are unemployed. Whatever the researcher's findings, the reduction of relief chronicity is surely one of those global aims that has countless variables within it.

What is interesting, and all too familiar, is the assumption that nonspecified casework service will affect relief chronicity, without reference to hundreds of potential variables that might be called into play in a group of public assistance cases. Have we not yet accepted that despite service amendments to the public welfare law, casework service without increased money from some source cannot help reduce the public assistance caseload in this country?

This study of chronic relief recipients had as its avowed purpose for casework practice the lowering of public welfare costs. We should not be startled at this as a defined goal, since it has been with us a long time, but neither should we gloss over it indiscriminatingly. The connection between social services and social control —for example, in this case in which social workers aimed to get people off relief, albeit through casework service—is untenable when compared with other professional goals of helping, supporting, enabling, rehabilitating, and so forth. Social control is one of those moralizing goals that we must deliberate. If we adhere to it, it must be enunciated for what it is. We may have kept it hidden too long, because students have discovered it and are beginning to embarrass us with their questions. To the degree that casework service supports a family in the throes of some psychosocial agony, particularly if impoverished, one could argue the case for keeping them as clients and not helping them get off relief. This was reflected in the study where casework services raised the costs of relief and increased the degree of dependence upon the agency. What may have been deemed a failure by the public welfare agency supporting the research might be viewed as a success by the caseworker. Where agency policies and practices are dysfunctional and obstruct the health and well-being of clients, does that agency system, then, become part of the caseworker's case? In this study, it is hard to see how there could be casework service without primary attention to the agency's policies, which would then be part of *the case* needing the caseworker's intervention.

A Comprehensive Program for Multiproblem Families (Marin, 1969) reported using a before-and-after study of child welfare cases, using as the experimental variable family-centered social work treatment. Again, the treatment components were non-specified but a thematic apperception test was used to measure needs for achievement, affiliation, and power—considered the motives most likely to affect economic dependency. One wonders about other measures of economic behavior such as employment opportunities, options for a comfortable way of life, health, education level, and so forth. When the environmental strains that seem self-evident are not studied at the time of input or outcome, it is hard to know whether problems in family functioning are causal or reactive, "due to lack of staff, other agency resources, and inadequate social policy" (and probably to the lack of precision in the definition of family-centered treatment). The study raised questions about the continuing usefulness of child welfare and other rehabilitative services, since no changes were found in concrete behaviors and environmental deprivation. Not knowing exactly the nature of the intervention, it is impossible to comment upon the findings, except to note that the reported lacks in resources, staff, and programs could hardly have been side issues in the search for explanations.

The Chemung County Study (Brown, 1968) illustrates all of the points cited describing this group of studies. Its purpose was to evaluate change in client functioning, using the St. Paul Scale of Family Functioning, of an experimental group of families known to the public assistance agency. Professional casework was the major variable under study here, and the findings indicated that there was no greater success in cases handled by professionals than in cases handled by the regular, nonprofessional staff in the control group. According to the researchers, "After two years of service to multi-problem families by trained caseworkers, operating with reduced caseloads and with special cooperation of the community's resources, but within the framework of public assistance policies and procedures, the demonstration group showed a small but statistically nonsignificant margin of improvement over the control group(s), which received only routine service from regular public assistance workers."

In this and comparable studies probably reflective of casework ideology, the implication is that the families in question are culpable, on-the-fringe, misfits, immature, and, at the least, dependent. It cannot be denied that such families are the most troublesome to the community and perhaps the most pathological in our society. Yet, as long as value judgments are implicit in the selection of the families to be studied, the community permitting conditions that foster pathology and stratification of classes should also be included as part of *the case* being studied. Whatever is said about families who cannot make it, as much or more can be said about societal institutions which have not provided the opportunities and wherewithal for all their citizens. Thus, a study of Chemung County families on public assistance is incomplete without reference to employment opportunities, school conditions, housing, recreation, medical care, police and sanitation services, and conditions of discrimination. Obviously, the more complex and demanding society becomes, and the fewer built-in supports of family life, the greater will be the necessity for families to rely on institutionalized supports. Is it even relevant to seek to keep families from using those supports or to help them achieve independence?

As the Chemung County public welfare agency is one of the institutionalized supports in the community, then its policies and practices have a great deal to do with the well-being and behavior of the client group it serves. To the degree that continuing eligibility is the primary determinant of "success" in a case, notwithstanding higher casework goals, then we might as well wipe out the goals of rehabilitation and self-fulfillment. As long as dependence on social services is viewed pejoratively, the worker and the client must respond to mixed messages, and the service will be doomed. The more one ponders the question of less-eligibility, the more one is drawn to the conclusion that the casework problem might indeed be the agency, which is itself dysfunctional.

In the type of cases studied in the Chemung County Study, what is progress anyway? To seek symbolic improvement in client situations as a result of casework intervention limited by narrow definitions of *the case* as a psychosocial object, the research design, the public welfare agency, the environmental deprivations of clients, and the professional qualities or social work style that was questioned, is to attempt vainly to evaluate progress in its pure form. When medicine fails to cure diseases like cancer, a research instrument is hardly geared to evaluating medical skill; more likely it pays attention to the unknowns in the disease itself. Since the problems under consideration were not subject to clinical definitions (in fact, we are not even dealing here with a disease which could be clinically defined), is it possible that we still do not comprehend the role of social casework in the overwhelmingly complex psychosocial systems in which it is involved?

The Community Service Society-Department of Social Services Collaborative Demonstration Project (Mullen and others, 1970) was similar to the Chemung County Study but used voluntary agency workers instead of public agency workers. It was concerned with the increasing number of families becoming dependent upon public assistance for economic aid, and the effects of prolonged dependence. The underlying assumption was that families needed help to cope with effects of dependency, leading to deterioration in their functioning and a chronic state of dependence. Although it was known that budgets were inadequate to prevent disorganization, it was assumed that CSS workers practicing casework would strengthen family functioning, help the families take advantage of employment and job training opportunities, and so forth. The goal of the project was to evaluate the effects of the collaborative service project, assuming that the experimental collaborative group (100 families) would have more desirable outcomes than the control group without a CSS worker. Measurements of change were derived from the family's self-reports and the impressions of a research interviewer. The findings indicated no statistical significance between the groups in areas such as length of time on public assistance, increased employment, improvement of housing or of marketing practices. There was a modest statistical difference noted in the families' view of help with individual and family difficulties. In regard to internal areas of family functioning—cohesion, relationships, and the like—there was no statistical evidence that the experimental group felt they were helped more than were the control group.

This study introduces a new consideration, since it presents only a limited description of the input of the DSS and, in fact, comments upon the actual lack of collaboration between the CSS and the DSS. The theme of the study was later modified to describe the professional casework given to public assistance clients, rather than the collaboration as previously envisioned. Thus, without reference to organizational theory, professional casework was viewed as a *thing* which could be practiced in isolation from both the positive and negative values expressed in the DSS program. To the extent that there was no statistical finding of significance between the effects of CSS and DSS service to these clients, one might conclude either that the CSS workers were not as effective as had been hypothesized or that the DSS workers were more effective than had been anticipated. Once again, we are confronted with a study that isolates casework practice from surrounding systems, this time, more from the agency system than from the contributing environmental institutions.

Group II: Client Field or Surrounding Systems. The studies in Group II lend themselves to different kinds of observations. They have less in common than did the first grouping, except that they did not expect the medical model of casework treatment to resolve problems which reflected broader systems influences.

Earlier in this chapter the *Pursuit of Promise* (McCabe and others, 1967) was cited as an example of research being prototypical of casework practice. In this study there was an effort to develop a *life model* of service, mainly expressed through activity groups for parents and children, the aim being to contribute to the development of autonomous ego functioning. The purpose of the study was to enhance educational achievement, which moved the program beyond the disease focus and the therapeutic ideal. Despite the fact that the school itself was not made an object of practice, there was an effort to comprehend the influences of the urban slum on the potential of promising young children. In a sense, this study moved away from the more rigid models of practice that we examined in Group I.

Review of *The Neighborhood Improvement Project* (Geismar and Krisberg, 1967) and *The Family Life Improvement Project* (Geismar and others, 1970) lends itself to a discussion of social work practice goals. In these two studies, as in the Pursuit of Promise, flexible modes of intervention and comprehensive views of the clients' real world were included in the designs. Thus, in these field studies, we do not have to struggle with the same concerns raised earlier. However, these studies do raise questions about practice goals and illustrate better than many studies some of the dilemmas to which we have already alluded.

The Neighborhood Improvement Project preceded the Family Life Improvement Project, but both were directed by the same researcher. The first study explored practice experimentally undertaken in a neighborhood known to have certain problem characteristics. On the other hand, the second study addressed a general population of young urban families considered, at first, to be representative of normal, theoretically problem-free families. The irony, in the case of the Family Life Improvement Project, was that Newark, the area in which the families lived, was not in itself problem-free and, as a city, had most of the socioeconomic deprivations possessed by the housing project in the Neighborhood Improvement Project. Thus, both study populations suffered from similar urban life pressures, although the researchers had moved on to address a universal rather than a residual population.

The Neighborhood Improvement Project was a sophisticated program of planned intervention to help a socially disadvantaged population. The client group was viewed as multiproblem families and the practice goal was to improve their family functioning. The researchers noted that the families suffered from economic deprivation, unemployment, lack of educational and occupational opportunities, inadequacy of health facilities and the absence of social and recreational outlets. The project attempted to reduce juvenile delinquency, family disorganization, and deprivation, and tried to solve these problems through neighborhood workers practicing casework. Similar to those in the studies in Group I, the client-worker transactions were presumed to be salient despite the recognized socioeconomic restraints in the lives of the people under study. The researchers describe the "subculture" of the multiproblem families not as deviant but as a functional way of life not optimally useful to promote the families' welfare and say that "understanding the reasons for existing ways of thinking and behaving does not mean viewing them as optimum methods." Thus, despite researchers' awareness of the deprivation extant, they were convinced that effecting behavioral change would make lower-class life bearable and contribute toward system change. Intervention was aimed at promoting the process of acculturation by educational techniques and opportunities for social participation.

Social worker activity focused on tangible problems, especially health, and on influencing families to use available community resources, in which the social worker served as a bridge between the family and community. Also, social workers concentrated on interpersonal problems and systematically promoted client independence, attempting to achieve clients' greater role responsibility through attenuation of social worker activity toward termination of service. All of this resulted in middle range help, better coping, and fewer crises—appropriate social work practice goals. There was a neighborhood open-door casework service, in which the project tried to remove the stigma from those receiving services for normal urban pressures. Failure cases raised questions as to caseworkers' skills, the severity of problems, lack of community resources, and the possibility of too-high expectations from treatment.

All in all, the practice model studied here seems to have some very positive qualities. The closer the practitioner works with the client in his own life style, meaning his neighborhood, the more likely his understanding of client needs, fears, capacities, and opportunities. This is all to the good; however, the difficulty with this project is its basic premise that the goal of service was to change behavior of what is still considered the multiproblem family. Is it possible that to some people the quality of the multiproblem family differentiating it from other families is that its functioning is made public through incursions by social agencies and other institutions, while most families can afford to keep their doors closed? One must ask, "Who decides the legitimacy of the social worker's expectations of socialization?" To the degree that social workers stand against social dysfunctioning rather than being available to help people in their self-actualization, clients will continue to suspect social workers —and with good reason. This has aspects of moralizing, which we inherited from the Poor Law days, and which by now should have a low place in our repertoire. How different is the eighteenth-century view of the poor as immoral from the present view that they are multiproblemed?

The Family Life Improvement Project set out to study family disorganization in process through longitudinal research on the social functioning of a random sample of young urban families. It was refreshing to examine a study that concerned itself with collecting demographic data that would throw light on significant socioeconomic issues. But, the second major purpose of the project was to provide multifaceted early intervention to modify developmental patterns to help families achieve adequate social functioning. The effects of this purpose in research efforts of this kind and the hypotheses underlying the design tell us more than do the findings. In this project there were five hypotheses that needed to be related to family life style and environmental influences, but were not. First, "as families grow older, problem functioning increases." One could hardly disagree in light of the fact that more children and the increasing influence of extra-family systems do make life more complicated. Second, "family disorganization originates in intrafamilial relationships." This assumes without fear of contradiction that family disorganization cannot be affected by external pressures. This is an issue today, when most of the influences on urban families are outside the family, since outside institutions have begun performing traditional family functions. Third, "severe family disorganization can be predicted by indices that include value systems and economic behavior." This still follows the basic assumption that the urban family controls its own destiny. Fourth, "the degree of malfunctioning is directly related to the marital pair's family of orientation." Even granting the assumption, one is forced by this hypothesis to ask how—through inheritance, unconscious identification, conscious imitation, or continuing social impact? Fifth, "early intervention designed to modify problem role patterns by situational intervention will reduce or prevent family disorganization." Here we confront the issue: is the goal of social work practice through any form of intervention to modify role functioning in order to prevent family disorganization or is the goal to help the family cope with, and find pleasure in, the world in which they live?

Although I agree with the view of this project that current services are remedial rather than preventive, serving the motivated over the nonmotivated client, and are shaped more by service pattern than by client need, it is difficult to grasp to what ultimate use even positively viewed means might be put. The study claims more functions for which the family is held responsible than families presently have for socialization in the city, and it is possible that researchers continue to see family life as failing rather than seeing society and family life as changing.

Looking at the research design itself, one can identify the dilemmas of the field at large. The project cites its situational intervention, but it only treats and studies interpersonal malfunctioning. One finding of this study shows that the total functioning scores skewed in the direction of greater adequacy including affectional ties than researchers expected. Also noted are poor health practices among the families and the impression that the presence of children reduces marital functioning and that child care worsens as families grew. It is important to know whether this is a phenomenon of family dysfunction or of social change as reflected by the urban poor; in cities children are an economic burden and, because of child labor laws, do not serve the economic function they once did in the city or on the farm. It is also relevant to know the day care and baby-sitting situation in the community. It seems the hypotheses are not broad enough to address fully the problem being studied and the findings bear this out.

The conclusion of this study might be a hypothesis for future study and a basis for developing a more functional type of practice.

It implies that the modern urban family greatly depends on the community in which it lives to satisfy its needs and that existing services, especially in areas of primary human need, were inadequate. In an area where economic and health problems are severe, caseworkers must broaden their case boundaries and attempt to make clinics, the Department of Welfare, and the employment office more accessible to families. To the degree that we concern ourselves wtih morality—that is, the good and bad of family functioning—we will overlook the true meaning of the cases, particularly when the dysfunction involved is related, in large measure, to unresponsive social institutions in the client's environment. It seems important to restate the question: Should the goal of social work practice be to change client behavior according to our image, or to help the client, by following his life style, to cope with the real and often nonserving world around him by changing institutional behavior? If we chooose the helping rather than the socializing goal, then we will be freer to attend to the improvement of services—to socialize them, if you will.

The Familycenter Project (Kühl, 1969) is from Copenhagen, and in a sense could serve as our proof of the pudding. Similar to American experiences, examples in Copenhagen showed "that successful improvement of dwelling, institutional, or employment conditions can essentially change the total situation of a family, but there also are cases demonstrating that some multiproblem families will need *continued* support in order to prevent a complete collapse and dissolution of the family." The researchers clearly described casework as a process in saying that "the support to the families in question has to be given in a very flexible and individual way, paying due regard to the total situation of the family." Compared to some of the American studies, this study produced more positive results. A comment made in the study might be the understatement of all time, noting as it does that "the argument must be considered that favorable social conditions in the community are necessary for all social rehabilitation work."

So we come to the conclusion of our review of two groups of studies, where the client-worker interactions were demonstrated and in large measure found wanting as a major solution to deviance in school behavior, dependence on public assistance, the condition of being a multiproblem family in a socioeconomically deprived area, and the state of unfulfilled promise. Considering the statement made by the Copenhagen study, we must ask if casework has promised more than it can offer. Is there still a need and a purpose for individualizing services? How might they be more successful? How might practitioners develop greater competence? Are changes to be sought in new modes of individualizing services, new patterns of manpower utilization, and revised conceptions of case boundaries including the client's field?

Group III: New Practice Modes. The studies in Group III branched out, attempting different modes of service, apparently because the researchers had asked themselves some of these same questions about the aims of social work practice. While the four studies do not include all the questions raised in this chapter and thus cannot provide insights for all the answers, they can give us some clues.

The Area Development Project (United Community Services of the Greater Vancouver Area, 1968–1969) addressed multiproblem families and studied family role breakdown, using the St. Paul Scale of Family Functioning, in the face of severe environmental deprivation. It is not necessary to deal with these issues again except to ask why this is such a popular phenomenon to study. Are such clients simply the most captive of audiences? The model of practice is somewhat new and interesting, for the project directors were concerned with overlapping, fragmented, nonfamily-focused agencies that were proven to be ineffective in helping families with complex problems. The researchers established two new modes of service provision. First, integrated family services, that is, five caseworkers from several agencies under one administrator, served 100 families. In some instances, social services were delegated to community agencies, and in other instances, they were coordinated through the efforts of the social workers in the experimental unit. The aim was continuity of service, which researchers hoped would be accomplished by the varied agency functions carried out by the project workers. Second, neighborhood services, where two social workers, social work students, part-time personnel and volunteers carved out a small area for the focus of their services. The approach involved participation of local citizens, stimulation of resources, development of demonstration services and operations of a neighborhood center.

In the integrated family services component of the Area Development Project, it was concluded that even though better service was offered, there were still limitations regarding what social workers could do with the service institutions and programs in the community. It was also concluded that each agency should take care of all the casework needs of the particular segments of the population they serve. Actually, the services in this project were not integrated as much as they were coordinated; selective services of selected agencies were made available to families through one social worker, but that social worker was quite evident in the client's immediate surroundings. Findings were stated quantitatively, that is, in number of contacts and hours of service. Unfortunately, there was no attempt to control for professional education, so we do not know which of the five workers were M.S.W. graduates; yet compared to the control group of 100 cases treated in the usual manner the demonstration project gave evidence of more effective service. But we do not know why, particularly since the effectiveness resulted from the social workers themselves.

Despite the limited success of this project, which could be a result of how casework was defined and the goal model approach researchers insisted upon using, there is much of interest in this demonstration which sought to change the multiagency impact upon already burdened clients. The social workers were neighborhood-based which meant they were close enough to the life style of clients to be in touch with their needs and desires. Finally, to the extent that the service repertoire was expanded in this project and social workers were not bound to family, child welfare, and other functional constraints, it is likely that the gaps in services were filled by the more flexible network of service delivery. In other words, where there were less discrete service patterns, people might have been less apt to fall between them.

The neighborhood service component of the Area Development Project provided open-ended, exploratory, nonintervenfive approaches to a defined neighborhood. The design suggested this as an alternative to treatment services, and the program included community development, environmental supports and helpful community relationships; the underlying assumption was that in a poverty subculture self-development, better resources, and more effective programs of service were needed. The findings indicated negative change in certain areas: citizen leaders moved, there was strain on the limited amount of leaders, and competition and conflict developed among groups until support was finally withdrawn from the project. Positive change was noted in increased neighborhood loyalties to area concerns and movement from absorption with family or group to cooperation with the larger group. The program was not oriented to individuals, but to conditions, and social worker roles were confined to organizing, advising, moderating, advocating, coordinating, and giving of staff services.

While this component of the Area Development Project did not assess individualized services, there are some principles to be drawn from its location in a local area as the base for service, its concern with community resources more effective in meeting needs than are traditional social agencies, its awareness that preventive intervention and citizen participation are necessary, and its use of flexible modes of service and a host of supportive, open-ended service programs. This project was really concerned about the role of the community worker at the local neighborhood level; and to the degree that neighborhoods are where our clients live and that community workers actually work with people and not solely with *conditions,* there might be some clues for individualizing workers as well.

Serving the Aging (Blenkner and others, 1964) was an experiment comparing the results of three different modes of service used by aged clients. Results were compared with data on nonapplicants to the agency, who had the normally expected incidence of problems and levels of adjustment. The project was addressed to the average older person in his own dwelling as an independent, self-directing member of the community. One is struck by the effort to follow the life-model, not the goal-model or the medical-model. As for measurement criteria, this study states that length of service does not measure effectiveness but utilization of service and its cost to the agency. Length of service has always measured this, and is not, as in the Experimental Study to Measure the Effectiveness of Casework Service, an indicator of dependence. The study makes another flat statement that preferred treatment should be that which accomplishes the desired results with the least time and effort. This principle of parsimony will be discussed further when we look at the Casework Methods Project. The most common problems for which applicants sought help were finances, housing, and living arrangements; and the least common were interpersonal relations. Although none of the three programs reached normative levels of problem incidence among their participants, the experimental programs did better than the control group, the single discipline, short-term service doing best. Again, we are faced with the dilemma. The problems facing the clients are the ones the agency cannot solve, and the interpersonal problems in which the agency is expert, may be either least among the client's concerns, or nonaccessible when viewed outside the normal environmental strains of his life. Do we then reserve casework skills for those people with interpersonal problems but with less severe environmental strains? But, we have traveled that route already; and in order not to backtrack when environmental strains are everywhere around us, we must confront squarely the issue of expanding boundaries so the case will include the client's milieu interwoven with his interpersonal relationships.

We might see *The Casework Methods Project* (Reid and Shyne, 1969) as a natural development of the study on the aging or as a response to the criticisms of traditional social casework practice. Whatever the motivation for the study, it has made a real contribution to the case for clarity of goals and procedures, and it has produced a number of valuable insights.

The underlying assumption in this study was that, "given limited resources, brief service is the only practical means of providing necessary help to growing numbers of people." By the end of this study, one is almost forced to conclude that brief service ought to be the treatment of choice as well. The researchers make it clear that the terms *brief* and *extended* are nondefinitive and that they are related only to each other and to other examples of long-term treatment. One wonders if the decision to limit interviews forces a new definition of casework, but neither open-ended nor time-limited services are themselves theories. It is likely that the use of new, limited goals in Planned Short Term Service (PSTS) will help us define relevance, sharpen skills, and reevaluate the purposes of casework. It is important to note that PSTS is not just shorter than open-ended, long-term treatment but actually different in its goals and procedures.

In the design the only hypothesis was that variation in treatment approaches would be associated with some variation in results; there was no intent to use absolute criteria. To be eligible for the study, the family had to meet the criteria of motivation, capacity, and opportunity, and had to be seeking help for a problem in family relations. The researchers' idea of a good case was a *workable* case. Thus, examining this study will not involve questions we raised about the other studies, most of which would have used *unworkable* cases according to these criteria. Here, we are simply addressing a different problem. The sample provided an ideal testing ground for certain hypotheses about casework practice. One such hypothesis is: "If extended treatment aimed at modifying patterns of behavior through insight-oriented techniques constitutes an especially effective mode of casework, as has been widely thought, then its effectiveness should be demonstrable in treatment of a group of clients . . . who appear particularly well suited for it. If such a treatment approach does not prove to be clearly more effective with this group, then its usefulness with less suitable groups can be seriously challenged. Similarly, if PSTS works well with families who are prime candidates for 'standard'—that is, open-ended— treatment, then our conception of what should constitute standard treatment may need some more thinking."

As for PSTS, it can be characterized as goal-directed and less likely to provoke client resistance. We must ask if cure is in the caseworker's mind alone, and if people really want to gain insight. PSTS highlights the contract between social worker and client, and its aim is shared, explicit treatment objectives. Thinking seems to be more in evidence in PSTS, as the recapitulation of experiences addresses itself to cognitive review of gains and goals, and access to autonomous ego functioning after the case is closed. It was noted that assignment of cases to PSTS seemed to limit the generality of the caseworker's goals, even though it did not appear to produce any strong tendency for goals to be cast in specific terms. Pressed by time and limited goals, the whole process was quickened, brought into focus and made direct and active. There was more reliance on logical discussion and less on open-ended exploration, although there was more insight-oriented intervention in PSTS cases than had been expected.

Once again we find social worker style an important variable. Here, as in other instances, caseworkers seemed to confuse knowing all with doing all; and in continued service cases, social workers did not use summaries to help them conceptualize what they were doing. Apparently this was a symptom of open, noncognitive treatment. In general, social workers found it harder to work with PSTS than with CS (continued service) cases. And the fact that PSTS was found to be more effective is not paradoxical; a mode of treatment can work best for clients and still be difficult to apply. It is hard to think, focus, act, and deal with immediacy.

The findings indicated further that for the intact, middleclass families in the study, PSTS families made more progress than CS families, and their gains proved to be as durable. Also, the PSTS structure affected the caseworker's activity in reference to timing, treatment planning, goals, mobilizing effect, and style. The broader the goals, the more diffuse and the less effective the treatment. Here, the findings related to CS workers' concentration on underlying problems not susceptible to modification through casework treatment. PSTS was found to have a salutary effect on clients in that it elevated their motivation and hope, enlarged their capacity for extra effort and provided realistic goals for change. As the study notes, "PSTS client's expectancy that positive changes might occur within a brief period of time may have generated a set of conditions that helped bring such changes about."

So, treatment as an *end* was diminished through PSTS, and CS was carried well beyond the point of diminishing returns. One cannot help but wonder what would have happened in the studies of Group I had PSTS been used instead of CS. Despite the narrowness of the designs of these studies, clients might have been helped a modicum. It has been demonstrated that PSTS is more effective than CS, costs less, and certainly has more realistic goals and methods which could be applied in more places to greater numbers of people. One ironic observation is irresistible: *brief,* after all, is only a construct invented as an opposite to *extended*. We invented the extended mode, in the first place; it was never a basic truth.

Is there a way in social work education to keep the students' minds open so that they will not have to worship old icons twenty-five years from now? Perhaps that is the key to professional education—to teach students to ask questions and not to accept ideologies. The days of inculcation should be over, so now we must educate students to pose their own questions, to themselves, as to how things are structured, and even to us.

The Midway Project (Schwartz and Sample, 1970) is the last of Group III studies we will examine. In a sense, it is the payoff study, for it is about manpower utilization. Assuming that we could perfect the casework process, it would be useless if we could not deliver it wherever it was needed; unless we can deliver our "perfect" techniques outside the family agency or the treatment clinic, they will be relegated to the few, practiced by the few, and noticed by the few. It is a professional death wish that when a choice must be made between restriction of service through lowering caseloads and utilization of technical or nonprofessional manpower, we so often choose service restriction. The Midway Project suggests that we are no more faced with a Hobson's choice as far as manpower is concerned than we are as far as brief versus extended service is concerned. In fact, the pressure of reality might force the practice into a mold more relevant for this society, with its particular kinds of problems and particular kinds of people seeking help and individualizing services.

The purpose of the Midway Project was to develop and test ways of improving the organization and utilization of public assistance staff. Most of the social workers in this country work in that setting, and it carries the major burden of unfilled and unrewarding jobs. This project aimed to fashion a more rewarding technique for the entire staff in contact with clients, more effective in providing needed services and more acceptable to an informed community. The study focused on the social worker's job. Traditionally, supervisors have mixed roles as managers, consultants, trainers, and caseworkers, but their particular roles in public assistance are often as managerial and control agents. As the researchers point out, all social workers and supervisors at Midway worked at what they were not prepared for; even, or especially, professionals got to be supervisors, and they were neither qualified nor happy in this role.

The general form of the research problem was to test the proposition that the administration of public assistance may increase its efficiency by increasing the specialization of work in providing client service. Also, since a division of labor tends to increase the necessity for coordination, it was proposed that a team form of organization provided both specialization and coordination, for planning and control. This was a field experiment and not demonstration research. These researchers claim, as opposed to some in the first group of studies, that an experiment exists only when the problem is well structured and the variables clearly defined, when the input is established, when measurement criteria are perfected, when field and study subjects are under control, and when risks are known. That view is only correct for the physical and technological sciences; in the Midway Project a long-range program of research providing spin offs was desired, and researchers were comfortable with the vagaries of practice they had to study.

Underlying all the assumptions in the Midway Project was the idea that psychosocial impoverishment cannot be substantially eliminated by any one form of direct individual or family social treatment. Scaling down expectations—and keeping them close to reality—the study states that a reasonable expectation might be that a client's methods of coping with a problem, as shown by his actions, have undergone important changes or have been activated for the first time. It was expected, and found, that basic problems remain the same but are less intense when the caseworker has helped the family in its ability to deal with a problem. Accordnig to the study, positive change or improvement takes into account *efforts* to achieve change even if such efforts have not resulted in change. In fact, the study takes limited goals even further in suggesting that casework might sustain the client at a present level of functioning. The notion of action rather than verbalization, as pointed out in the study, is particularly relevant to apathetic clients and to those who lack verbal skills; to record effort and not objective change is to stay closer to the client's life style.

The diehard who is not ready to accept the demonstrability of greater effectiveness in the team situation because no absolute improvement in functioning was demonstrated must at least accept that the model has shown there is a world of possibility out there, if we only had the imagination—and professional security—to plunge in and devise a variety of manpower models. The key is increasing the explicitness of individualizing practices, in clarifying the goals, in articulating the concepts, and in adapting casework to the real world of today. For if we can get a model of practice to work, we will need more and more manpower, most of whom will not be professionally trained. That is the major challenge to be faced—how to use all levels of manpower differentially and to the limits of their capacity, no matter what their level of training.

Implications for Practice

First, there is the unresolved question of goals of practice which the field of social work must address. It is one thing to say that practice goals are as individualistic as the case requires them to be, but it is quite another thing to say that casework practitioners can do everything. Perhaps, out of our professional developmental strains, we have developed grandiose pretensions. We went through long decades assuming that a reasonable practice goal was personality change, and, even today, a significant number of caseworkers continue to reach toward that goal of practice. In our recent past and undoubtedly still present as a goal is the notion of social change, where it is presumed that practitioners as practitioners are able to change institutions, mores, laws, and public attitudes through politicalization of social work means. Neither of these are reasonable goals of direct practice because they are not necessarily what people need from social workers, nor are they teachable as skills in schools of social work. Another kind of goal seems to plague us, although it is now over a hundred years old, and that is what can be called social control, sometimes expressed as socialization. This is a moralizing theme in practice which has appeared in several of the reviewed studies. Can we not consider more reasonable goals of maintenance, of helping to enhance clients' lives, of tuning in on their life style rather than insisting that they tune in on ours? Perhaps the very use of lofty expectations for change in so many of these studies has contributed to their limited results. To wit, we should remember that when we go to a doctor he does not tell us never to return; he does not assume we are dependent when we use his services several times a year—that is what he is there for. Is that not why agencies exist? Why are we so anxious to free people from our services, to *cure* them, and to let them go?

The second broad implication has to do with the definition of casework practice itself. Casework is an individualizing process; it is not a specifically defined treatment procedure. Casework means making the case or sorting it out from the mass, or differentiating it from others which are never alike. When defined in this way, the case may be viewed as narrowly or as broadly as is required by the components of the case. Looking at casework this way does not confine the practitioner to separate use of individual and group methods. If the case requires group methods, family treatment methods, office interviews, consultation with the school principal, joining with the Welfare Rights Group to deal with the public welfare administration, and so on, all this is individualizing practice, in this view, which is a systems view, for it takes into account the interlocking salient systems that radiate from the person. The anchor concept is still person-in-situation; only the systems framework has given us the conceptual tools to really make use of both sides of the hyphens instead of bowing to the situation and addressing the person.

The third general implication is about knowledge; throughout the studies the researchers expressed concern about the generality of casework knowledge. It is true that the specificity they sought was missing, and knowing it was, they insisted upon using specific, objective criteria for evaluation. The unit of attention in social work is general. What could be less specific than person-in-situation? Persons can be classified along so many variables, and situations are ever changing. Social workers may rarely see the same arrangements of elements in cases, which is one reason why the idea of casework as an individualizing process is so helpful. Clearly, the more broadly we define the boundaries of the case, or the unit of attention, the more general will our knowledge, and our repertoire of skills, have to be.

We already know the alternative—traditional, clinical type practice, where specific symptoms reflected specific states of psychopathology, where there was a quid for every quo. Practitioners had only to know about the client in his narrowest dimensions; skills were all bound up in the interview and in the relationship; and goals were identifiable and plausible—if not feasible. Were those the good old days when we *knew* that anxiety hysterics suffered from sexual repression, when obsessive compulsive mothers had children with school phobias, when a psychosis was really a psychosis and not an adaptive state? Clinical definitions of problems determined that treatment would be defined clinically. Specific, yes—but did it work? Did cure through casework methods really occur? What happened to skills that addressed sexual repression in this age of sexual expression? What happened to symptomatology as a sign of motivation, when ego psychology came along and viewed it as a sign of adaptation? What happened to the good old days of simple virtues and explicit morality? Even if one were to grant that those days were virtuous and moral, they are gone in any event.

The world has opened up, loosened up. Can anyone classify behavior today? Are beards, beads, and helmets clinically definable, or do they reflect a new life style? Is the pot smoker a delinquent? Is the student activist neurotic? Is the Welfare Rights Group out of touch with reality? When we cannot even define with any specificity who the enemy is in Vietnam and what that endless war is about, can we truthfully say that we are living in an age of specificity? No, the linear, cause and effect days may be over in our lifetime, and we may have to learn to live with generalities as best we can. Do doctors do better when they seek the cause of the common cold or of cancer or of heart disease? Does anyone know the causes (and cures) for delinquency, illegitimacy, addiction, child abuse? We have only one specific in front of us, and that is poverty, the cure for which is money, and as a nation we seem not to seek specificity there.

We may not know much about prediction and specific tendencies, but we know an awful lot about an awful lot. We know how to help people maintain themselves in this chaotic world, to cope, to find some pleasures and to improve their lot somewhat. Our educational task will be to organize our knowledge and to conceptualize our practice, to concretize what we do, and to articulate it and transmit it to others. But we will be pursuing an old-fashioned goal if we, in our uncertainty, turn inward and seek certainties than do not exist, except perhaps in our faded family albums.

Implications for Curriculum Development

In stating that a need exists for educating professional graduate students for responsible practice we mean that the time has come when we must hold them accountable for independent practice and thinking about their actions. We can no longer afford the luxury of educating students for beginning practice, when BA graduates are at that level. The few master's graduates we have must assume great responsibility for caseloads, for case-finding, for figuring out the dimensions of cases, for training of nonprofessional teams, and so forth. In order to achieve this level of accountability, students must articulate what they are thinking and doing, and there must be less reliance upon social worker styles. So far, the master's program does not have the goal of examining and questioning what workers are doing while they are doing it.

This is not to suggest that professional practitioners withdraw from direct practice, but only that they become adept at coping with enlarged case boundaries, which require massive use of nonprofessionals. Assuming that such will be the practice reality, schools of social work must prepare for it. For example, doctoral residency programs could provide the student with field work in a clinical setting so that he would learn about clinical practice. Or, the student might be placed in a public child welfare office covering a large section of the city, and be assigned the task of planning the best utilization of three professional child welfare workers and some nonprofessional workers on the protective service staff to serve the thousands of known and unknown cases of child abuse in that area. Such an assignment would test the mettle of a professional social worker. And how many professionals could do it?

Since every school has its own curriculum and culture, it is inappropriate to suggest specific approaches to the goal of social work education proposed in this chapter. However, field work is one area in the curriculum that needs attention. Rather than assign each student x number of cases, each student would be assigned an area—a city block, a floor in a housing project, or whatever geographical area made sense in a particular setting. This form of field work would give the students the opportunity to learn about the influence of client systems upon client functioning, about client life style, health, and pathology. The student's case was still families, but he would work with families in their life context, not as welfare clients known mainly through case records and pent up hostility to the welfare department.

Of course, we all agree that field instructors must teach conceptually and that they must develop autonomy in their students; this is an old, endless story. And need it be said that students in field work must learn as wide a repertoire of skills as it is possible to teach them? The student in direct practice must know how to work with individuals using one-to-one family and group modes of interaction.

In the classroom these days a lot of rapping goes on as students ask for encounters, for us to "communicate" and be on a first name basis, and the like. Their cry for tapes and films and experiential illustrations is pretty tough on the teacher who has prepared a careful plan of study. The students are more sophisticated than they used to be, and as long as pedagogical methods are not confused with course content, it is still possible to teach—even while communicating on a "feeling level" and "experiencing the content."

To the degree that the knowledge base of social work practice is broad and general, students feel fragmented, especially when they take courses in the university at large. General courses contain such broad content that perhaps a beginning seminar is needed, like a final one in many schools, which seminar helps students to develop and structure the varied course content, so they can fit each course in its place. Even practice students probably should deal with some of the issues discussed in this book, even if they are not ready to understand all the implications for their practice. A further help for students is integrated courses such as those with cross-methods, and those which combine methods with the teaching of social policy, social science, human behavior and research. As for research, the loudest and clearest message of this book is that practitioners must be research-minded and must learn to design appropriate studies and ask the right questions.

Professional education must aim to teach students how to learn to keep their minds open. Students should not have to worship their teachers' ideology, particularly, since their teachers probably adopted it twenty years earlier. Students must learn what there is to know, but also that knowledge changes as the world changes. The best to be hoped for is that twenty years from now, our present students will not need a book such as this in order to examine themselves and what they have been doing, sometimes with little effectiveness, for twenty years. If this confrontation creates a crisis for us, let us take heart from the crisis intervention theorists, who claim that in every crisis is a hazard or an opportunity; let us seize the moment and see in this crisis an opportunity.

11

Once More, With Feeling

Helen Harris Perlman

A *multiproblem dilemma* confronts us as we look at these studies once again. We face problems within the studies themselves, the practices they have examined, the opinions and proposals of the commentators; and we must consider the consequences of the studies, their import for planning professional education for social workers in the next few years. To deal with this dilemma we can utilize a principle underlying good problem-solving—partialization, which is an effort to select from a complex of problems a few that seem manageable, are characteristic, and are expected to have some permeating effect upon the large problematic system.

Although the studies on which we are commenting encompass work with small groups as well as individuals and families and this section is on microsystem interventions, I shall, in the hope of achieving precision and clarity, limit my discussion to casework. Casework is the process in social work which has recently been under closest examination not only by its denigrators but also by its

concerned representatives. It has had more critical scrutiny by research studies than have other social work methods. It warrants
our sober attention lest more evidence accumulates suggesting that
this form of help has little significance for the people to whom it is
addressed.

To begin with, let us note that it is important that casework
practice be placed under the microscope of research. Perhaps the
lenses of that microscope are not finely ground enough and the
specimen-weighing scales are not finely calibrated enough to catch
the subtleties which may be of moment. But casework help has
been a socially supported endeavor, costly in time, energy, and
money, so it is only sensible that we begin with whatever crude
instruments we possess to gauge its efficacy and outcomes. Moreover, such assays have considerable potential value to the present
and future teaching and practice of casework. They may be upsetting, but they may also open doors held shut by custom and
convictions.

One thing learned from these studies is that caseworkers
have oversold themselves and their influence and its possible or
probable outcomes. They have promised, both implicitly and explicitly, especially in the public family and child welfare services,
that if enough caseworkers existed with enough time and skill, people
would be taken off relief, moved out of ghettos, rehabilitated, and
so on. The 1962 amendments regarding public assistance services
were probably based on these assumptions. What had not been
faced—has it been faced today?—was that no amount of individualized help, skilled and competent though it is, can be more than
individualized help. It can do no more than deal with one person
or family who, at a given time and place, is suffering the effects of
what may be an endemic social problem. Lack of money, jobs, medical
resources, adequate housing—these are social problems made up of
complex socioeconomic-political factors. No amount of reparative
or restorative work person by person, family by family, can affect
poverty (though it may affect a poor person) or slum rot (though
it may affect a badly housed family). Other forms of social action,
not casework, are required for problems that inhere in the social
fabric.

Yet so deeply does the puritan ethic of personal responsibility persist in us that professional as well as lay persons have continued, often unconsciously, to believe a person, by some combination of will, get-up-and-go, and casework, can clamber out of the disadvantageous social situation into which he was born or forced. Some people can and some do. It is also true that some by their own actions slip into the quagmire. But the quagmire is there, and social casework is not the form of social action that can or will clear it out.

"In the past we have tended to persist indefinitely in attacking problems and in dealing with situations in which casework service was not the answer. We are coming not only to recognize the futility of persisting in situations which are beyond the scope of casework help but to realize also our social responsibility for revealing the inadequacy of social casework in these instances, in order that interest and effort may be directed toward social action. . . . Let us cease to be the great pretenders. Casework . . . cannot substitute for certain other lacks" (quoted in Perlman, 1969). That was Charlotte Towle, one of casework's spokesmen, writing in the 1930s. Still, for many reasons that cannot be examined here, casework remained social work's major mode of help. When at last, in an economy of abundance, people began looking at the remaining invisible poor, there arose a cry of shock and indignation that caseworkers had not done anything about massive, rapidly festering social problems.

We are all agreed that we have taken too long to grasp that social situations exist beyond the scope of casework help and that social casework is inadequate in these instances. Some of us still seem to blur out the difference between a social problem and the individual who suffers. There is yet another facet to this problem of our unwitting pretense. The person who suffers a social problem may want help with it; he may want to escape it, get rid of it, be provided with what he lacks, to have his deficits filled in. He may need and want someone to provide him with resources and with what he thinks he needs and to advise, guide, and counsel him, too, because as a human being he has problems common to all men. But money, employment, housing, health are first things for all of us. If social conditions are such that these primary things cannot be had or if the caseworker cannot make them available or if they do not yet exist in the community, then the victim of a general social problem feels he has been helped only negligibly. Yes, his caseworker was a nice person, he didn't mind talking with her, but what help or change was seen or pointed to or valued? When people's basic needs dominate their thoughts and their lives, a helper must be able to provide means by which deficits can be eliminated. If he does not, hope for, and experience of and assessment of change will be minimal, probably insignificant by present statistical measures.

Although, technical faults may be found here and in these studies, nevertheless, it is clear that each was individually and carefully designed, according to preconceptions and hypotheses regarding the particular problem to be tackled, the maximal conditions of testing, and the expected outcomes. But the process being studied—casework—was not designed at all. There is no evidence that the caseworkers sat down and asked themselves exactly what services or provisions people with needs and deficits would want and find useful, nor did they ask what reasonable results might be anticipated. Or what, if any, special emphasis or forms of psychological influence toward change might be called for and utilized. Or, what the client's perception of service might be and, consequently, what clarifications and agreements would have to be reached. And so on. Instead, one repeatedly receives the impression that caseworkers are turned loose on clients, adjured to do casework or give casework, as if casework help were a thing to be bestowed upon a person or an immutable process, or as if casework help bore small relation to the nature of the material with which it is involved.

The nature of the material with which one works by the process called casework is an individualized sociopersonal unit, one person or several, who are in some problematic transaction with a complex of social circumstances. That complex of persons with problems and those transactions determine what the focus of attention should be, what goals may be reasonably sought, and what kinds of interventions may achieve them. When a group of cases must be dealt with, some diagnosis or assessment of the particularities of the group is needed in order to design a blueprint for action. If the process is casework, each person or family is individualized within that group diagnosis. To say that a group is multiproblem or on relief or disadvantaged is not enough. One must also ask: what are the expected deficits and discrepancies between what the person wants and needs and what he has or can get, the expected disturbances or distortions of his perception, say, of the establishment representative, the social caseworker, in the light of his past experiences? And further why can't the people in this group cope unaided with their problems? Why don't they use the resources open to them? And so on.

In brief, a project that sets out to demonstrate the effectiveness of a process must assay the material and conditions with which that process is involved. Caseworkers take this requirement as an article of faith in their work with individuals, though there too it is more honored in the preachment than the practice. But examination and assessment of the probable needs, motivations, and capacities of a group of persons selected because of presumed commonalities have not occurred in these studies. Thus, the treatment offered or the forms of intervention provided have not been designed by if-then propositions.

There is little evidence such design occurred in these studies of the effectiveness of casework; the most recently published study, the CSS-DSS Study, illustrates this lack. Those studied in this project were families going on relief for the first time. Caseworkers and researchers shared the assumption that this event would provoke a crisis in their lives. However, most of these families had lived in acutely precarious financial circumstances for some time prior to their acceptance of money; it is possible that going on relief was a small triumph, a release from anxiety and stress. If crisis were indeed the experience for most of these families, the casework design should have required immediate contact between caseworker and family at the white-hot point of felt hazard and disequilibrium. Actually the amount of intervening time was usually over a month. Crisis theory posits the impossibility of maintaining the intense feeling of need induced by crisis, and some leveling off is inevitable; thus, after a month on relief, the families' interest in casework intervention may have greatly declined.

Even if we allow for this possibility, we have no indication that what the professional caseworkers did was designed by the action theory of crisis. If it was, the study does not note it. If it was not, what was the use of the assumption that the families were in crisis? The casework services in Girls at Vocational High likewise were undesigned; they were business as usual for a group of already poorly functioning, distrustful, unmotivated girls. That was over a decade ago, but evidently, the intractable belief that casework is a package of services and techniques that can be delivered persists despite efforts to dislodge it.

It is not enough to say that casework is an individualizing process; legal and medical practices are also individualizing processes when they focus on individual cases; so are numerous other professional helping processes. We must clarify (1) the individually felt problems falling within the area of responsibility of social work as different from those which are the usual concern of other professions and (2) the conditions under which the method called casework is an appropriate social work mode and to what end casework may be utilized.

Within the purview of the whole profession of social work fall problems of person-to-person, person-to-group, group-to-group, and person/group-to-social circumstance interactions. Typically they are problems in daily social interchanges and transactions and in interpersonal relationships as experienced in their social roles. When a person (or family) finds such problems insurmountable by his own efforts or resources, he may seek or be proffered help to deal with them. Such help may make available the means by which his resource deficits are supplied or may stimulate his personal capacities for dealing with his situation effectively and satisfyingly or may do both. This help, casework, is a process focused on the person's felt need and is guided by assessments of his motivations, capacities, and resources. Its purpose is to enable a person (or family) suffering from a general social problem or a uniquely personal one to suffer less, to cope better, and, as a result, to feel able to deal with his tasks and relationships with increased confidence, steadiness, and satisfaction.

Focused on these purposes, the casework process does not even scratch a general social problem. It affects only this person or that family victimized by the social problem. True, in the course of helping an individual or family one often deals with and perhaps causes change in some large social systems which create or bear upon the individually experienced problem. Perhaps a whole school system is the cause of a single child's misery, his truancy, his failure to learn. His caseworker must attempt to deal with those persons and rulings that affect his problem. If the caseworker is successful, an environmental change has been achieved for one child. But the large system is likely to remain unmoved and intact. A caseworker may deal with the persons and forces that affect his client who is a patient in a large hospital system. This doctor, that nurse, this occupational therapist may be brought to a whole new way of dealing with his client-patient. But the caseworker cannot claim to have changed the system except in the individual instance. A by-product of the caseworker's efforts may occur if the individual case stimulates some general consideration toward change. But this occurrence is more rare than we piously hope and certainly cannot be counted on. In sum, the caseworker as a policy or program changer operates for his client; he is a case advocate. This is quite different from being a policy advocate who takes the system as his treatment target.

The basic condition for one person's use of another's help is that he both knows and feels he has a problem. He hurts, and he wants to be rid of that hurt or stress. The problem that he identifies, that he feels, and that he wants to be rid of is the crucial point of entry and connection between a client and his caseworker. Where his emotion is, there his motivation is. This point, not the social problem predefined by the caseworker or the researcher, is the starting point for giving help and taking help. It is not clear that this consideration governed the proffering of casework help in the situations under review here.

As one looks across the wide and varied range of people and problems dealt with by the process called casework the issues in education for social work interventions, even at the so-called micro-level, show themselves to be large and complex. In the effort to grapple with problems of what every caseworker should know, whether professionally educated or trained on the job, and what, in addition, only some caseworkers need to know, I put forth the following, tentatively, for consideration.

There are three main ways by which one can solve a problem or achieve some bearable relationship to it: by getting the material, tangible aids which meet present needs, such as money, a job, better housing; by having access to necessary social services so that they may be utilized in coping with the problem, such as homemaker help and child care facilities; by getting therapeutic guidance aimed toward changes of perception, affect, attitudes, and action so that the impact of the problem is decreased or the problem is dealt with more effectively than it was previously and the person's sense of mastery is increased in relation to it.

Each of these modes is contained within the problem-solving process of casework. Many cases call for all three sorts of help. Basic to each of them, to be taken account of by paraprofessionals and skilled caseworkers alike, are these elementary considerations: How the applicant-client sees his problem and what he wants to be helped to do about it should be the determinants of the caseworker's beginning actions. (Exceptions to this flat statement occur chiefly in situations where an individual's or family's "clear and present danger" necessitates unasked-for interventions.) The need the client feels, the help he desires, the capacities and resources available to him should be the primary material for diagnostic assessment by the caseworker and the design for next steps in treatment.

Such next steps may simply be the relief of stress by the provision of necessary and symbolically vital means. Thereby a person may be freed to look ahead, to reconsider, to plan beyond the day. By the same token, all the compassionate support and reasoned guidance in the world cut little ice when one feels, and is, deprived of basic needs. Unless the person is relieved of need-created stress, he tends to remain mired in frustration. Skills cannot replace goods in these instances. And although the client may be convinced of and grateful for his caseworker's goodwill and intent, he scarcely feels that any real help has been given him for the problem he finds central and omnipresent.

Among the multideficit clients who make up the populations studied here are those who long ago resigned themselves, hopelessly, to making do with the money, housing, clinic care provided by the relief agency. The caseworker may see many other problems which effort and time might modify or even solve. But if this client has so armored himself that he does not find such problems uncomfortable or if he has so little hope or energy that he cannot rouse himself to grapple with new ways and means, he will find little use in the caseworker's discussions about them. This client exercises the same right to live his life, problem-ridden though it may be, as he wishes, as do all other persons who do not "take relief." He may talk about his problems to his caseworker, but he also talks about them to his neighbors. Such talk for momentary relief of tension does not necessarily lead to the self-mobilization and directedness that are the precursors of change. With this client caseworkers may be misled, assuming that "communication" marks "relationship" and that relationship leads to change. It may; but the primary and insistent question must be: to what problem-solving ends?

The psychologically debilitating and hope-lowering effects of chronic marginal subsistence have long been observed and commented on by practicing caseworkers (Towle, 1965; Perlman, 1957, 1960, 1968a), and research data have long been available to support these observations. For example, the 1964 study by Ripple of almost four hundred continuers and discontinuers who had made voluntary application to several family agencies found that clients with external problems and resource deficits are likely to continue with the casework agency if environmental conditions are restrictive but modifiable and that they are almost certain to discontinue if environmental conditions are restrictive and unfavorable (Ripple, 1964). These were clients of voluntary agencies making voluntary application for help. Clients of public assistance agencies are not free to discontinue their agency relationship, at least not bodily, but they may successfully absent themselves in mind and be unmotivated to use help other than money grants. And researchers questioning them as to whether they were helped by the caseworker's efforts at guidance regarding problems other than material deficits may draw a complete blank. Helped? How? In what way?

Another question of design presents itself to caseworkers and researchers alike. If provision of material means and survival resources is what most disadvantaged persons want and need, were the studies which used experimental and control groups with trained caseworkers on the former and regular relief workers on the latter actually examining casework versus no casework? Or were they examining two forms of casework: one in which untrained caseworkers utilized all available tangible resources to meet their clients' material needs; the other in which trained caseworkers did that plus assume that counsel, guidance, supporting attitudes and relationships would motivate the clients and enable them to cope with their problems of need or other problems or both? At least one study (Mullen and others, 1970) speculated that the regulars, knowledgeable as they are about community resources, were perhaps more effective in finding resources for their clients than were the professional caseworkers assigned these cases. Thus, if what the usual client felt he needed was the provision of life-sustaining necessities and such services as he could not buy, why should he have reported that he was more significantly helped by the trained caseworkers than by the regulars? Why was it expected that some psychological influence exerted by the professional caseworker could ameliorate or obviate such immutable social deficits as persisted in these families? Or that deficit needs met by one kind of caseworker would be more valued than those met by another?

Related to this is the fact, long recognized in casework theory but apparently insufficiently noted in practice, that we cannot assume a client's participation in his problem-solving simply because he sees and even complains of a problem. He must want to do something about it. Further, he must want to do something about it in partnership with the caseworker and to work toward realistic outcomes. He and his caseworker must have had to come to some openly discussed agreement about what business they have together. Their business cannot just be heartfelt talk or compassionate comments—though these are involved. It is about some difference or change the client would like to have happen in his daily life. This necessity for agreement between client and caseworker has been stressed in some psychiatric literature as early as the 1950s and in casework writing since at least 1960 (Menninger, 1958; Perlman, 1960, 1961). One wonders why it has been consistently ignored or blurred out in practice when caseworkers have undertaken to deal with people deficient in means and resources? Have we been so full of our good intentions that we have not considered how our presence and efforts are read and understood by those to whom we proffer services?

People may also need individualized help when needed services are inaccessible or when they are unable to use available educational, medical, legal, substitute family-care, and other services. Generally, caseworkers are aware of these organized means, for they have created and manned many special agencies which provide for the needs of families, children, and the aged. Caseworkers know, too, that people often have difficulty connecting with and using these services, either out of fear, ignorance, or distrust, or because such services tend to be impersonal, bureaucratic, bound by routines and rules geared more to organizational efficiency than to people's needs. Thus, caseworkers have long recognized their function as linkers or as brokers between individual persons or families and socially organized and supervised services.

Two sides of this operation may need casework help: he who needs the service may have to be prepared to understand how the resource relates to his need, to want the resource, and to behave in such ways as to get it and make use of it; those who give or represent the service may have to be prepared to bend and shape their approaches and operations to the particular situation or psychology of the needy person. These aids come under the heading of "environmental modification," long considered a vital part of casework's helping means, vital, yet more honored in mention than in action.

It is probable that most professional caseworkers hold the fact-to-face interview with the client (single person or family) to be the central core of practice. Linking the client to the services he needs and lacks tends to be seen as a side issue. True, the caseworker frequently makes referrals to resources, but he often does not pave the way for the client to be received or explore what mental or emotional obstacles may stand between the client's knowing where to find help and actually going out to get it. Certainly one finds little attention given to such efforts in caseworkers' spoken or recorded accounts of their work. The brokerage operations called environmental modification as practiced in casework have scarcely been designed at all. Ways to influence the thoughts, feelings, and actions of the client have been formulated, at times in exquisite detail; ways to influence people who constitute the proximal environment of the client (except those who are part of planned family treatment) and whose actions and attitudes affect the outcome of the client's problem-solving efforts have had little or no description or formulation. Anyone who has been in casework practice knows firsthand the difficulties and frustrations in trying to reach some of the people who control the services needed by one's client, to persuade them to consider the case particularities, and so on. If such contacts and connection operations are difficult, irritating, and time-consuming for a caseworker, how much more difficult are they for a client to manage on his own—unauthorized, inarticulate, and scared as he may be?

Because environmental modification has been considered a side operation in casework, because it has had no governing principles (beyond common sense) of methodology, and perhaps because it takes the caseworker out of his professional habitat and into the uncontrollable area of other people's territories, it has had little prestige and status in professional casework. Thus, it has had little attention beyond lip service in education for practice. Where can we find case material to show a student that what a caseworker said and did with collaterals effected a change in the ongoing social transactions between his client and some part of the client's milieu? Where, with all the cries about delivery of services, have the principles of such delivery been articulated? Or is it assumed that this is simply a conveyor belt matter?

Since the principles governing environmental modification, or social brokerage, have had small attention in professional theory and training and have no design, it is not surprising that in the special projects under study here the professionally educated caseworker did not do better with it than did the untrained caseworker. The fact is that in most of the client groups studied this need to find or create (or both) services and resources and to make them accessible to the clients was one of the most pervasive and frequently encountered needs. For our failure adequately to conceptualize environmental modification and thence to give it place and prestige in casework education we are, caseworkers all, culpable. It is possible that this field of transaction between people and the increasingly complex and impersonal systems that govern their daily lives, if developed in theory and practice, may become one of social work's unique areas of expertise.

Beyond environmental modification, a most vital factor in the help-giving failures recorded in these studies was the actual lack or insufficiency of needed and wanted resources and services. As the Chemung County Study shows, both the control and the experimental groups lived at a substandard economic level. Child care services were not to be had by mothers able and willing to work. And, as the CSS-DSS Study shows, employment was scarce for those who were ready to work. Improved housing was virtually nonexistent. So the unasked but compelling question underlying a number of these studies is not whether professional casework is effective, but, rather, can professional casework—its counsel, guidance, and efforts to influence behavior—substitute for adequate food money, a job, or suitable housing? The answer need not be sought by research. It is obvious.

Now the third type of casework help must be considered. It may include the provision both of economic sustenance and of welfare services and opportunities. But, beyond or in addition to these it takes as its center of attention the need and wish in the client himself to change. Such change may involve shifts or modifications in the client's attitudes, his affects, his actions, any or all of these, sometimes minimally, sometimes radically. Its focus is upon the client's use of himself and his rewards or frustrations in carrying one or more of his problematic social roles. Its goal, shared and agreed upon by client and helper, is some consciously sought change in the person's self- or other-management (or both) as it relates to the problem with which he wants help.

To move toward the goal of some behavioral change in one's self in relation to some identified problem the person gives himself to the expressive, reflective, considering, and choice-making work that constitutes problem-solving. With the support of the caseworker's empathy and concern, with the focus, guidance, and counsel the caseworker may afford him, the client grows to relate responsively to his helper, to see himself as actor in and upon his problem (not just its victim), and increasingly to exercise his own present or potential powers in problem-solving.

How usual is this striving for personal behavioral change in chronically disadvantaged populations? We speak here of populations, not of individual persons, who occasionally arise, buoying our hopes, and are the exceptions which prove the rule. Such persons are rather unusual, to say the least, as is borne out by casework practice experience, observation of common reactions, and research on conditions governing human behavior (Bradburn, 1970; Department of Health, Education, and Welfare, 1968). When one's eyes are fixed on outside dangers, they usually do not look inside; when one thinks of one's self as a chronic victim of fate or, worse, of the whims of presumably powerful people, one scarcely conceives of one's self as a changer or as needing to change; and when one discovers that talking one's heart out feels good but does not diminish one's troubles, the motivation even to talk dwindles rapidly. Thus, in order to be an active problem-solver, a person must have within himself or his social situation (or both) reserves of energy, hope, and trust which enable him to consider changing his behavior or perspectives. The marginal man whose existence has been hand-to-mouth and chronically demeaning rarely has such reserves to call upon, nor does he have reason to trust someone who represents the society from which he feels outcast. Thus the preconditions for using help with self-to-social tasks or interpersonal problems are minimal in the populations with which the reviewed studies dealt.

The paradox becomes manifest: this kind of helping, by which persons are moved to change their affects, attitudes, and action in the casework process taught to and learned by the professionally prepared caseworker. It may be argued that such caseworkers are overtrained for situations where the predominant problem is actual and felt material need. Perhaps, too, they have been undertrained in the recognition of those chronic socioeconomic circumstances that nullify people's psychological adaptability.

To help people examine and modify their usual ways of coping with their problems, to help them face and deal with the deficits, discrepancies (emotional and cognitive), and disturbances (intrapsychic and transactional) that undermine their social functioning, these are the kinds of help about which most concepts and principles in present-day casework theory are formulated. They involve complex knowledge of psychodynamics and fine skill in the management of the affectful and verbal interchanges of casework treatment. It is the sort of helping that students who choose to become "professional" and to specialize in the casework process most value and respect. Moreover, large numbers of people coming to social agencies and to other human welfare institutions where caseworkers operate (schools, clinics) want just such help with problems they themselves have identified as intra- or inter-personal (or both). So it cannot be tossed off as irrelevant to social work's cause and functions.

It is possible that this kind of help is not necessary or even suitable for the first-aid, basic-provision requirements in the population with which these studies were involved. Even if, in individual instances, the socioeconomic deficits are indeed caused by problems of personality, the present and pressing consequences require our first attention. It is possible that the need for and use of skilled caseworkers must follow the establishment of that base of socio-economic security from which the beleagured client can dare to look about him with the modicum of hope necessary to engage himself in change. I suggest that the use of professionally educated and process-skilled caseworkers for the population in these studies or demonstration projects grew out of that often unconscious but almost immutable belief that the cause of social malfunctoining lies in faults of personality.

And now, uncomfortably, I face a dilemma of my own creation. I have long hoped that one of the contributions that professionally prepared caseworkers could make to the growing numbers of paraprofessionals, volunteers, and undergraduate degree holders in social work would be, through formal or informal teaching, to transmit the ideas and principles that govern good human relationships, to expound understanding of usual and also deviate needs and motivations, to guide what the untrained caseworker does with his clients and how he does it. How will the professional caseworker be equipped to do this teaching unless in his own schooling and practice experience he has learned to differentiate needs and people and thus to consider differential treatment designs? So one must turn, if too briefly, to see what changes need to take place in the educational programs that prepare professional caseworkers.

The idea of personal pathology or character-faulting tends to be given strong support by traditional courses in personality development, and it often governs the thinking of class and field teachers who were themselves thus indoctrinated. Thus assessments are made in terms of personality classifications, and subsequent treatment plans focus upon changes in the person's feelings, on the further assumption that changes in affects and attitudes must precede changes in behavior. But both practice and research reveal that consciously attempted behavioral changes may change feeling, and that feelings and attitudes also change quite unconsciously through changes in the conditions with which one lives. Freudian theory for all its range and brilliance is not enough. It does not account for the impacts of value systems or ethnicity or variant social class and culture upon the growing child. Except as extrapolated by Talcott Parsons, for example, it does not examine the transactions between emergent personality and role sets and rules. Except by subtle implication (and all-too-brief courses in an all-too-brief graduate program can scarcely explore these subtleties) it does not take into account the powers or defects of cognition or the affect-changing potentials of action.

Nor is it possible to expand personality theory (Freudian or other) simply by additive means. Systems theory, for instance, cannot just be tacked on, nor can one expect that the present-day plethora of ethnic and social class studies will yield, by addition or substitution, a unified, coherent explanation of man-becoming in a changing environment. An integrated theory of human development and behavior is yet to be hard won. Behavioral science is struggling and floundering with this task. Perhaps the most that the teachers of social caseworkers can do is to keep themselves and their students alert to the categories of variables by which the person in a situation may be affected and explained, and then try to organize the seemingly most useful parts of emergent theory into some coherent, applicable whole. One must risk taking a position, it seems to me, rather than presenting a potpourri. Unless the student of casework is taught to assess not only the person but also the dynamics of his social transactions and milieu, unless he is taught to ask not just what is the matter with the client but also, or instead, what keeps him from being able to cope, then his understanding of cases is both constricted and skewed, whether he chooses to work with the rich or the poor.

Along with the problems of the adequacy and fit of our explanatory theory are some problems of values. Misconceptions of values may affect the efficacy of the professionally educated caseworker when he deals with long-disadvantaged people. Like all social workers, caseworkers believe in equality of opportunity. It goes against the grain somehow to entertain the idea that one sort of opportunity should be offered to economically deprived and educationally disadvantaged persons and that another, more prestigeful, should be offered others. The result is an undifferentiated helping process proffered to populations who are different from one another in telling ways.

One of the persistent problems in professional education has been the often wide gap between what the student learns in the classroom and what he learns in the field. Field learning usually is the most deeply absorbed learning because it is experienced, not just intellectually digested; thus, a major concern is that there be congruity between class and field at a graduate level. Yet this is often not the case. The reasons are manifold, and some of them involve cost and administrative considerations which are almost insuperable. Congruity between class and field emerges and continues only as a product of mutually reached agreements among class and field teachers upon the essential, basic concepts and principles to be repeatedly stressed.

The acrimonious arguments about whether class or field is "ahead" have no place here, or value either. Some field teachers teach only what they were taught; so do some classroom teachers. Some field teachers are in the forefront of innovative practice; some hold to the ironbound traditions of their agencies. Some classroom teachers, out of continuously assessing and observing current practice, are theory builders; others remain good (or poor) interpreters of theory. Good, bad, ahead, behind, the important goal is that class and field together offer the student a learning experience that may be found in the microcosm of the single case and in the macrocosm of governing principles and generalizations, that may be transferred from one case or agency to another; or, if this goal is not feasible, that the criteria for nonapplicability be articulated. The field teacher repeatedly must help the student to see that "this place" is not the universe of social work and thence to identify in what ways his practice is affected and differentiated here. The classroom teacher repeatedly must help the student to pick apart the generalizations that govern practice, to critically examine them for fit and congruence and applicability. Otherwise the graduated professional caseworker goes forth bravely but naively to apply familiar methods to unfamiliar and often quite different settings and situations.

Questions there are aplenty for our continuous pursuit in both class and field, and, as Carol Meyer suggests in the previous chapter, we must encourage students to pose them insistently. They will be such questions, one hopes, as rise not out of hostility or cynicism (was it Oscar Wilde who said that a cynic is one who knows the cost of everything and the value of nothing?) but out of concern to find answers that, imperfect as they are, will bring us close to being effective helpers.

Essentially, teachers of casework, the practitioners they train, those who plan and implement special treatment projects, and those who study their effectiveness must firmly take hold of the idea that the casework process is skillful only insofar as it is differentially designed; that such design follows upon assessment of the nature of the person(s) in situation(s), what the person(s) wants, is capable of, and has accessible to him by way of resources and social opportunity. Survival needs call for means to survive. Self-realization needs emerge and become insistent when survival needs are met and can be counted on. Casework intervention may be at either level of need-meeting, but neither one can be expected to substitute for the other "successfully."

A further implication for social work education is that it is possible that some typology of people's personal-social functioning problems may yield a typology of caseworker preparation differentiated by priorities of need, emphasis, goals, and thence by methodology. Perhaps for the first two kinds of individualized help, the provision of life essentials and the facilitation of connections between clients and the resources they need, the education of caseworkers may be given at preprofessional levels. Within such programs there would need to be taught and exercised all the modes by which empathy and concern are conveyed by the would-be helper and the ways to test and recognize a person's wish for and readiness to try to help with problems of an interpersonal or psychosocial nature. The latter kind of help may be the form of casework for which the fully "professional" caseworker is educated and trained.

Beyond his clinical sophistication and skills one would hope that the professional caseworker would be identified by several other abilities: to precisely formulate the questions of theory or application or values that are continuously a-boil within social work and its several helping processes; to bear uncertainty and tolerate differences at the same time as he must act within one framework of thought and one style of action; to mentally weave the connecting threads between the instance and the generality; and to hold himself to some systematic ways of viewing people and their problems and assessing and designing action that differentiates target-focused problem-solving from buckshot trial and error. "Effective intervention" may then frequently be the outcome of casework help. Certainly it will then be more susceptible to adequate study and measurement.

12

Continuum in Education for Social Work

Werner W. Boehm

This chapter, drawing on the reviewed studies, identifies their implications for a continuum in education for social work. Obviously, the studies were not made with changes in social work education in mind; however, this goal seems appropriate if one accepts the premise that studies of social work practice must be considered by the social work educator for their implications for changes in education. In this case, an even stronger argument can be made for the examination of practice research from the vantage point of education because these studies emphasize the effectiveness of the casework method, the oldest of the several intervention strategies in social work, and the one that can rightly claim to have received the greatest attention in the training of social workers.

In a sense, this book reflects what many of us have often hoped would happen, namely, a tough-minded and searching collaboration of the thinking of practice researchers and educators to bring about better links between practice and education. Our joint endeavor seems guided by our conviction that education can benefit from the findings of practice studies and that practice should change in the light of research results. Rather than arguing as some do that education must follow practice or that education should be ahead of practice, it seems more realistic to advocate the existence of a creative tension between practice and education which causes them to stimulate each other. The premises of the following comments deal with the current nature and characteristics of education for social work. It would have been preferable to fashion a philosophy screen similar in purpose, but not necessarily in content, to the one created for the Curriculum Study of the Council on Social Work Education.

Premises and Implications

First, education for social work is a complex of programs consisting of formal and informal training components. The informal components are agency-based in-service training and continuing education. Formal education, located in institutions of higher learning, is provided on the associate, baccalaureate, master's, and doctoral levels. The several components of social work education, both informal and formal, can be or ought to be viewed from a systems perspective. That is, they should be interrelated in such a way that each level and type of education bears a defined relationship to the other, and that together they form a comprehensive whole which like each of its constituent parts has its own integrity. In reality, at present, such a system of education for social work does not exist.

Second, the purpose of education for social work, stated in broad terms, is to prepare personnel for the performance of functions in the realm of social relations in a variety of social institutions, particularly in health, education, welfare, and in the judicial system. Generally, social work personnel, regardless of level of training or level of competence, can be categorized in terms of functions they perform as direct service practitioners, supervisory and consultative personnel, planning, policy, administrative, and coordinating personnel, teachers and trainers.

Third, the common functions of social work personnel include development and implementation of social welfare policies, creation and administration of programs and resources, coordination of such programs and their delivery to the consumer through direct services geared to the needs of individuals and families, with a view to maintaining or enhancing their social functioning or preventing their social dysfunctioning in the face of existing or emerging societal or personal problems. The notion of practice contained in these premises is intentionally much broader than the one frequently found in current literature. For purposes of this discussion, the term practice is not limited to activities of direct service personnel but applies also to personnel engaged in policy, planning, and administrative activities.

Fourth, the fact that the studies under consideration appear to focus primarily on the effectiveness of casework could lead to the conclusion that inferences drawn from these studies are applicable only to the teaching of casework. However, these studies, in some instances explicitly and in others implicitly, go beyond casework. They contain suggestions for the service structure of which casework is part, for program resources at the neighborhood and community levels, and even touch upon the generally prevailing sociocultural, economic, and political circumstances which have some bearing upon the needs of the consumer.

In general terms and without specifying variations in method and outcome, from study to study, perhaps the single most important finding is that comparing control with experimental groups reveals only modest progress in a number of areas of family functioning. In some studies the changes which occurred were statistically not significant. In other studies positive change was found to be associated with differences in the utilization of personnel combined with reduction of the number of cases per social worker. Planned short-term contact was found to be more effective than long-term continued service in more than one study.

Of central importance for this chapter is that numerous studies have pointed out that factors other than casework intervention may have had some bearing on outcome or should be considered in a study of outcome. Some of the noncasework factors identified as worthy of consideration are the degree of knowledge of a family of existing resources in the community; the quality of housing available to families; adequacy of economic resources; availability of and ease of access to effective community resources, such as day care and homemaker services and treatment opportunities for psychological problems; the presence or absence of social legislation such as abortion legislation which might further or impede family cohesiveness; and, the level of economic prosperity and economic security prevailing in the region or country as a whole at the time the studies were made.

In addition to this set of factors, educational implications also flow from a consideration of the target group and the characteristics of the intervention itself. For instance, Ludwig Geismar reports that intervention with young and potential multiproblem families at an early stage did lead to some improvement, especially as a result of intensive efforts. This suggests that if intervention has a preventive cast, is intensive, relates timing to degree of problem development and addresses itself to populations at risk, the chances for improvement are enhanced. As Geismar suggests, these studies cannot help but produce inferences for service structure, agency program and policy, and delivery systems. In similar vein, Edgar Borgatta, David Fanshel and Henry Meyer comment, in a study completed some years ago, "Many important outcomes of casework services may depend less on understanding and effecting changes in clients as persons and more on understanding and effecting change in their social environmental situation. For such understanding, knowledge about families, peer associations, community institutions, and many forces and obstacles will be necessary. The professional skills required to change such factors may implicate the agency as an organization and, indeed, the whole complex of social welfare and civic institutions in the community" (Borgatta and others, 1960). Although not everybody wishes to equate casework with changes in clients as persons, as the above authors seem to do, there can be little argument with their suggestion that in our quest for change we must widen our range. But the recognition that we must draw the net wider to catch the factors relevant for change should not lead us to abandon the dimension which we have come to call casework. Whatever the term connotes now, or will connote in the future, the notion of eliminating a process of help because it is not the only dimension crucial in producing change is at best illogical and, at worst, irresponsible. Instead we must realize that in education, as in practice, many factors must be viewed singly and in relationship to each other. Their relative weight in producing change and specific outcomes sought need to be stipulated in behavioral terms; Helen Perlman and other caseworkers have said repeatedly: *casework cannot be expected to substitute for a lack of material and psychosocial resources.*

Framework for Content

The preceding comments highlight a seldom addressed problem about the relationship between practice and education. To say that practice and education should be linked is little more than mouthing a platitude; if there is to be a relationship, we must ask what impact education should have on practice and vice versa. From the vantage point of education, it is important to determine whether education should teach what practice does, whether practice activities should be viewed against broader principles which they might illustrate or reflect, or the like. If professional education means more than presenting the student with information in an article, book, or report; if it means extracting from existing materials pertinent concepts and principles which can be described, analyzed, applied, tested, and changed, then a framework is needed which provides education wtih a means of getting at practice data in systematic fashion. We have attempted to conceptualize the disparate elements which have been discussed in the preceding section and unite them into one schema, the purpose of which is to provide the educator with a convenient tool to examine practice data systematically.

The schema consists of four components: the characteristics of the population to be served; the nature of the resources and service facilities available; the nature of the intervention system, its objectives, process and methods; and the roles to be performed by the social worker, that of planner, coordinator, administrator, or direct service provider. This framework makes it possible to arrive at educational content suggestions for learning in class and field and to examine ways of distributing this content on several levels, bearing in mind the desirability of a continuum and a systematically planned relationship between formal and informal education. What is being presented here is not a blueprint for social work education, but a guide or an approach toward thinking about appropriate structures, levels, and areas in the social work education complex. Understandably, bias and ideological preferences are not absent from such an undertaking. One such bias has already been expressed, namely a point of view of practice which includes not only direct service but also planning, policy, and coordinating function; and the following points of view expressed are not necessarily those of other social work educators or practitioners.

It is evident the populations served in these studies were lower income groups. Therefore, the question may be raised whether the findings are applicable only to lower income groups. To put it differently, if the typical family agency client who is somewhat elevated in socioeconomic status, as in the Casework Methods Project, and the private practitioner's cleint who tends to be still more elevated had been the foci of more studies, would the results have been different and more encouraging? To put the question in these terms avoids asking a more fundamental question.

The question that must be answered is whether social work as a profession chooses to address itself to lower socioeconomic strata by design, and whether by so doing it plans to leave other strata of the population to the ministrations of other professions or unattended. Is such a position compatible with the notion of a profession which must be available to all strata of the population, even though it may not at a given point in time be able to serve all strata? And is not a profession obligated to strive for the competency needed to work with all population segments? Such questions must be raised, despite the fact that currently the major effort of social work practice is devoted to lower socioeconomic groups. However, it is one thing to give service priority to one group among several, and another to make one group alone the exclusive target of professional concern. Consideration of this issue, which is particularly urgent these days and which cannot be solved through research endeavors but requires value judgments, helps us deal with the pressure to reorder the profession's priorities by working with the poor.

The resolution of the issue has important consequences for social work education. Although different social workers have different viewpoints on the matter, a profession cannot claim to be a profession unless it is available actually and potentially to all segments of the population. This does not preclude giving, at any one time, priority to a population group with a history of deprivation—a group which warrants particular attention and high priority in the provision of services. This position is more consistent with the ethos of a profession than is the position which claims social work should be the profession which serves the poor, no matter how noble this may sound.

If it is decided that social work should be a profession available to all segments of the population, the implications for education are different from those based on a decision that social work is the profession for the lower socioeconomic strata. If the former position is followed, the social work curriculum on several levels should contain sociocultural material describing and differentiating several socioeconomic groups from each other while, at the same time, being comprehensive in its coverage. Such material should also dwell upon the particular vulnerability of certain socioeconomic groups, such as the poor and ethnically different, compared to groups belonging to the majority color or majority religion. Furthermore, the social work curriculum should address itself, in describing the populations coming within its purview, actually or potentially, not only to sociocultural characteristics and the understanding needed of subcultures in the larger sociocultural context, but also to socioeconomic characteristics of different population groups and the political forces which differentially impinge upon their well-being. Thus, a comprehensive approach, bringing within purview of social work all population groups, enables us to distinguish among population groups by identifying the characteristics of the different segments of the population. Through comparative studies of such characteristics as opposed to focusing on only one segment of the population, we could show effectively how the socioeconomic structure, the culture and the politics of the nation combine to make life more difficult for the poor than for the nonpoor.

Such an approach to the curriculum puts us in a position to utilize not only knowledge but observation and experience to enable the students to become aware of, and sensitive to, the different social expectations to which different segments of the population are asked to respond. Students could thus become sensitive to the differential constellations in the multiple causation of stress and problems which affect the different segments of the population and the varying ways in which different population groups express their responses.

Increasingly, as studies emerge about the nature and extent of the vulnerability of the poor, we are beginning to see that we may have created other vulnerabilities, including some for the rich, in this country. Are we not permitting life styles to develop in the suburbs and elsewhere making it possible for well-to-do people and their children to become alienated from the culture and to engage in behavior which is class-connected, yet different from the class-connected behavior of the poor? The useful, but for our purposes somewhat crude, sociological concept of social deviance which some of the studies employ, may have less value in the future because we seem to be learning that nonconformity to community norms is perhaps much less widespread than anomie, normlessness, or internal consistency of private family norms. If such views are judged pertinent, educational consequences should ensue not only for content but also for method of teaching and learning. Thus, examination of personal experiences on the part of the student may become a more widely used and appropriate tool (Butler, 1970).

Considerable knowledge is available about the developmental stages of man, and knowledge is accumulating about the vulnerability of the family and of individuals during critical periods in their life span. This knowledge often draws on and combines concepts from sociology and psychology with maturational concepts. This is appropriate for studying systematically and comprehensively the several population groups which could be examined from a developmental vantage point; at the same time, these groups could be studied both for their similarities and their differences, thus combining the sociocultural, socioeconomic, and political approach with the developmental one.

Such treatment is not compatible with the social problem

approach frequently advocated. In the context of the question—
which population should the profession serve and therefore what
should students know about the population groups the profession is
serving—it appears that the social problem approach may not give
students a comprehensive picture of both the social vulnerability
and the social potential of all population groups. Social problems
shift in definition and public attention and their recognition or non-
recognition is often as bound up with politics as with a given state
of scientific development. Moreover, social problems tend to be
seen by the public and even by professional groups as afflicting
primarily the lower socioeconomic groups. The fact that the social
problems which are identified or studied as such have a high incidence among the lower socioeconomic strata may well reflect a
reactionary bias on the part of social scientists. It would seem that
the phenomena called a social problem usually are not identified
and studied as such even if those who are afflicted call attention to
them. Study or remedy, or both, seems to occur only when the un-
affected realize that the existing equilibrium is threatened. However,
it may be possible to incorporate the social problem approach as
one dimension in a study of the total population, if social stratification data can be used and knowledge of the incidence and prevalence of social problems becomes available, bearing in mind that
social problem definitions usually do have ideological overtones.
Such an approach should open the door to the production and use
of social epidemiological data which currently seem to be missing
in social work curricula and, in general, are insufficiently available.

Now that we have considered the population served within
our schema, we can move on to the social resource structure. Political and socioeconomic aspects are closely intertwined when it comes
to consideration of the social service structure. Here the appropriate
role-relationship of federal, state, and local levels must be considered
as well as the relationship of the public to the private sector. The
scope of services, their modes of decentralization and coordination,
and the delivery patterns needed on the local level to make them
easily accessible to the consumer call for examination of the relationship and function of federal and state programs and the desirability
of compacts among states to facilitate program development by cir-
cumventing the artificial boundaries of county, state and federal

levels. It is not clear whether our present structures provide a reasonable division of labor among the several levels of government or a functional relationship between the public and the voluntary sector. Several ideologies will probably emerge within the social work profession and different patterns must be considered, for it is clear that planning in this realm is urgently needed.

Therefore, the student must know something about the nature of existing and future patterns and the differential role of social work personnel in them; plus, he must have an opportunity to test the effectiveness of such patterns. For example, since the proposed programs for income security are created under federal auspices, it seems reasonable to assume that the role of the social worker will be that of planner and policy maker. He would perform as expert and consultant in conjunction with economists, political scientists, and the like. Different program proposals have differential impact not only on the level of economic support they provide but also on the individual dignity they ensure, enhance, or diminish.

If income maintenance programs are geared to minimum support, the social worker on the local level would be freed to provide nonfinancial services such as information and advice about community resources; and consumers could be helped more effectively than they are now to find health, education, recreation, and other services essential for satisfying living. In contrast, state level programs would set guidelines for effective delivery on the local level, thus making social workers on the state level administrators, planners, and consultants.

The students also must understand the structure and function of related human service institutions such as education, health (mental and physical), the professions operating in them and the changes in function and structure these institutions are experiencing. By the same token, more attention must be given to the social welfare system itself, its linkage with other social institutions and its changing nature. The difficulty in clarifying the boundaries of the social welfare institution may be less important than its key characteristics examined on comparative terms and viewed against the experience of other societies. Much more seems needed to determine how social work as a profession operates or behaves and what similarities and differences exist in it, as it functions in health (mental and physical), in the educational and the judicial systems, and in welfare proper.

The emergence of new combinations of systems, not only public and voluntary, but also nonprofit and profit-making, in the provision of social, health, educational and recreational services, warrants an examination of widely held notions which may or may not be true. We must review the validity of the old proposition that social and other human services should be provided through non-profit organization from the vantage point of efficiency and of social work values which point to such considerations as effectiveness, ethics, and quality control.

The focus on the needs of population groups either by socio-economic stratum or by developmental stage, or a combination of the two, affords a promising approach to the identification of services needed for satisfying living, such as day care or homemaker services and other family support services. Some of the reviewed studies imply, and recent literature on social planning suggests, that several categories of services are needed by each population group in varying combinations, with varying intensity, at different times. If comprehensive coverage is desired and if the notion is accepted that, actually and potentially, the total population falls within the purview of social work, then we must try to accommodate the difference in population needs rather than focus on the specific needs of a segment of the population.

If such considerations are plausible and valid, it seems that social work education must review institutional structures—their nature, relationships, and auspices: private-public, profitmaking-nonprofitmaking—through descriptions as well as analysis. New programs not yet tested or sufficiently described in the literature must be assessed, and trends emerging from new administrative combinations and federal encouragement, such as tax incentives available to industry to embark upon service ventures, must be considered. This segment of the curriculum, if examination in value-policy terms is intended, may contain conceptual material and, also, dwell on factual description and analysis.

Since these programs tend to intermesh by plan or by happenstance vertically as well as horizontally on the local level, they must be seen as a structural system, not isolated as discrete events. Such an approach to this material enables the student to increase his knowledge and affords him an opportunity for attitudinal development and sensitivity to values, because he is confronted with what is and what may be, with the compromises and power coalitions reflected in current or emerging programs, and how the continuation or discontinuation of programs is related to political factors. It is important, for instance, to know whether a climate of social experimentation is likely to flourish during periods of prosperity, whether certain parties in power and certain election strategies are likely to bypass or utilize traditional state-city power combines as has been revealed in the differential treatment of the Office of Economic Opportunity in the Kennedy, Johnson, and Nixon administrations.

Production analyses which afford opportunities for the study of the impact of politics on program are usually absent from the current social work curricula. They must be introduced in order, as a minimum, to enhance the sophistication of students about the political dimension of social welfare. Such an experience would hopefully make students aware that the creation and continuation of needed social programs requires knowledge of the political process and an acceptance of political activity as one dimension of the professional role. Economics is a related and equally neglected dimension in program creation, maintenance, and change. The tax structure at the state level, the allocation of tax resources, and the federal administration's fiscal and monetary policy all have some bearing upon program creation and continuation.

We are not suggesting here that social work students must possess the subject matter of economics and politics, in addition to everything else. What is meant is that professional education must find new ways to secure from related disciplines, such as economics and political science, those concepts and facts relevant to the functions of the professional. But it is doubtful if this can be done merely by suggesting that a social work student take a course currently offered in the related discipline for such a course demands that he reach the performance level of subject matter majors or advanced students whose knowledge and sophistication far exceed his. The special courses taught social work students by experts from related fields who are also conversant wtih social work, at present, seem to be preferable, but for how long remains to be seen. This problem is by no means unique to social work; it is essentially a dysfunctional aspect of academic organization in which subject matter organized into academic departments does not meet the needs of professional education, which by its nature has a multidisciplinary base.

Moving on to the intervention system, we observe that the reviewed studies do not clearly seek to create blueprints for new service structures or to design intervention systems, but they have many implications for the need to clarify objectives of intervention and to define change goals clearly, selecting processes and methods appropriate to these goals. We cannot here develop a blueprint for a comprehensive intervention system, but we can offer suggestions. Three findings emerge from the studies: casework, as traditionally conceived, is appropriate in some instances and not appropriate in others; methods other than casework may be needed in conjunction with casework; and clarification and specification of treatment goals are necessary.

In some instances, stabilization at a given level of functioning seems appropriate; in others, amelioration is sought and, in still others, prevention of further dysfunctioning seems desirable. These are general goals, which must be refined to show us what treatment activities to engage in. For instance, breaking down family relationships into categories of instrumental functions, as Geismar has done, and differentiating those from expressive functions of family interaction serves a useful purpose for both research and casework intervention. However, for the latter to be effective, still more subtle and more specific areas of functioning must be developed.

The following questions flowing from the preceding considerations suggest a variety of educational approaches. First, are existing service methods such as casework and group work appropriate separately rather than in amalgamation? The studies seem to suggest the former. Second, can processes be identified within the casework method which range from the cognitive to the affective and also vary in complexity, or should casework be considered a monolithic whole? The studies seem to suggest the former. In the studies, use has been made of advice, referral, and information-giving as well as of counseling—both the ego supportive and modification variety.

Third, are skills considered to be part of a traditional social work method, namely casework, the exclusive property of that method, or are they part of the needed equipment of all social workers regardless of method specifications? Among these are skills needed for referral, consultation and teamwork, for case cooperation, fact-gathering and inference drawing from facts. The studies do not answer this question, but it would seem that these skills can be differentiated and abstracted from the methods and become the skills of the social work *generalist*.

Fourth, can we assume that principles of casework apply to all population groups regardless of socioeconomic status or developmental stage? And, if so, do social workers, in dealing with different population groups, merely use different techniques, but derived from the same principles? The studies do not address themselves to this question. They do suggest, however, that we ask whether different methodological approaches used for different groups in the population operate not on the same set, but on different sets, of principles. If so, the training of students must be modified and the current philosophy of casework which postulates similarity of principles and differentiation in application (from setting to setting rather than among population groups) must be challenged.

Fifth, is it possible and desirable to add to the current and sought-after breakdown of social functioning into role requisites of family members another dimension which deals with role requirements and with the personal aspirations of individual members of the family or with family aspirations as a whole? Such a dimension would obviate the possibility of sociological bias, which could lead to the assumption that societal or group norms are the only or primary goal to which families must adjust, forgetting or underplaying the importance of individual or family norms which, at given times, may be at variance with societal norms. A pluralistic society such as ours, despite repressive efforts and practice, values and seeks to make possible a strong climate and opportunity for self-expression and individualization without endangering cohesion. If this be the case, intervention goals could and should be much less societally determined, more tailored to individual needs and geared to the wishes and preferences, norms and values of individuals and families. Undoubtedly, ideological differences on this score do exist among social workers and among members of other professions. Increasingly, we learn that social control and social change are not alternatives for professional function but components of a continuum of activities. When conflicts exist, it is important that they be brought into the open rather than kept underground, because the position held by the professional will undoubtedly influence his behavior on any level, from planning to direct service. Such considerations must find their way into education, and will, if we teach not only existing practices and structures but also call attention to problems, issues, trends, and values reflected in behavioral choices.

The last component of our schema is social worker roles, which, as suggested earlier, can be divided into those of planner, administrator, and direct service provider. Within each role, a number of functions or tasks have to be performed. For instance, in the planning role, the social worker may, as an expert or consultant, work with the physical planner who needs to be socially informed. This same worker may also serve as an analyst of policy, as a program developer, and may serve, in conjunction with or independently of, other planning occupations in community organization. He may be closely related to the political system, as an expert or consultant; or may be operating in a bureaucratic structure on the federal or state level, a national or regional developmental and planning body of a voluntary nature; or, in keeping with recent developments, may hold a line or staff position in business.

In the past, social work has not produced practitioners for planning and policy roles in any large extent, and, currently, is only beginning to train personnel for such roles. This probably accounts for the paucity of information about educational content for this role. The primary value favored by social work, namely, concern with the self-development of the individual, causes content which may be found in other fields, both existing and emerging, to be melded into a configuration appropriate for social work rather than other fields. Hence, the unique characteristics of such a configuration, rather than its component parts, are the contribution that both practice and education make to the social sciences.

As functions are clarified, so will educational content be; thus, education and practice must join hands to do the job. A suggestive and imaginative set of functions for the planner is provided by Alfred Kahn (1969): planning for social problem-solving, for recognized components of social welfare, and for coordination of social components; planning for new program areas assigned to social work and for new social fields as they are developed; adding, at an accelerated pace, social components for social concerns to economic and physical planning domains; and, making modest or major efforts to coordinate economic and social planning in several ways.

The knowledge needed by the administrator is not primarily contained in social work but, for some time, has been drawn from related fields. Recent social work studies (Gurin and others, 1970) suggest the need for analytic and interactional skills in the performance of the tasks of administrative personnel. The best developed educational content lies in the descriptions of the direct service role, and the studies under consideration are most explicit about it. Within this role, a gradually increasing number of functions is being identified. There is recognition that, in addition to intervention activities focusing on interpersonal relations, there should also be concern about the social situation, social factors, or social conditions which affect families.

Furthermore, it is apparent that a variety of personnel on several levels of skill is appropriate, including technicians who provide information, referral, and advice service as well as personnel skillful in intervening on the interpersonal level. Both considerations, one broadening in scope of intervention and the other breaking the intervention roles into functions of differential complexity, warrant consideration for inclusion in the curriculum. The recent creation of new programs under the auspices of the O.E.O. and new services such as homemaker and day care programs, Head Start, neighborhood and legal services point to the need for personnel skilled in providing information and advice for specific programs, in facilitating access to existing community programs and referral services, and in engaging in case advocacy. A thoughtful and well developed schema is presented by Kahn (1969). Kahn's studies and the reports on recent practice development suggest the desirability of thinking about direct service as a series of more or less interrelated functions. Drawing heavily on Kahn's suggestions and relating them to suggestions contained in the studies, it is now possible to consider the following direct service roles or functions: first, the social work technician who provides advice and information and gathers facts; second, the social work general practitioner who provides liaison and basic counseling in relation to specific, concrete services such as foster home placement, homemaker, day care, after-care arrangements, and referral service to specialized community programs. The general practitioner is a first-line case service provider; he coordinates the services, provides accountability, and furnishes case advocacy as appropriate. His is what has been called the social brokerage function. Third, there is the social work specialist who provides counseling, focusing on interpersonal problems, psychotherapeutic case services, consultation to other community services in health, education, and the like, and as expert is available in relation to other human service utilities. Among his functions could be included policy advocacy which would call for review and revision of agency policies found to be dysfunctional in relation to outcome (as opposed to case advocacy which focuses on inappropriate performance of existing services).

Each of these roles or functions requires different educational preparation. Considerable difference of opinion will undoubtedly be engendered by educational proposals which assign less than the M.S.W. training to the general practitioner. Whatever the outcome, a proposal such as this cuts across current practice settings and their stranglehold on functions and roles, and possibly even opens the way to a new conceptualization of casework and group work methods. Such a conceptualization would not seek to fashion similarities in approach and process between the two methods. Instead, it would ask whether the problems of individuals and families are more likely to receive effective service if there is a combination of processes currently assigned to the rubric of casework or the rubric of group work, as well as the invention of new processes currently not belonging to either method.

Educational implications arise in the recognition of the need to focus on social and environmental factors as well as on interpersonal ones. While this suggestion is not new in social work, its implementation in education and practice has lagged behind partly due to theoretical limitations and partly due to the vague meaning attached to the terms *social* and *environmental* which tend to be used interchangeably. At times, social refers to the conditions and circumstances with which a given family must contend, such as poor housing, marginal employment, and inadequate income. Occasionally, the term social refers to the relationship between and among members of the family and significant others outside the family. Often, the term social is equated with large societal factors or problems such as poverty, racial discrimination, unemployment. Not infrequently, the term social refers to the community service structure and the nature of the service supply, its adequacy or inadequacy. Absence of clarification of the many meanings attached to the term *social* makes it very difficult for social casework to carry out the social dimension of its psychosocial mission. If the term is broken down into its different meanings, and different designations are given to the several possible properties of the term, progress can be made in teaching, learning, and, thence, in practice. To contribute to this clarification we suggest: the term social should be reserved for the interactions between and among members of the family and significant others. The conditions which operate in each family and deal with the nature of housing, life styles, economic behavior and resources, and habits of living (including food, clothing habits, and child-rearing patterns) might be called the *social situation* or the *family culture*. Factors dealing with the nature of the service structure and the social utilities available to the family in the community and which are needed to maintain the family on a level of effective functioning or to bring it to a desired level of functioning might be called the *social resources structure*. This includes child care and family services, health and educational services, and the like. Finally, the large unsolved problems in society which have inevitable repercussions on family functioning such as poverty, racial discrimination, unemployment, urban blight, and pollution might be referred to as *societal problems*.

Differentiations such as these might ultimately help us to clarify and, more important, to devise appropriate intervention approaches and strategies geared to the several levels suggested by the current term social. It would then be part of the social worker's job to clarify in what way the family's problems are related to the social situation, the resources structure, societal problems, and in what realm or realms intervention is needed, in addition to, or instead of, direct intervention in the social realm of the family.

Stages

It is not appropriate here to dwell on the education of trainers, teachers, and researchers, for the studies do not contain direct implications for this category which usually warrants doctoral-level training. In the preceding pages suggested educational content was identified or derived from the reviewed studies by devising a schema which focused on the populations served, the resources structure, the intervention system, and the professional roles of social workers. No attempt was made to relate the educational content thus obtained to levels of education; thus, the present section proposes and explicates a continuum of social work education. Current developments in the United States suggest that a continuum in education for social work should range from the associate degree to the doctoral level, and that, in conjunction with in-service and continuing education, social work education should constitute a systematic whole. Unfortunately, this is more easily said than done. At present such a continuum or any continuum is not in existence, if by continuum we understand a planned progression from one level of education to the next with each level not only serving as a prelude for the next but also constituting an educational component with its own integrity. However, recent developments in education, paralleled by some developments in practice away from traditional settings, bid fair that a continuum can be created or is emerging. The educator then faces the challenge of planning educational programs which can be interconnected. Current programs have their own integrity but are not related to the next higher or lower level. Moreover, current programs do not necessarily systematically and in order of increasing complexity contain elements previously identified.

In light of the foregoing, we postulate that a continuum needs to reflect the following principles: each level has its educational integrity and is a self-contained unit; each level is a way station to the next level; and each successive level is more complex, in terms of educational content, than the previous one. These principles, which may or may not be applicable or upon examination may even turn out to be undesirable, enable us to construct an ideal type of continuum. An ideal type is not necessarily the best or the most realistic arrangement, but it makes possible the examination of problems and issues of a continuum in the context of current educational and practice reality. Before proceeding to develop such an ideal type, some characteristics of a continuum must be identified.

First, education for social work has a class and field component on all levels. Second, a movement from lower to higher complexity is reflected in the material taught in class and the learning experiences provided in the field, the latter ranging from participant-observation to direct responsibility. Third, formal education for social work must be supported by a system of in-service training and staff development as well as continuing education. In-service training should be linked to generalized formal training that can be provided on any level and should be geared to specific job functioning.

Continuing education should aim, once a given level of formal education has been achieved, to help the student bring himself up to date on new developments in knowledge and skill or on changes in practice or to fill gaps in his previous education. Continuing education, too, might not limit itself to classroom instruction but might also contain a combination of field and class experiences, just as staff development need not limit itself to didactic approaches.

Fourth, all education, whether formal or informal, has as its goal the development of skill, which expresses the integration of knowing, believing (attitudes and feelings), and experiencing. Skill can exist on several levels of complexity, and the integration of knowing and feeling with doing, while in many instances idiosyncratic, can be learned. We know that the best way of effecting integration is to provide the student with learning experiences demonstrably based on knowledge, attitudes, and values. This viewpoint appears to be heavily supported by new developments in learning psychology such as the work of Bruner; it seems to be consistent with claims of behaviorists and has been held in social work education for some time. Skill has several levels of complexity due to the complexity of knowledge and attitude on which skill is based, and, in large measure, to the nature of the task for which it is needed.

We can here suggest areas of content (knowledge, attitudes, and skills) which can be developed on each of the three levels of the formal education continuum, by referring to the four categories constituting the framework identified earlier and to the educational content suggested in discussing each of the four categories: populations served, resources structure, intervention system and social worker roles.

Knowledge of population characteristics is provided on the undergraduate level, including the two years of college leading to the associate degree. Knowledge about population characteristics and the sociopolitical and economic dimensions that have some bearing on these populations' well-being could be imparted early. Increasingly, such material is offered in experimental colleges and improvement in the quality of high school education makes it possible for students seeking an associate degree to profit from such material.

The attitudinal component is sometimes neglected on this level or on subsequent levels. It is important to realize that the method of teaching more than the selection of content itself may have some bearing on attitude development. Discussion groups and learning experiences related to material contained in short stories, novels, movies, or the daily press (because it reflects certain debatable viewpoints) could link cognitive and factual material to the development of attitudes. The coming together of the two and the further development of attitudes can then take place in the field through participant observation. Associate degree training could aim to prepare technicians who serve as aides, referral agents, information providers, and the like, and who would also engage in selective activities of fact-gathering.

On the associate degree level, students could also learn about the network of programs and service structure and the interrelationship of programs with each other. Assessing the effectiveness of structure and service delivery systems should probably take place at the baccalaureate level, but at the associate degree level some of this learning could take place in the field, being reinforced and facilitated by overview courses dealing with the several social institutions in which social work and other human service professions operate.

Moving on to the baccalaureate stage, more sophisticated learning would take place. Interdisciplinary approaches to those population groups which are particularly vulnerable and the consequences of programs and policies in existence could be among the goals. The focus would be on the relationship of knowledge areas to each other. Information pertaining to the relationship between cultural, political, economic, and epidemiological factors as they affect the needs of population groups, demographic data, and the like would help the student emerge with a more sophisticated understanding of the characteristics and life styles of populations. He would be able to differentiate between societal values and norms and between group norms and deviance which is societally defined as opposed to deviance from family or individual norms. The student would be more sophisticated regarding the service resources structure, obtain a clearer picture about the advantages and disadvantages of linkage between national, state, and local programs, and possible ties between public and voluntary programs, profit-making and nonprofit-making ones.

In the field, the student would have direct responsibility as a provider of access to information and referral agents, as an access facilitator, and, perhaps, as a case advocate. Thus, he would be able to see how classroom courses pertain to professional activities in the field. Being trained to perform as a generalist would prevent him from specializing in any one method of help. He would have to limit himself to essentially factual approaches to rendering service as well as to cognitive components on the identification of problems. These activities would enable him to increase his understanding of and his sensitivity to individual needs.

The next stage would be the master's stage. Nothing at this point can be said about the optimum or desirable duration of any stage, since developments are underway to reduce the length of the college program and consideration is being given to the length of time needed for the master's program. Obviously, this question cannot be answered effectively until there are clarity and agreement about the content of the master's program. We suggest that the master's program consist primarily in developing a high level skill of practice in the direct service methods (direct service specialist) as well as in the other practice methods, namely, administration, planning, and policy making (which includes community organization). The social work student would have an opportunity to learn about theories which furnish concepts and principles needed to engage in practice skills. Consequently, the focus would be less on understanding and more on application of knowledge to develop competence.

Concepts drawn from psychology, social psychology, sociology, organizational and systems theory, and the like, and the theoretical underpinning for the development of analytical skills available from such fields as philosophy and history seem appropriate. The social work student would be given an opportunity to develop various practice skills by identifying both those which are profession specific, namely, generic skills needed by the practitioner of any method, and those which are method specific with a view toward having a much greater opportunity to specialize in a method of service and to develop competence on a higher level than is currently possible. Such a plan warrants the creation of new types of field experiences. While resembling those of the traditional master's program in objective, such types of field expeirence would also use the practicum idea suggested by the curriculum study. Thus, opportunities to acquire a high degree of analytic and interactional competence through practicum experiences would be placed under educational auspices.

The master's stage would not exclusively focus on the development of competence but would enable the student to become familiar with the workings and structure of related professions, with the history of his own profession, and with emerging societal and professional trends. This training would nurture a taste for social criticism and would produce a desire for flexibility of educational planning and frequent program reevaluation. Hence, the master's program would contain a strong dose of interprofessional content, much opportunity to work in related professional and academic fields, and, at the same time, possess a well-defined social work core.

The place of doctoral studies is deliberately omitted here, not because the doctoral level should not or could not be considered part of a continuum, but because the studies under review do not permit direct inferences to the doctoral level. However, any consideration of the place on the continuum of doctoral studies requires consideration of the objective of the doctorate. If its objective is to produce a practitioner with advanced competence (D.S.W.), the advent of the baccalaureate level social worker will force a much closer examination of the future role of, and educational content for, the current master's degree in social work. In what ways should M.S.W. role and content be different from that of the doctoral level? By contrast, if the objective of doctoral training is to produce a researcher-theorist (Ph.D.), a more clear-cut differentiation of training on that level from that of a practitioner on either or both the M.S.W. or D.S.W. is possible (Boehm, 1968).

A continuum such as the one suggested or any other which may emerge would provide both opportunities and constraints. Opportunities obviously reside in the articulation of levels of education and the student's chances for steady progression from one to the other. The constraints lie in the need to create specific and well-contained programs for each stage, something which is, perhaps, not possible and not even highly desirable if value is attached to the current educational practice whereby any undergraduate major, not just a specific social work one, is considered appropriate preparation for the master's program.

The ultimate role of each level of education cannot be determined unless we move from the ground up rather than from the middle, down and up. Many claim that any type of specific preparation, the differential quality of teaching to the contrary notwithstanding, constitutes as good a liberal education as any other. If so, the social work major would offer an advantage over baccalaureate education in a field other than social work, but the characteristics and content of the next level of social work education would have to undergo profound change. If the concept of general education and the concept of specialized education increasingly represent a difference without a distinction, the problem disappears and the advantages defined above become compelling, because in addition to laying the groundwork for the following stage, each preceding stage will constitute a self-contained program preparatory for a level of practice.

Much more needs to be said about the characteristics and content of each stage of the continuum, however, the absence of specific educational and curriculum suggestions in the reviewed studies makes greater specificity difficult and inappropriate. Hopefully, the principles and suggestions for content developed above can guide the creation of a continuum translatable into educational programs. Further, it now seems unwise to be more specific about the continuum since some of the knowledge areas needing consideration are at an uneven and, in some respects, an underdeveloped stage. Moreover, an impression is emerging that on the master's level scientific theory and research skill must be joined by emphasis on such components of the curriculum as program and practice issues, policy choices, value alternatives, and moral issues. These may have to play an important role in social work education of the future.

Each stage of the continuum, as suggested earlier, should ideally be related to in-service training and continuing education. That a systematic relationship between these two modes of education does not now exist should not prevent its creation. The rapidity with which knowledge and experience accumulate, not only in social work but in related human service occupations, the likelihood of legislative changes particularly in the financial assistance pattern in the foreseeable future, and the almost certainty that a post-industrial society will require a greater deployment of manpower in the human services—these conditions combine to point up the need for the creation of a partnership between agency complexes, higher education, and national professional and functional associations, with a view to creating in-service and continuing education programs which are well articulated with those provided on the three levels of higher education.

Classroom, Field, Community

We have previously suggested that improved skill is the desired outcome of education on any level, and that skill has been conceived as the coming together and expression of cognitive and attitudinal learning. Educators seem to agree that the best way to acquire skill is through learning experiences which consist of appropriate activities on the part of the learner; and this is one reason why the arrangement of a class-field linked pattern of education has been recommended for each stage of the continuum. This position should not be misunderstood to mean that learning experiences that call for doing should take place exclusively in the field. Doing can mean analyzing or reporting or thinking or any human activity that is responsive to an intellectual, emotional, or experimental stimulus, or, in the case of social work, to a combination of these. These inputs can take place in the class as well as in the field and frequently do. It would be a mistake to assume that learning experiences in the classroom call for intellectual efforts and learning experiences in the field, for emotional and experiential work. These kinds of activities have their place in either milieu. The criterion for selection of one or the other milieu, class or field, is not the nature of the learning experience but the appropriateness of either milieu for the content to be learned. In social work, we have, at times, realized that the utilization of both is appropriate. While it is true that the classroom lends itself more to intellectual endeavors and the field setting more to experiential ones, we find, on close inspection, that affective experience coming to grips with feelings occurs in both places and that intellectual learning also occurs in the field. More thought must be given to ways of reducing the unnecessary polarization of class and field. There is a development occurring in social work education—the first section of this chapter refers to it—which calls for a reconsideration and revision of possibly stereotyped notions about the proper place of class and field in social work education, referring to the fact that field becomes increasingly an educational laboratory and part of the university structure. Three trends seem to point in this direction.

First, in the direct service methods, field opportunities are increasingly sought in university-based experiences or provided by university-based field instructors, or both. The quest of many a school of social work for the practice center is another attempt to bring the agency closer to the university, either by taking a portion of its work into the academy or by creating a new type of relationship which essentially has the same result.

Second, schools of social work increasingly set up agencies virtually for the purposes of field learning. They utilize new and experimental programs such as satellite learning experiences in conjunction with traditional ones, with learning experiences provided by nonsocial work personnel and overall field instruction entrusted to a school-based faculty member who may or may not have remote control over the quality and content of learning.

Third, for the learning of skills in policy, planning, and

administration, the classroom increasingly may become the focus for integration of experiences, of feeling, and of knowing, and do exactly what is expected from the field. It is not surprising that, in one school, integration seminars held in the classroom have been developed for the planning track of the curriculum. By contrast, in the direct service track, efforts are under way to lay the groundwork for combining the activities of field and class instructor and making one person responsible for them.

These developments may foreshadow a blurring, if not an elimination, of the difference between class and field. If this is correct, new ways must be found to ensure closeness or, better, exchange between practice and education. This centripetal tendency is paralled by a centrifugal one: there are pressures to make much more use of the *community* for learning experiences. Once the romantic glow has been taken out of the suggestion to utilize community programs and indigenous personnel indiscriminately simply because they provide problem-related experiences, and after educational accountability has been assured, there is no reason why the use of community programs and persons cannot enrich and even vitalize education for social work. The issue is not whether such programs or persons should be used, but how their contributions can be related to already existing and, at times, more traditional contributions in such a way as not to destroy the integrity of the educational enterprise but to strengthen it. Community programs which have been developed under O.E.O. auspices in the social service, legal, and health fields have indeed enriched student learning where imaginative use has been made of them in the context of a sound educational program. By bringing such programs into relationship with the university, new educational values for students can become available and student learning can be expanded. This, of course, cannot be done without considerable investment of faculty time. When students can become familiar with traditional as well as nontraditional service delivery systems, not only relevant learning may ensue but perhaps a meaningful relationship between the university and the community can develop.

Integrating Education and Practice

As such developments occur there is no question but that education for social work will prepare personnel less well equipped to fit into traditional practice structures than has been the case until recently. It has been argued that if education in social work is too far removed from traditional practice roles, it will be difficult for graduates of these programs to find positions; or if they do get employed in traditional agencies which still are and probably will continue to be the major employer, they may not be able to function effectively. If this be so, we need to give renewed thought to the philosophy underlying social work education. Few would argue that education for social work should train for practice as it exists at any moment in time (as if practice were static), or that it should train for the patterns of practice of the future (as if these were always knowable). To put the issue in those terms is to create a false dilemma. Instead, it seems opportune to reiterate that education for social work can and should do no more than provide generalized approaches to problem-solving, not devoid of techniques but emphasizing the former rather than the latter. If this be the case, it should not be too difficult for graduates of social work programs to find their way in traditional and nontraditional practice, and in-service training and continuing education can become powerful resources to make this possible. Perhaps this philosophy of education explains why leaders in practice and education, who have been trained for a different kind of social work, have managed to move with the times and are able to engage soundly in innovation.

Events and points of view will inevitably alter the relationship between education and practice. In some instances, there will be tension and even conflict—a situation not necessarily undesirable. It can be viewed as a healthy phenomenon if one accepts the mutuality of the relationship between practice and education, with practice convincing education that it must be related to reality and education convincing practice that habitual service patterns may no longer be commensurate with existing knowledge and emerging needs. If both practice and education can accept the notion that changes in the socioeconomic and political structure in this nation and the world may require new professional roles, new patterns of practice, that change is likely to be the characteristic of our time for the next several decades, that human services will become increasingly essential for effective living for the total citizenry, then an attitude will result that accepts change as a desirable condition for the continued vitality of both practice and education.

In conclusion, two important reports on higher education have recently been published by the Carnegie Commission on Higher Education. One deals with the duration of university education, especially on the undergraduate level, and the other deals with policies for medical and dental education (Carnegie Commission on Higher Education, 1970). This report suggests that medical educators consider two models, in addition to the current Flexner or research model which emphasized biological research, and stresses the importance of science as the base of medical education. One is the health care delivery model in which the medical school, in addition to training, does research in health care delivery, advises local hospitals and health authorities, works with community colleges and comprehensive colleges on the training of allied health personnel, carries on continuing education for health personnel, and generally orients itself to external service. The other is the integrated science model in which most of the basic science and social science instruction occurs on the main campus or other general campuses and is not duplicated in the medical school which provides mainly clinical instruction.

Many an opinion to the contrary notwithstanding, schools of social work have not followed the medical or Flexner model, but have been much closer to the health care delivery model. Perhaps the time has come for us to consider adapting this model for social work. In doing so it is appropriate to bear in mind circumstances which set schools of social work apart from other types of professional education and give social work an advantage over them, which circumstances are the traditional concern in social work education not only with knowledge but also with the role of viewpoint, value, attitude, and professional ideology. It is hoped that this concern, rather than being sacrificed to the knowledge component of competence, will be more vigorously translated into learning experiences in the future on the premise that neither knowledge nor value are sufficient but that both are necessary for the creation of competence.

This chapter owes its existence to impressive and painstaking research into practice. There is no one who would not welcome and support more research into the phenomena of practice, particularly the appropriateness and effectiveness of modes of professional intervention. Nevertheless, while more research is needed, we must not overlook both the knowledge and experience extant about the phenomena with which social work deals both within the profession and related disciplines. Professional education is not a function of level or degree but a function of our success in enabling students to integrate the scientific and humanistic strands of learning.

Heliocentric Perspective on Social Work Education

Donald L. Feldstein

Werner Boehm points out two basic approaches for viewing the social work educational program. The first, the geocentric view, puts the master's degree curriculum at the center of the universe of social work education; other parts relate themselves to that center to a greater or lesser degree. The second approach is that social work education must be viewed from a heliocentric perspective, that is, that social work education itself is at the center of our universe, and the various levels contribute to lesser or greater degrees. It is in this context that we can examine issues pertaining to the continuum in education for social work with reference to what may be learned from practice for that continuum.

The preceding chapter connects the studies to formulations for a social work curriculum. But when it comes to the continuum, any significant approach discussed now must suffer from a lack of direct relation to practice. There are intrinsic difficulties in viewing what is now going on in practice and concluding, "Let us decide what should be the continuum or how to build linkages." Apart from theoretical difficulties, there are no studies yet of baccalaureate social workers or associate degree community service technicians in practice. In fact, there are hardly any such workers; we have to create the work force, then study it. We cannot conclude from the reviewed studies the proper role for people on different levels and for what we can educate.

There is today no significant body of experience on the use of personnel from the different levels of social work education. Some of the present studies, it is true, refer to the use of baccalaureates and other people without graduate social work education. These people, however, are not social work educated on their respective levels. All we can do is extrapolate from this kind of experience, from the experience of VISTA and the Peace Corps, and from the various experiments being done with paraprofessional and indigenous personnel to guess at what social work educated workers might do at similar levels. There is no way out: we must create new programs in social work education and then use the market and the experiences which emerge to build, to change, and to admit our mistakes. For better or worse, we start with education.

Boehm sees social work education built around a study of the populations served, the social resources structure, the intervention system, and social worker roles, and offers these divisions as constructs for all social work education. Boehm talks primarily about these four basic areas and the degree to which their content belongs on each level of social work education. He does not assume, as some other authors have, that one can separate content areas by levels, so that on level X content area Y is placed and that on level A content area B is placed. His approach seems to be holistic—that we must pick from the four content areas that which is appropriate to each level and that something from each of these areas belongs at each level, which is a sound way to approach the continuum.

In Boehm's discussion of populations served, an important and perhaps a controversial point is made. It is not necessarily correct to say, as Boehm does, that today social work concentrates on service to the poor. Certainly, we talk about it much more than we did before 1964, and there is a thrust in that direction, but it seems that in terms of allocation of professional social workers, we still have a way to go in serving the poor. None of this objection negates Boehm's fundamental point—namely, that social work education has to be a study of all people, not just poor people, black people, or any subdivision of people. Boehm personalizes the argument of selectivity versus univeralism in social services. Should the social services conceive of themselves institutionally as specialized services for specialized segments of the population, or is society and the poor more benefited if we address ourselves to all the people? As others have said, services for the poor tend to become poor services. We demean the profession and cheat the special groups we mean to serve if we say that social work is that profession which addresses itself to the poor: social work must address itself to society. There are various priorities in different times in different places within society, but we must learn about all people, just as we must learn how to use and create institutions for the whole society.

Boehm says that his definition of practice includes more than what has been traditionally included, and he believes his definition is important and true even though it may not be generally accepted. In this respect, many of us may be suffering from what the sociologists call multiple ignorance. This is similar to the person who says, "I'm perfectly happy to live in an integrated community, but I can't because all my neighbors are not yet ready for this, and they don't want to." And all the neighbors have gone through the same process, saying, "I'm ready, but the other fellow is not." It seems that this premise has been accepted. Social work practice is, in the minds of most social workers and social work educators, now accepted as including the areas of policy, planning, and administration that Boehm mentions. Thus, we do not have to keep fighting this battle; people are now asking for the next step. It's all very well to say that these are components of social work practice—but in what way? How do we incorporate planning, administration, and the like into practice and what must be done by practitioners? The field of practice and education is looking for answers to these questions. We have passed the point of philosophical argument and should be working on the *how to*.

To Boehm, three findings related to the intervention system emerge from the studies: clarification and specification of treatment goals are necessary, methods other than casework may be needed, and casework as traditionally conceived is appropriate in some instances and not in others. Therefore, he concludes that education should proceed on the assumption that existing service methods are appropriate separately rather than in amalgamation. He also sees a group of skills, now considered part of casework, which could become part of the repertoire of a social work generalist.

The studies do suggest that what caseworkers did was sometimes effective. But we cannot justifiably claim that what was effective were the specific casework skills which would not be taught as part of a generalist's education. In fact, one could just as well claim that it was precisely those skills which helped and that if the social workers had had available noncasework skills which would be part of a generalist's repertoire, they would have been even more effective. The studies can reinforce a bias to eliminate specific methods in favor of a single social work method as easily as they can reinforce a bias to maintain specific methods such as casework. How to develop special competence in given areas with a single social work method, though it can be done, is not the business of this chapter.

So much for the backdrop—the educational package to be distributed over the continuum. Boehm enunciates three basic principles regarding the continuum. One is that each level in the continuum must have a wholeness of its own, must have its own reason for existence, and must be a coherent piece. Second, each level in the social work continuum must be a way station to the next level; and, third, each level in social work education must be progressively more complex than the preceding level. Few would argue with these three principles, but they raise certain problems in implementation.

We are furthest along in observing the first principle. Certainly, the master's degree programs have an integrity of their own; the technical programs, the associate degree programs, at least the better ones, also have an integrity of their own. The level which meets this criterion least is undergraduate education in social work, which is due to historical factors and to the problem of creating coherence for one program in a larger liberal arts college system.

However, this unity is coming because it is in the nature of organizations to be concerned about their own integrity. As baccalaureate programs develop an internal integrity, they will hopefully not lose sight of their broad mission to contribute social welfare content to the entire university.

The more difficult principles are the second and third, the degree to which each level is a way station to the next, and the degree to which each is more complex than the previous. Boehm does not offer a specific prescription for how a program may be a way station to the next. For instance, by way station we may mean that each level is a prerequisite to the next. Thus, will it be necessary for someone to graduate as a baccalaurate social worker before he can enter a master's degree program? Must all people who enter doctoral programs in social work be masters of social work? This is not what most of us mean; it's too narrow and restrictive an interpretation. Do we mean, then, that each level is simply *desirable* preparation for the next? That is too simple a solution because desirable can mean almost anything or nothing, as long as each level does not have any negotiability toward the next level. Graduate schools of social work have been weak in their past approach in this area; they have always insisted that the best preparation for social work study is liberal arts, have pushed undergraduate programs in social welfare toward liberal arts, and yet have never made liberal arts a prerequisite for entering graduate school. People come out of education or engineering or English or whatever with equal access to the graduate school because the graduate school is a self-contained program with integrity at its own level. The insistence on keeping the baccalaureate programs in social work liberal was a way, apart from the merits of the case, of keeping them in their place.

But now we have a new reality—significant, strong, viable undergraduate programs developing an integrity of their own; and graduate schools must face this issue. They can move in several directions. They can make the one level prerequisite, and people without this background for graduate education will have to do makeup work; they can maintain their policy of admitting any baccalaureate degree holder but give advanced or special standing to the graduates of baccalaureate programs in social work. Or, instead of giving a waiver or advanced standing to such graduates, they can create new tracks within their graduate programs for such people. However, they must address themselves to this issue because it is crucial. In several experimental programs, graduate schools are working with their own undergraduate programs in a continuum and developing linkages—five-year packages, for example—all within the same university. We are not going to lick this problem until we have a rationalized approach to the linkage question between levels that transcend individual universities. The fact that one graduates from one master's program does not prevent him from applying to, and being accepted by, a doctoral program in another university. Similar articulation must develop between the baccalaureate and the master's degree, and between the associate and baccalaureate degree. This is our priority concern in the continuum.

As one reads Boehm's suggestions for the content of M.S.W. education, the question of way stations or prerequisites comes sharply into focus. He wants, quite legitimately, learning of "concepts drawn from psychology, social psychology, sociology, organizational and systems theory, . . . analytical skills available from such fields as philosophy and history . . . [familiarity] with the workings and structure of related professions . . . [and with] emerging societal and professional trends," along with the development, through practice, of competence on a high level. Graduate schools of social work will never achieve such objectives until they themselves follow through on the suggestion they have successfully sold to undergraduate education: that a strong liberal base be a prerequisite to social work education. Thus, while baccalaureate social work education may not be a necessary prerequisite to graduate social work education, liberal education is. The commitment to educate humane professionals with a social philosophy demands such a commitment.

The third principle that Boehm enunciates is that each level must be more complex than the last: this recommendation is made difficult by a complicating factor in social work history; it is easy to make each level more complex than the last when you are building upward. When you have a master's degree program and you create a doctoral program, the doctoral program is naturally more complex than the previous level. But, when you start with a master's degree program and then create programs below, there is a strong tendency to build from the top down, instead of from the bottom up. You tend to say—given the master's degree program—what less complex may we teach on the associate degree level? And that exercise becomes very sterile. In spite of the fact that we are building chronologically from the top down because our master's degree is our strongest level today, we must maintain the principle of building from the bottom up. We must start with the lowest level and ask what is appropriate, what can students handle, and what should we be teaching at this lowest level, even if it includes a lot of what we have been teaching at the upper level. And then the upper level has the responsibility to change and to move in accordance with the principle of increased complexity that Boehm mentions.

Boehm performs a tremendous service when he includes among the ingredients in his continuum several elements we often forget. When we talk about the continuum, we usually mean associate degree programs, baccalaureate programs, master's programs, and doctoral programs. But Boehm reminds us of informal education, continuing education, and in-service education. Any intelligent approach to creating a continuum must take these three into account. The recognition of informal education is vital if our profession is to provide access for many now excluded. It is not a choice, as some radicals in the new careers movement would have us believe, between accepting and believing in credentials on the one hand and opening the door on the other hand. It is perfectly possible to believe in a formal educational system as the best system, at present, for bringing large numbers of people to a point where we can give them approval for practice. However, this acceptance of formal education does not preclude the possibility that any number of individual persons may be able to come to a similar point through informal experiences. The formal system must then find ways of crediting and bringing into the mainstream those people who have achieved a certain level through informal educational methods and mechanisms and who can challenge that level. Different people in the community have to be brought in at different levels in the continuum, depending on the education and informal experiences they have had. For instance, community colleges may be the main conduit for transferring informal learning to the formal educational mainstream and for passing its products on.

As we build linkages in the continuum, continuing education (Boehm's second addition) is going to grow stronger and more important than it is today and yet will almost disappear as continuing education. It will increasingly merge with part-time credited education toward whatever degree the student is pursuing. Keeping continuing education as a separate, noncredited track has dangers because it has been corrupted from two sources. One is practitioners who express contempt for the formal education system. They say, "These people on the job have to learn something real and useful. We can't fool around with all the nonsense you teach them in school with your formal courses. So let's set up this separate course, give it to them to learn, and forget about credit, so they can get to work." This viewpoint insults the educational system; either the charge is not true or the educational system for credit ought to change.

The second source of corruption is educators who approach continuing education in a way demeaning to the individuals to be taught. "Now," say educators, "we can't really give these people credit because we're not going to give them that kind of content, and we can't really do the planning that goes into it. But, it's OK to set up a limited continuing education course as long as we're not giving credit for it, as long as it's only a certificate to state that they took the course. We are not putting our university on the line and the value of its credits on the line." This viewpoint insults the students. Increasingly, our clientele will demand that the continuing education they enroll in be for credit: it will have to be relevant and real, and of the same quality as any other university program we offer. So continuing education, not in its present form but merged with part-time mainstream courses for credit, will begin to be more and more important in building a continuum.

The third ingredient Boehm talks about is in-service education. Maintaining in-service education is crucial to the ability of social work education on every level, including the technical, to be sufficiently generic. When we forget in-service training, our programs become vocationally oriented and poor. This is not just true in our field. Community colleges with computer programs and technical training programs may invest several million dollars in new computers of the latest generation. They put their students to work on them; and when the students leave two years later and try to get jobs, a new computer is out which they know nothing about, and they are technologically unemployed. The community college is embarrassed at having invested several million dollars in those computers, so keeps using them and turning out people who are technologically unemployable. This is a dramatic example, but the point is that, even in a technical field like computer training, we must train people more generically than we now do. We must teach them principles of computer programing, so that in field work and in in-service training they can adjust quickly to whatever machine they are assigned. Even on the technician level, we must recognize this principle in social work education. We must train people for a changing world, and the vocational training in social work has to be generic enough so that people can shift and change and move. Keeping in mind that in-service training is part of the continuum and can give people the specifics they need gives us the opportunity to construct university education properly.

The Boehm chapter addresses the question of what educational content belongs at what level. In spite of his general commitment to a holistic approach, Boehm seems to suggest that the associate degree student needs content essentially in only two of his four suggested content areas: the populations served and the resource system. But if the associate degree graduate is the technician, he needs to learn skills as well. In Boehm's educational schema, the baccalaureate social worker gets a generalist degree, for he is a general practitioner and needs content in all the areas. The master's degree practitioner is application centered, says Boehm, and therefore present or future specialties may be appropriate. In his formulation for the baccalaureate, some of the appropriate content, and specifically the professional content, is played down.

It seems we have crossed a bridge, and our ability to recognize that crossing determines how intelligently we can approach the rest of the continuum. Rightly or wrongly, after due process, our national association has decided that graduates of approved undergraduate programs in social work may become full professional members, be listed in the same professional directory, pay the same dues, and be subject to the same code of ethics. We have said by that action that the baccalaureate degree in social work is the first professional degree. If this is not so, then we should soon hear about it from the profession. If this is so, then we have to strengthen and upgrade what Boehm prescribes in terms of how much professional orientation, how much socialization to the profession, and how many application-centered programs baccalaureate social work students need in their curriculum. One formulation of the social work roles appropriate to the baccalaureate social worker is not unlike Boehm's summary (drawing on Alfred Kahn), but is freer and more inclusive. This piece, by Barker, Briggs, and Daly (1971), suggests that the baccalaureate generalist can engage in the full range of social work practice except for the independent establishment of a social diagnosis, critical judgments, and determination of interventive modes to be employed. For these, he should consult with a master's degree practitioner. This formulation is a bit conservative, but certainly baccalaureate social workers can and should be prepared to do that much. The master's curriculum, as prescribed by Boehm, is sound but fails to relate to the issue of whether and how it might differ for baccalaureate social workers and for others.

Finally, it is impossible to exclude the doctoral program from an examination of the continuum. In looking at linkages, we must consider the doctoral program a possible element in a new continuum model. For instance, one alternative may be that, as in many fields, people will go from the basic practice degree (baccalaureate) to the advanced degree (doctorate) with the master's being simply an incidental degree along the way. The master's would then be part of the package of courses toward a doctorate, as is true in most graduate education. We must also look at the doctorate in terms of how much time is needed to reach certain objectives of advanced training. Others have made the point that for many of its objectives the master's degree program is a particularly asynchronic one. For what most social workers do, two years of postbaccalaureate study is too much; for what we would like to claim we do, whether in social policy or in clinical practice, two years is not enough. So if we look at a revised package, we must consider the doctoral program as an ingredient in the recipe.

The following is another formulation of what content belongs on what level: associate degree education covers the gamut of content areas which Boehm suggests but covers them without the breadth of conceptual knowledge which makes possible the autonomous expertise or professional judgment demanded on the other levels. In other words, the associate level is not the professional level, but the technical level, though it covers the same content areas. The baccalaureate social worker is, as Boehm suggests, the basic generalist-practitioner. The thrust of education at that level should be toward preparing the generalist as a full practitioner; the program can, if it is well thought out, be both liberal and professional. The master's and doctoral programs, to be completed in various amounts of time depending on the specialized areas desired beyond the basic profesisonal degree, could then emerge in a number of different combinations. It may take two years to become a good supervisor and trainer, three years to become an expert advanced clinician, and four years to do something else. Time may also vary depending on the nature of one's undergraduate education. In addition, we must reconstruct patterns of graduate education, based on objectives, both for advanced clinical practice and for the planners and teachers in our field.

Graduate education in social work should insist on some liberal base. Where students bring none, they should have to make it up by informal experience or by additional courses. However, the liberal base students bring to graduate education should also be examined. Students should receive graduate credit for whatever they have above a certain minimum. Hopefully, someone with a baccalaureate in social work will not be competing on equal grounds with someone with a baccalaureate in English or in history. This rough and tentative formulation suggests only the beginnings of a rational and sound approach, and a somewhat different approach in different schools in different parts of the country, to a continuum in social work education.

The readiness for change and the willingness to give up old habits are greater than any of us realize; educators and practitioners are ready to move. But, at this stage, we must find out how to proceed intelligently without throwing out the baby with the bath water. If we can provide some guidance, the field and social work education will accept it.

Concluding Note

Edward J. Mullen, James R. Dumpson

Social work emerged from the 50s with confidence concerning its effectiveness. As a profession, it sought expanded opportunities and resources to demonstrate this competence. The 60s witnessed a marked increase in those opportunities, and social work set about to demonstrate its relevance. Out of this confidence social workers boldly exposed their practice to the critical scrutiny of scientific evaluation and assumed that such evaluations would assist them as they refined their technologies and expanded their knowledge. They assumed, too, that these evaluations would clearly demonstrate the effectiveness of their interventive efforts. As the findings from these evaluations became available, it was evident that interventive impact was not so easily demonstrated. As pointed out in the preceding chapters, the researchers, for many reasons, were rarely able to conclude that a program had even modest success in achieving its major goals. In fact, it appeared that the more traditional, estab-

lished programs were the most difficult to validate. And now, the
profession is confronting the evidence from these assessments and,
in the context of its experience, is attempting to understand the
meaning of these findings.

Throughout the preceding pages, the evidence has been reviewed and inferences drawn. Suggestions have been offered for the
reorganization and development of social work practice and education, and the general directions are now clear. Social work must
give priority to tackling what has been defined as the macro and
mezzosystems, and the human needs and problems they generate.
Basic to achievement of this goal is development of strategies for
effecting social policy development on the macro and mezzosystem
levels. The broad social problems of poverty, racism, and general
social injustice must be addressed; but it is clearly evident that
these problems cannot be properly addressed simply by interventions
directed toward individuals experiencing these problems. The studies
reviewed in this book clearly attest to the futility of attempting to
resolve our major social problems through microsystem interventions.

This is not to suggest that microsystem problems should not
be the concern of social work. People do have personal problems
which do not directly emanate from the mezzo and macrosystem
levels. For such microsystem problems, the profession must have an
armamentarium of knowledge and skills applicable for effective intervention. The profession must continue the responsibility it has
for intervention on this level, even while it tests and retests the relevance of its knowledge base and the effectiveness if its skills. However, it must carefully distinguish between microsystem problems
and macro- and mezzosystem problems and determine the kind of
understanding and skills required for effective differential intervention.

An additional priority that emerges from reviewing the
studies discussed in this book is the urgent requirement that social
work invest resources in expanding its understanding of social and
human problems. Without increased understanding in these areas,
ability to effectively intervene is severely limited. Intervention built
on limited understanding or invalid propositions about the nature
of target problems and needs will have little effect. The time has

come for enlarging the parameters from which the knowledge basis of social work is drawn by utilizing knowledge developed in many relevant established scientific disciplines as well as in the emerging applied sciences. We must attempt to systematize the incorporation of this new knowledge into social work as it becomes available. These efforts must accompany, if not precede, the investment of resources in creative, systematic program development and innovation. Program interventions must be built on a reliable understanding of the nature of the target problems and evolve from clearly defined values, defendable assumptions, and realistic goals. The profession can no longer be content to rely on traditional methods and practices and the knowledge and understanding on which they are based, but must creatively develop qualitatively different approaches which reflect expanded knowledge and new understanding.

Priority must also be given to a reexamination of the manner in which the profession and society have structured and organized themselves for the delivery of services and social intervention. We are struck with the observation that what was being observed in many of the reviewed evaluations was the dysfunctional nature of social agencies. Rarely did the organizational structure reflect concern for the fundamental nature of the problem presented, the level on which the problem had its primary source, or the manner in which it intertwined with other levels. The manner in which the programs reviewed were organized and structured reflected a lack of comprehension of the variety of levels on which intervention must proceed. If effective interventions are to be developed, then the role, structure, and processes of existing social agencies must be rethought. Many of the problems and needs of concern to the profession may better be addressed by a qualitatively different type of organizational system—a system that will more rationally utilize the resources available. Within this context, it seems relevant to question the validity of a social agency addressed to social problems and needs limiting itself to the input of a single professional discipline. Given the complex nature of social problems, it seems that intervention systems would be more effective, if they used knowledge and skills from a variety of professions and disciplines. Finally, development of program, to be sound, must be based on systematic feedback. We stand convinced that program evaluation must be built into all major organized interventive efforts, and feedback should be part of the ongoing processes of all agency systems. Professional accountability demands systematic evaluation. We should not have to rely on infrequent reports of field experiments to learn of intervention effectiveness.

Social work education must find ways of responding to these critical needs, and social work educators seem to agree that traditional curricula are no longer sufficient. Already, models of social work education are evolving which reflect the relationship between microsystem problems and mezzo and macrosystem problems, and the demands this relationship imposes on the helping professions. It seems evident, as suggested by Werner Boehm and Donald Feldstein, that social work educators must develop a rational educational continuum posited on an understanding of intervention tasks. Such a development is certain to increase the emphasis on, and importance of, undergraduate social work education. Graduate education, within that context, must prepare a different type of practitioner than it currently does, a practitioner skilled in planning, administration, research, and specialized intervention. This volume offers many suggestions for curriculum design which need not be repeated here. But as the curriculum moves in these new directions, we expect that, as Walter Walker suggests, methods must be found for enhancing the competence of social work faculty by drawing on a range of disciplines and investing in relevant faculty development programs. Such programs must seek the integration of a systems framework into the profession's view of social problems, needs, and interventions.

A final observation: a priority requirement for social work is the need to make explicit its values, goals, and goal criteria. Nearly all of the researchers, as well as the contributors to this book, noted the general lack of definition of underlying values, goals, and goal criteria in the studies reviewed. To what extent this reflects the state of affairs in social work education and practice deserves consideration. Without such specification we can hardly expect meaningful effectiveness.

References

ALLPORT, G. "The Open System in Personality Theory." *Journal of Abnormal and Social Psychology*, 1960, *61*, 301–310.

ARONSON, S., AND SHERWOOD, C. "Researcher Versus Practitioner, Problems in Social Action Research." *Social Work*, 1967, *12* (4), 89–96.

BALLARD, R. G., AND MUDD, E. H. "Some Sources of Difference Between Client and Agency Evaluation of Effectiveness of Counseling." *Social Casework*, 1958, *39*(1), 30–35.

BARKER, R. L., BRIGGS, T. L.. AND DALY, D. B. *Educating the Undergraduate for Professional Social Work Roles*. Syracuse: Syracuse University School of Social Work, 1971.

BEHLING, J. H. *An Experimental Study to Measure the Effectiveness of Casework Service*. Columbus, Ohio: Franklin County Welfare Department, 1961.

BEVERIDGE, W. I. B. *The Art of Scientific Investigation*. New York: Random House, 1950.

BILLINGSLEY, A. "Education for Strategic Uncertainty in Social Welfare." In *Education for Social Work with "Unmotivated Clients."* Waltham, Mass.: Florence Heller Graduate School for Advanced Studies in Social Welfare, Brandeis University, 1965.

255

BLENKER, M., JAHN, J., AND WASSER, E., *Serving the Aging: An Experiment in Social Work and Public Health Nursing.* New York: Community Service Society of New York, 1964.

BOEHM, W. W. "The Nature of Social Work." *Social Work,* 1958, *3* (2), 10–18.

BOEHM, W. W. "Common and Specific Learning for the Graduate of a School of Social Work." *Education for Social Work,* 1968, *4* (2), 15–26.

BORGATTA, E., FANSHEL, D., AND MEYER, H. *Social Workers' Perceptions of Clients.* New York: Russell Sage Foundation, 1960.

BOULDING, K. "General Systems Theory—The Skeleton of Science." *Management Science,* 1956, *2,* 197–208.

BRADBURN, N. *The Structure of Psychological Well-Being.* Chicago: Aldine, 1970.

BRIAR, S. "Clinical Judgment in Foster Care Placement." *Child Welfare,* 1963, *22*(4), 161–168.

BROWN, G. E. (Ed.). *The Multi-Problem Dilemma.* Metuchen, N.J.: The Scarecrow Press, Inc., 1968. Also reported in: WALLACE, D. "The Chemung County Evaluation of Casework Service to Dependent Multiproblem Families." *Social Service Review,* 1967, *41*(4), 379–389.

BUNGE, M. "Metaphysics, Epistemology and Methodology of Levels." In WHYTE, L. L., WILSON, A. G., AND WILSON, D. (Eds.), *Hierarchical Structures.* New York: American Elsevier, 1969.

BUTLER, R. M. *Social Functioning Framework: An Approach to Human Behavior and Social Environment.* New York: Council on Social Work Education, 1970.

CABOT, R. C. "Treatment in Social Casework in the Need of Criteria and of Tests of Its Success or Failure." *Proceedings of the National Conference of Social Work,* 1931, *58,* 3–24.

CARNEGIE COMMISSION ON HIGHER EDUCATION. *Higher Education and the Nation's Health.* New York: McGraw-Hill, 1970.

CHASSAN, J. B. "Statistical Inference and the Single Case in Clinical Design." *Psychiatry,* 1960, *23,* 173–184.

COHEN, P. C., AND KRAUSE, M. S. *Casework with Wives of Alcoholics.* New York: Family Service Association of America, 1971.

CORNFIELD, J. "The Frequency Theory of Probability, Bayes' Theorem and Sequential Clinical Trials." In MEYER, D., AND COLLIER, JR., R. *Bayesian Statistics.* Itasca, Ill.: F. E. Peacock Publishers, Inc., 1970.

DAVIS, K. "The Perilous Promise of Behavioral Science," "Research in the Service Man." A conference sponsored by the House of Representatives' Subcommittee on Government Research, October 1966.

DEPARTMENT OF HEALTH, EDUCATION, AND WELFARE. *Perspectives on Human Deprivation.* Washington, D.C.: United States Department of Health, Education, and Welfare, 1968.

EDINGTON, E. S. "Statistical Inference and Non-random Samples." *Psychological Bulletin,* 1966, *66,* 485–487.

ETZIONI, A. *The Semi-Professions and Their Organization.* New York: The Free Press, 1969.

EYSENCK, H. J. "The Effects of Psychotherapy: An Evaluation." *Journal of Consulting Psychology,* 1952, *16,* 319–324.

EYSENCK, H. J. "The Effects of Psychotherapy." In EYSENCK, H. J. (Ed.), *Handbook of Abnormal Psychology.* London: Pitman, 1960.

EYSENCK, H. J. "The Effects of Psychotherapy." *International Journal of Psychiatry,* 1965, *1,* 99–142.

EYSENCK, H. J. "The Effects of Psychotherapy." In EYSENCK, H. J. (Ed.), *Handbook of Abnormal Psychology.* London: Pitman, 1969.

FLECK, A. Address presented to a staff training program in District of Columbia, Department of Health, January 1966.

GANTER, G., YEAKEL, M., AND POLANSKY, N. *Retrieval from Limbo.* New York: Child Welfare League of America, 1967.

GEISMAR, L. L. "Implications of a Family Life Improvement Project." *Social Casework,* 1971, *52*(7), 465.

GEISMAR, L. L., AND KRISBERG, J. *The Forgotten Neighborhood: Site of an Early Skirmish in the War on Poverty.* Metuchen, N.J.: Scarecrow, 1967.

GEISMAR, L. L., GERHART, U., AND LAGAY, B. *The Family Life Improvement Project.* New Brunswick, N.J.: Rutgers University, 1970 (unpublished draft report).

GEISMAR, L. L., LAGAY, B., WOLOCK, I., GERHART, U., AND FINK, H. *Early Supports of Family Life.* Metuchen, N.J.: Scarecrow, 1972.

GLASER, B. G., AND STRAUSS, A. L. *The Discovery of Grounded Theory.* Chicago: Aldine Publishing Co., 1967.

GURIN, A., in collaboration with ECKLEIN, J., LAUFFER, A., JONES, W., AND PERLMAN, R. *Community Organization Curriculum in*

Graduate Social Work Education: Report and Recommendations. New York: Council on Social Work Education, 1970.

GUZZETTA, C. "Concepts and Precepts in Social Work Education." *Education for Social Work,* 1966, 2(2), 40–47.

HALL, A. D., AND FAGEN, R. E. "Definition of System." *General Systems,* 1956, *1,* 18–28.

HOLLIS, F. *Casework: A Psychosocial Therapy.* New York: Random House, 1964.

HYMAN, H. *Survey Design and Analysis.* Glencoe: The Free Press, 1955.

JETER, D. R. *Children Who Receive Services from Public Child Welfare Agencies.* Washington, D.C.: Children's Bureau Publication, No. 387, 1960.

JETER, D. R. *Services in Public and Voluntary Child Welfare Programs.* Washington, D.C.: Children's Bureau Publication, No. 396, 1962.

JETER, D. R. *Children's Problems and Services in Child Welfare Programs.* Washington, D.C.: Children's Bureau Publication, No. 403, 1963.

KADUSHIN, A. "The Knowledge Base of Social Work." In KAHN, A. J. (Ed.), *Issues in American Social Work.* New York: Columbia University Press, 1959.

KAHN, A. J. "The Design of Research." In POLANSKY, N. A. (Ed.), *Social Work Research.* Chicago: University of Chicago Press, 1960.

KAHN, A. J. *Studies in Social Policy and Planning.* New York: Russell Sage Foundation, 1969.

KAPLAN, A. *The Conduct of Inquiry.* San Francisco: Chandler Publishing Co., 1964.

KERLINGER, F. N. *Foundations of Behavioral Research.* New York: Holt, Rinehart, and Winston, Inc., 1964.

KOGAN, L. S., HUNT, J. MC V., AND BARTELME, P. E. *A Follow-Up Study of the Results of Social Casework.* New York: Family Service Association of America, 1953.

KOGAN, L. S. "The Short-Term Case in a Family Agency." *Social Casework,* 1957, *38*(5),(6),(7), 231–238, 296–302, 366–374.

KOGAN, L. S., AND SHYNE, A. W. "Tender-Minded and Tough-Minded Approaches in Evaluative Research." *Welfare in Review,* 1966, *4*(2), 12–17.

KRAUSE, M. S., BREEDLOVE, J. L., AND BONNIFACE, K. I. "An Evaluation of the Results of Treatment." In COHEN, P. C., AND KRAUSE,

M. S. (Eds.), *Casework with Wives of Alcoholics*. New York: Family Service Association of America, 1971.

KÜHL, P-H. *The Familycenter Project, and Action Research on Socially Deprived Families*. Copenhagen, Denmark: The Danish National Institute of Social Research, 1969.

LAGAY, B. "Assessing Bias: A Comparison of Two Methods." *The Public Opinion Quarterly*, 1969/70, *33*(4), 615–618.

LAGEY, J. C., AND AYRES, B. *Community Treatment Programs for Multi-Problem Families*. Vancouver, B.C.: Community Chest and Councils of the Greater Vancouver Area, 1962.

LEVINE, A. "Evaluating Program Effectiveness and Efficiency." *Welfare in Review*, 1967, *5*(2), 1–11.

LEVITT, E. G. "The Results of Psychotherapy with Children: An Evaluation." *Journal of Consulting Psychology*, 1957, *21*, 189–196.

LEWIS, C. J. *An Analysis of Knowledge and Valuation*, Paul Carus Lectures, seventh series, 1945. LaSalle, Ill.: Open Court, 1947.

MC CABE, A. R., SELLIGMAN, A., PYRKE, M., BERKOWITZ, L., KOGAN, L., AND PETTIFORD, P. *The Pursuit of Promise: A Study of the Intellectually Superior Child in a Socially Deprived Area*. New York: Community Service Society of New York, 1967.

MAAS, H. "Group Influences on Worker Client Interaction." *Social Work*, 1964, *9*, 69–79.

MANNIX, D. P., AND COWLEY, M. *Black Cargoes*. New York: The Viking Press, 1962.

MARIN, R. C. *A Comprehensive Program for Multiproblem Families—Report on a Four Year Controlled Experiment*. Rio Piedras, Puerto Rico: Institute of Caribbean Studies, University of Puerto Rico, 1969.

MASTERS, W. H., AND JOHNSON, V. E. *Human Sexual Response*. Boston, Mass.: Little, Brown and Company, 1966.

MELTZOFF, J., AND KORNREICH, M. *Research in Psychotherapy*. New York: Atherton Press, Inc., 1970.

MENNINGER, K. *Theory of Psychoanalytic Technique*. New York: Basic Books, 1958.

MESAROVIČ, M. D., AND MACKO, D. "Foundations for a Scientific Theory of Hierarchical Systems." In WHYTE, L. L., WILSON, A. G., AND WILSON, D. (Eds.), *Hierarchical Structures*. New York: American Elsevier, 1969.

MEYER, H. J., BORGATTA, E. F., AND JONES, W. C. *Girls at Vocational High: An Experiment in Social Work Intervention*. New York: Russell Sage Foundation, 1965.

MILLER, J. G. "Living Systems: Basic Concepts." *Behavioral Science,* 1965, *10*(3), 193–237.

MILLER, J. G. "A General Systems Approach to the Patient and His Environment." In SHELDON, A., BAKER, F., AND MC LAUGHLIN, C. (Eds.), *Systems and Medical Care.* Cambridge, Mass.: Massachusetts Institute of Technology Press, 1970.

MILLIKAN, M. F. "Inquiry and Policy: The Relation of Knowledge to Action." In LERNER, D. (Ed.), *The Human Meaning of the Social Sciences.* New York: Meridian Books, 1959.

MULLEN, E. J., CHAZIN, R. M., AND FELDSTEIN, D. M. *Preventing Chronic Dependency.* New York: Community Service Society of New York, 1970. Also reported in MULLEN, E. J., CHAZIN, R. M., AND FELDSTEIN, D. M. "Services for the Newly Dependent." *Social Service Review* (in press).

OLSON, I. "Some Effects of Increased Aid in Money and Social Services to Families Getting AFDC Grants." *Child Welfare,* 1970, *49*(2), 94–100.

PARSONS, T. *The Social System.* New York: The Free Press, 1951.

PERLMAN, H. H. *Social Casework: A Problem-Solving Process.* Chicago: University of Chicago Press, 1957.

PERLMAN, H. H. "Intake and Some Role Considerations." *Social Casework,* 1960, *41*(4), 171–176.

PERLMAN, H. H. "Can Casework Work?" *Social Service Review,* 1968a, *42*, 442.

PERLMAN, H. H. *Persona: Social Role and Personality.* Chicago: University of Chicago Press, 1968b.

PERLMAN, H. H. (Ed.), *Helping: Charlotte Towle on Social Work and Social Casework.* Chicago: University of Chicago Press, 1969.

PERLMAN, H. H. "Are We Creating Dependency?" In *Perspectives in Social Casework.* Philadelphia: Temple University Press, 1971.

POLYANYI, M. *Personal Knowledge.* Chicago: University of Chicago Press, 1958.

POWERS, E., AND WITMER, H. L. *An Experiment in the Prevention of Delinquency—The Cambridge-Somerville Youth Study.* New York: Columbia University Press, 1951.

RAWLS, J. "Two Concepts of Rules." *The Philosophical Review,* 1955, *64*(1), 3–22.

REID, W. J. "Target Problems, Time Limits and Task Structure," a paper presented at the Annual Meeting of the Council on Social Work Education, January 27, 1971.

REID, W. J., AND SHYNE, A. W. *Brief and Extended Casework.* New York: Columbia University Press, 1969.

REIN, M. "Social Planning a Search for Legitimacy." In MOYNIHAN, D. P. (Ed.), *Toward a National Urban Policy.* New York: Basic Books, 1970.

RICHMOND, M. *Social Diagnosis.* New York: Russell Sage Foundation, 1917.

RIPPLE, L. *Motivation, Capacity, and Opportunity: Studies in Casework Theory and Practice,* Social Service Monographs. Chicago: University of Chicago, School of Social Service Administration, 1964.

RODMAN, H., AND KOLODY, R. "Organizational Strains and the Research-Practitioner Relationship." In GOULDNER, A., AND MILLER, S. M. (Eds.), *Applied Sociology.* New York: The Free Press, 1965.

ROSENSTEIN, A. B. *A Study of a Profession and Professional Education.* Los Angeles: School of Engineering and Applied Science, University of California, 1968.

ROSENTHAL, R. *Experimenter Effects in Behavioral Research.* New York: Appleton-Century-Crofts, 1966.

SACKS, J. G., BRADLEY, P. M., AND BECK, D. F. *Clients' Progress Within Five Interviews.* New York: Family Service Association of America, 1970.

SCHWARTZ, E. E. "Strategies in Public Welfare Administration: The Field Experiment." In *Trends in Social Work Practice and Knowledge.* New York: National Association of Social Workers, 1966.

SCHWARTZ, E. E., AND SAMPLE, W. C. "First Findings from Midway." *Social Service Review,* 1967, *41*(2), 146.

SCHWARTZ, E. E., AND SAMPLE, W. C. *Organization and Utilization of Public Assistance Personnel: The Midway Office Field Experiment.* Chicago: School of Social Service Administration, University of Chicago, 1970.

SHERWOOD, C. "Issues in Measuring Results of Action Programs." *Welfare in Review,* 1967, *5*(7), 13–17.

SHYNE, A. W. *A Study of the Youth Bureau of the Community Service Society.* New York: Community Service Society of New York, 1959.

SIEGEL, N. "A Follow-Up Study of Former Clients: An Example of Practitioner-Directed Research." *Social Casework,* 1965, *56*(6), 345–351.

SIMON, H. A. *Administrative Behavior: A Study of Decision-Making Processes in Administrative Organizations.* New York: The Free Press, 1957.

STUDT, E. "Social Work Theory and Implications for the Practice of Methods." Paper presented at the Annual Program Meeting, Council on Social Work Education, January 24, 1968.

SUCHMAN, E. A. *Evaluative Research.* New York: Russell Sage Foundation, 1967.

SUSSMAN, M. B. "The Measure of Family Measurement." In CHILMAN, C. S. (Ed.), *Approaches to the Measurement of Family Change.* Washington, D.C.: U.S. Department of Health, Education, and Welfare, Welfare Administration, 1966.

TOREN, N. "Semi-Professionalism and Social Work: A Theoretical Perspective." In ETZIONI, A. (Ed.), *The Semi-Professions and Their Organizations.* New York: The Free Press, 1969.

TOWLE, C. *Common Human Needs* (rev. ed.). New York: National Association of Social Workers, 1965.

TRUAX, C. G., AND CARKHUFF, R. R. *Toward Effective Counseling and Psychotherapy.* Chicago: Aldine, 1967.

UNITED COMMUNITY SERVICES OF THE GREATER VANCOUVER AREA. *The Area Development Project Monographs I, II and III,* and *The Red Door: A Report on Neighborhood Services.* Vancouver, 1968–1969.

WALLACE, D. "The Chemung County Evaluation of Casework Service to Dependent Multiproblem Families." *Social Service Review,* 1967, *41*(4), 379–389.

WARTOFSKY, M. W. *Conceptual Foundations of Scientific Thought.* New York: The Macmillan Company, 1968.

WILSON, D. "Forms of Hierarchy—A Selected Bibliography." In WHYTE, L. L., et al. (Eds.), *Hierarchical Structures.* New York: American Elsevier, 1969.

WILSON, R. A. "Evaluation of Intensive Casework Impact." *Public Welfare,* 1967.

YATES, A. J. *Behavior Therapy.* New York: John Wiley and Sons, Inc., 1970.

Index

A

Abortion, 87, 213
Administration, 91, 92, 111–112, 147
AFDC families, 25, 70
Anomie, 217
Area Development Project (ADP), 16, 31, 33, 99–100, 135, 136, 159, 163, 177–179
Attitude scale, 20, 24

B

BARKER, R. L., 249
Bayesian analysis, 52–53
Behavior therapy, 9
Behavioral sciences, 156
Behavioral theory, 160
BELL, W., 104
Bias: epistemological, 72; experimenter, 61, 66
BILLINGSLEY, A., 149
BOULDING, K., 12
Brandeis University, 39
BRIAR, S., 149
BRIGGS, T. L., 249
BRUNER, J., 229

C

CABOT, R. C., 2, 14
Cambridge-Somerville Youth Study, 2, 3
CARKHUFF, R. R., 9
Carnegie Commission on Higher Education, 238
Caseload size, 106, 114, 134, 138, 139, 167
Casework, 13, 16, 20, 36, 114, 191–209; intensive, 25; practice of, 159; service in, 6, 7, 20, 23
Casework Methods Project, 14, 17–18, 28, 31, 32, 34, 60, 62, 101, 124, 136, 159, 180–183, 215
Causal inference, 52
Chemung County Study, 4, 5, 18, 31, 34, 104, 113, 137, 159, 162, 163, 164, 169–170, 202
Child abuse, 188
Child care, 175, 198, 203, 227
Child welfare services, 19, 20, 70, 94, 178
Civil rights movement, 117, 120
Collaboration: interagency, 135, 142,

263